A WALK TOWARD JESUS

Coming Through the Wilderness

Pamela S. Valerio

xulon PRESS

A Walk Toward Jesus
Coming Through the Wilderness
by Pamela S. Valerio

Printed in the United States of America

ISBN 9781609578206

Unless otherwise indicated, Bible quotations are taken from The King James 1611 Version.

The Word definitions are from Collins Gem Webster's Dictionary New Edition 2002, Harper Collins Publisher Great Britain

Word study definitions are derived from Strong's Exhaustive Concordance, Crusade Bible Publishing Nashville, TN 37209

The Well A Church of Fellowship
Home Based Fellowship where we "Don't Preach We Teach!"
Email: wmcs123@yahoo.com

Take note that the name satan and related names are not capitalized. We choose not to acknowledge him, even to the point of violating grammatical rules.

Edited by: Konsensus Publishing Services
Back cover photo by: Patricia Magilke

www.xulonpress.com

Dedication

This book is dedicated to my children, Carl Presa, Steven Ybarra and Amber Trevino so that you may always have a simple go to book for understanding what a relationship with Christ is truly all about. The words in this book are alive in me and it is my prayer that they come alive in you. Never give up on Christ, no matter the situation. He is always there. All you have to do is "seek," and you will find Him "knock," and He will open the door for you "ask," and He will reveal Himself to you. In those times when all seems dark, never fear, for He is with you always. I simply love every one of you equally!

To my son-in-law, Nick Trevino, a man whom I witnessed going from the gang life to being a servant of God. Nick, I pray you continue to allow God to transform you into who He has called you to be. Listen intently to that simple, small voice that is God's.

To the lost world who has yet to know Christ, may you find Him before it's too late.

Contents

Acknowledgements

The author acknowledges that teaching from the people listed below was helpful to the author. Some of the teachers are still contending for the faith, while others stood for truth in past generations.

I give all glory and praise to God, as I am humbled to compile such a work as this. He has truly sustained me through it all.

Howard Katz, a man I have never met in person, but to whom I am truly thankful, for having an "ear" to hear while sitting under the great teachings of Glenn and Robert Ewing in Waco, Texas. Thank you for your faithfulness in Christ. It was due to your faithfulness to the office of a teacher, that a wonderful teaching was passed down to me, which set me on the journey that allowed God to "tune in" my hearing, and give me "sight" to see what His Word has to offer. Even if we never meet in person, I want to express my gratitude and thankfulness to you, for being a humble servant of God. Thank you for listening when God said, "teach my son, teach!" That you have surely done.

Pastor Martin Wisenbaker, my uncle. I never really knew you while growing up, but God had a plan and purpose for us that we now share, these many years later. I cannot express how thankful I am to you for having that "ear" to hear, while sitting under the teaching of Glenn and Robert Ewing in Waco, Texas. Thank you for your faithfulness to Christ and for all the past studies, future studies, and the fellowship in Christ that we share, and will continue to share. It is due to your faithfulness in passing down those generational teachings that I have continued on the path God has called me to be.

Pastor Joshua Valerio, my husband, for whom I can never fully express my thankfulness. It was through one simple action, so long ago, that God used you to lead me to a place to know that there was so much more to Christ than I had known. All I had to do was seek Him and He would begin to build His character in me. That simple act set me on a journey with Christ that began in 1996 and continues to this day. I simply love you and appreciate all you have done for me, and with me, through our journey of marriage and relationship.

My parents, Edward and Rose Wisenbaker, part of the generation that prayed for their children, their grandchildren, and now, their great-grandchildren. I cannot thank my mother enough for starting me in life by taking me to church, and enrolling me in Sunday school classes, which she also taught. You two have always been there when I had questions, giving me the advice that was desperately needed at the time. I simply love you two and will always appreciate what you have done for me in my life by teaching me that there is a God, that He does exist. What better gift can a parent give than that? There is none!

It appears God works most strongly in my life through people I never met in person. There is a woman who lives in Tennessee, Cindy D. She is a woman who understands her calling, who God has placed in my life to pray with, when the Lord gives either of us a dream or vision. Cindy, it was through you seeking the Lord, concerning two dreams He had given me, that brought the third and final confirmation to my life that this work needed to be completed. Thank you for being a woman of God and a supportive friend! I truly appreciate who you are in Christ.

To Martin Wisenbaker, Ed Wisenbaker, Rose Wisenbaker, Rose Ann Lamb, D.L.Creamer, Amber Trevino and Cheryl Baldwin who helped in editing this work. I want to express my thankfulness and gratitude for helping in such a tremendous way. You are truly awesome people!

Introduction

W̲e all desire to know the reason why things happen in our lives, especially when life-altering events take place unexpectedly. As I share my walk with you, my hope is that you will get a glimpse of why such events happen.

In the beginning of my walk with Christ, I struggled with those "why me" questions because I had a lack of understanding. This lack will keep one in a guessing game that will never allow one to grow spiritually. I also realized that many people were in this same boat, even some church leaders.

No matter what church I walked into, I found some people asking the same questions about God that I did. That lack was my first clue that the churches God sent us to were in a spiritual desert. I did not understand that in the beginning. I began to catch on shortly after my husband and I were falsely accused of trying to take over one of these churches. That did not stop us from searching, it just added to the mix of questions I already had. If seeking God in the Body of Christ results in accusations, what was the point of attending church?

I had to settle down within myself and get alone with God. If parts of the Body of Christ were fed spiritually, the answers to those questions would have been readily available. People who come to spiritually fed churches would find compassion and not accusations. What I experienced on my search for understanding was accusation and ridicule by some church leaders, while others, I found, were putting on church performances.

Where was the life transforming truth? I understand now that those who have built their own "temple" will push you out, in an act of rebellion, in order to save their own self-established church. I know now that life-transforming truth is found when you seek Jesus and develop a relationship with Him. The Church is there to present the message. It is up to the individual to seek out the truth, in "spirit and truth."

I did not want to go through the motions of "church" and pretend I had some big knowledge of God, though as you read, you will see I almost fell into this trap. I sought to know the deeper things of God so the Holy Spirit could operate through me effectively. I did not want to pretend to operate in these gifts. I also did not want to go church for a spiritual emotional high either.

Healing is vital in the Body of Christ. The healing I am referring to is healing of the heart that cleanses the mind and brings a healing to the soul. There exists today, a disconnection between the people of God and their ability to walk in the calling God has placed in their lives. I experienced this first-hand and wandered aimlessly, seeking help from those who appeared to have that connection. The only reference point I had to go by was sitting still in a Catholic church as a child. Therefore, this new experience of speaking in tongues, a feisty pastor in the pulpit, praise and worship teams, and altar calls were all new for me. Later, I realized that I must seek Jesus and patiently wait for Him to answer me. God sent us on this journey for a reason and I praise Him for sharing those answers with me, as only He could.

I truly believe He has called me to put together this work. First, to help readers understand what building a relationship with Christ is all about and what it will take to allow Christ to build it. Second, I want readers to realize that mental wounds of their heart are blocking their connection to God.

I believe that one must live through the circumstance first, in order to testify to them later. A transformation by the molding process has to occur in order for one to testify to the mercy, grace, and love of Jesus Christ. Having suffered emotional wounds from those I thought were close to me, and enduring two serious, inexplicable, life-altering events, caused a long period of asking God, "why?"

Through seeking God for understanding, He provided me with tremendous guidance and studies. Once I "ate from this plate," it all became clear, and all the "why me" self-pity questions were erased. If I had to say which was the biggest revelation of them all, I would reply, "Walking with Jesus is first, a solo event, then a group event." In the beginning, I tried to do it the other way around and the devil played havoc with my emotions.

I am a simple person, led to put together a simple book for that person who needs a simplistic look at what God can do in the life of a believer. I wanted this to be a book one can read and say, "Yes, that's what I was looking for!" and "Oh! Now I understand that" or "Yes! That is how God is really working in my life!" Those "life to the bone" moments that will lead you on a journey to truly grasping onto Jesus consistently. When the faith Christ gave you begins to grow you literally feel your feet beginning to sure up underneath you. You will begin to walk in faith as you recognize how He works in your life. When tribulations come, you will hang onto Jesus and know what to do in the midst of the storm.

This is a personal story, a personal study, a real journey. I believe it will be a real spiritual awakening for you just as it was for me. It is my personal walk, as I walk toward Jesus, to get to know who He is in my life daily. It is my walk through a wilderness, and coming through to the other side. Once realizing that "His ways are not our ways," and believing that, things began to move quickly. Be blessed in His holy name, amen.

Part One

The Basics

Y ou will recognize a teachable spirit by what one chooses to skip and how one chooses to hear. How well do you receive correction? Are you willing to change to who God has called you to be or do you cling to who you have made yourself to be?

A person with a hungry spirit will always hunger and thirst for righteousness. They will always make the necessary corrections because it is truth they desire and not self-righteousness.

Proverbs 27:7 says, "The full soul loatheth an honeycomb; but to the hungry soul every bitter thing is sweet."

No matter where you are in your walk toward Jesus, always have a teachable spirit.

CHAPTER ONE
What Brought Me to This Place
A walk in the wilderness

One of my distant relatives wrote a book about a great tragedy in their life. In one of the chapters, she wrote, "Life before and life after." I can relate to that statement, because I have experienced a permanent life altering injury. While my injury is tragic for me, it in no way mirrors her horrible tragedy, as she lost her husband and children in a house fire. What each of our tragedies had in common was that they were permanent, life altering, and they came out of nowhere.

This is my "life before and life after" story, and the fruits of the studies that sustained and saved my life during a time of great pain. By sharing with you, it is my hope that you will relate my story to your life, be sustained, or even that your life will be saved.

Some of the chapters in this book are from a study the Lord had me do in 2000. Some are from my personal writings through the years. Some chapters in this book were sermons preached and lessons taught many years ago. I believe the Lord is using this book to ensure these truths are passed along to the present and future generations. Borrowing my distant relative's statement, "Life before and life after," I am led to share this part of my life with you.

Before the Study: 1996-2000

Before the study, my life was simply "trekking along." When I first began dating Josh, the man who would become my husband, he brought me to an Assembly of God Church. Before that, I had never set foot into any church other than a Catholic church.

Initially sitting in the Assembly of God church, I began to realize there was more to God than what I had thought in the past. I realized how few Scriptures I knew. Until then, I knew only that Jesus was my salvation, and that God had given me a gift, but I did not know what to call it. I certainly did not know what to do it. It became clear to me that it was time for me to grow spiritually. What I did not realize would be the roads God would allow me to go down, and the people I would meet along the way.

As I began to catch on to the "church thing," I started praying certain popular prayers, because it seemed like the in thing to do in church. I would say bold statements such as, "Bring it on, Lord!" or "Devil, you aren't anything!" I began to copy what others were doing in the church **thinking** it was the right thing to do, but **knowing** in my heart it was not.

Today, because of the Lord's refining fire, I know better than to say such statements, or pray prayers just because they are popular. But back then, my heart and my flesh began to do two very different things. My heart was saying, "Hey! No, no, no!" However, my flesh was overriding that and saying, "Yes, yes, yes." I wanted to appear as if I knew what I was doing in church, but I was gaining conviction that this was fakery. Instead of following the Holy Spirit, I was following man's actions so I could fit in at the church.

Ultimately, we ended up leaving that Assembly of God church when a new pastor was hired, with whom we disagreed. For a while after that, we attended a few home fellowships, but attended nothing on a regular basis.

Then life dealt us a shocking jolt of reality. In 1998, my husband's life was suddenly on the line.

It began with a common cold that turned into a condition called Thrombotic Thrombocytopenic Purpura or TTP. There are five risk factors for TTP, and my husband had four of them. (The one risk factor he did not have was that he was not a pregnant female.) From what I understand, his spleen produced a foreign antibody instead of an antibody to fight the cold he caught. This foreign antibody started attacking his blood cells and platelets. This attack on his healthy blood cells and platelets was killing him.

Prior to getting sick, his co-workers were trying to lure my husband back out into the world. He was tempted to go with them to the bars at lunchtime or after work, but God had plans for him. Those plans did not include becoming a drunkard.

Suddenly, one day he experienced flu-like symptoms. After about 6 days of not feeling well, I took him to the doctor. He was told he had the flu and was given the "go home and rest; call me in the morning," diagnosis. Two days later, I was calling an ambulance because he could not form a coherent sentence. The paramedics said he was having mini-ischemia attacks, or MIA's. They took him to St. Luke's Hospital in downtown Houston. It was the Memorial Day holiday weekend.

The Physician's Assistant (PA) doing the work up on Josh came back in and said, "The MRI showed some dementia in the brain, but we are still waiting for the blood work results." They admitted Josh to the hospital, but said he would have to wait until Monday to see a doctor due to the holiday weekend. (A few days later we were told no dementia was found, it was only a shadow on the film.)

My mouth went into overdrive at the thought of losing my husband because some doctor was on holiday. I said to this PA, "You had better start calling some doctors in NOW!" I did not care that they were on vacation; they needed to be there now!

He started making the phone calls because, by that time, Josh's blood work had come back, and they knew it was serious.

After admission, he received his first Plasmapheresis treatment that night. His blood work showed his platelet count to be 3000 when the normal range begins at 150,000. If the treatment did not work, they said there was nothing more they could do for Josh. His dad sat with him that first evening. I had a young son to worry about, and could not stay overnight with Josh. In addition, I could not afford to let the house go to pieces, and felt I needed to keep a balance between home and the hospital. I was glad that his father offered to stay with Josh and was grateful for the help.

Another reason I did not stay that night was that I knew Josh would be okay. Two weeks prior to him getting sick, the Lord had given me a dream about the whole thing. I had to place my trust and faith in God that what He had shown me was that Josh would be okay.

I was never a person to allow anyone to help me, but at that point, I let go and let God and others help me. I dropped everything and stood on complete faith. When we do this, to some, it looks very odd. I was sad and scared, but I knew deep inside that he would be okay, and I just needed to stand still.

I mowed my grass a lot at this time because it kept me from doing what I wanted to do, and kept me focused on what God instructed me to do. Josh had a lot of time alone with God and realized that he was being sifted. He spent 3 weeks in the hospital, and it took 3 months to recover, but as God showed me, God was faithful in doing what He showed me in that dream. Through it all, his doctor told him he could never drink any type of alcohol because having had this condition it would thin the blood. God made sure he kept Josh close to his calling by allowing him to be sifted.

After Josh recovered, we resumed our journey to find a spiritual home by visiting various local churches in our area. We began to recognize a pattern God was working through our lives and learning His voice as we progressed along. Soon, we found ourselves doing home studies instead of attending a regular church service.

In 2000, I began to spend a lot of time alone with God. I would take my son to school, clean my house, and get dinner prepared early. By 9a.m. sharp, I was in the Word and, at times, just in my home alone praising God. I felt God drawing me in, and I was so captive in His presence and plan for me, I became consumed with Him. I did not watch television. I rarely answered the phone. When I was praising God, I could not even hear people knocking on my back door. I hungered for this journey, and deep inside I knew I needed to be faithful and continue on this teachable road.

During this alone time, I began to study the Bride of Christ. In late January 2002, I felt an inner desire to improve my strength, so I began to exercise passionately, driven from deep within. Every day for the next seventeen weeks, with no breaks, I exercised before each Bible study. It took about an hour to do the routine I developed, and the rest of the time, I studied God's Word. Then in June 2002, while walking down my driveway to get my mail, my life changed forever.

Life After the Study: June 2002 to Now

I had exercised for the day, studied, and had dinner cooking. I went out to get the mail, but on the way, my back muscles seized up, stopping me dead in my tracks and barely able to move. The pain was severe. With very slow baby steps, I managed to get back into my house, and went right to the couch. My husband was already on his way home from work and I made a call to my mother, asking her to pick my son up from school.

When my husband got home, I realized that my back was not doing its normal thing. The epidurals I decided to get while in labor caused a bad place in my lower back. If I overworked many days in a row, my lower back would swell and prevent me from being able to stand up straight.

In 1996, in desperate need of a chiropractor, I found Chiropractic Wellness Center in Humble, Texas. Dr. Marvin Watson, his wife and his staff are some of the most caring individuals I have the pleasure of knowing. They truly take the time to get to know who their patients are, a rare thing in the medical world. However, I knew that no amount of chiropractic care would fix what was taking place in my back. This was something completely different from what I had experienced in the past.

When my husband made it home, I asked him if he would help me off the couch, but at that second, his dad showed up and so we prayed over my back. I proclaimed that this injury would not stop me from moving forward in my search for what God wanted me to learn.

Josh met with his dad, and when his dad left, he came over to help me off the couch. That is when I realized that my back was in bad shape. I could hardly move and the pain was almost knocking me out. When I stood up, my left leg curled up a bit and I could not straighten it out. I had to grab Josh's neck and barely scoot along with my right foot. He got me to the bed, and I thought to myself, "Okay God, do your thing! Lord, heal me in the name of Jesus."

As I had learned in church, you leave these journeys in God's hands. For a period, I was just waiting on God to heal me as if I did not need to do anything else but sit and wait for my healing. The victory is only a fraction of our walk with Jesus. Because church focuses so much on that aspect, we fail to recognize when God allows a wilderness walk, to enter into our lives. Therefore, I did what most of us do, pray, sit and wait. God spoke to me a couple of years later about activation. Sitting and waiting for God to move is being idle and not actively walking in faith. It was not until then I realized God was sending me through a wilderness experience. The wilderness is a time of searching ourselves, admitting our faults, repentance and restoration. You will know you are in one if your situation is not progressing toward healing or changing toward a restoration, or both. Self-examination is vital in this part of our walk.

I was laid up in bed for a couple of months and things were not getting better. Josh took me to the doctor on several occasions, but it seemed as if they were clueless as to what was going on with my back. The x-rays showed nothing out of place. They would send me home with a prescription for pain medications and muscle relaxants.

During the course of the first year, my husband's company closed, and we lost our health insurance. I needed insurance, so we applied for state help until he found another job. The doctors on state health insurance pretty much did the same thing with me. They would set me up on a little physical therapy program working with exercise bands, give me more pain medication and send me home.

Thank God, my husband found a job quickly and we soon had regular health insurance again. I was able to find a regular doctor who really tried to figure out what was going on. Her bedside manner was fantastic. I was avoiding getting an MRI like a person avoids the plague because I suffer from panic attacks and anxiety. That stubborn will in me had to be broken and I fought it tooth and nail.

I ended up bedridden for about a year, barely able to do most things I had once done with ease. Getting along anywhere was a huge ordeal. I had to hold onto walls and doorframes to move about my house. My mother took my son to school and in the mornings would come over to cook me breakfast and to make sure I had enough water to drink. There I laid, holding on to the fact that God was going to heal me.

I needed to get an MRI, but I was having total panic and anxiety about it, which prevented me from getting it done. Therefore, I rested on, "God will heal me." I found out a couple of years later is that I had presumptuous faith. It is one thing to believe God can heal you, but it is presumptuous to believe God is going to heal you. **James 2:17 says, "Even so faith, if it hath not works, is dead, being alone."** Faith alone was my error, because the prayer of faith does not presume upon God to heal. It is a prayer that acknowledges that God will be faithful no matter what He chooses for you.

For a time, I saw a new chiropractor because Dr. Watson had moved his office and it was painful for me to drive my car that far. The chiropractor I found practiced Kinesiology. He convinced me I needed an MRI. All he did was curl my toes downward and pain shot through my back like a rocket. I realized that despite my fear of having a panic attack in the MRI machine, I could no longer put it off.

My chiropractor set up an MRI for me in mid-November of 2003. I felt I was coming to the end of myself, literally. The pain was washing over me. My left leg was barely working. I was not sleeping because of the pain and had cramps running up and down my legs and feet. It was a total nightmare. There were times when the pain was so severe that my body would just shake and a wave of fear would just wash over me. I would have to wake Josh up to help me because it was an overpowering feeling of helplessness. My husband would get up, kneel by my bedside, and begin to pray over my entire body. Prayer is powerful! My body would begin to calm down and that terrible spirit of fear would flee. He would climb back into bed and tell me, "Close your eyes. I will watch you until you are sound asleep." I walk up to him from time to time and say, "Thank you for all that you do."

On the Wednesday prior to getting the MRI, I decided to try to take a bath by myself. I filled the tub with water and slowly lowered myself into the water, praying the entire way down. My back locked up, and the levels of pain I felt exceeded every other pain I had ever felt. I yelled for my older teenage son, Carl, to come help me out. I had to get to a hospital and fast. There was no waiting for that Tuesday to roll around (which was about six days away). Carl called Josh to come home from work. He also called my parents to come as well.

Above everything else, I was feeling and going through, I knew deep inside that I had come to the end of myself, literally. I knew that this road was about to change. Josh got home and he called an ambulance, since I could not move, and my body was shaking from the intense pain levels and my mind was racing ninety to nothing, making me feel sick to my stomach. The paramedics put me on a backboard and took me to the hospital.

When I got to the hospital, I ended up getting sick and Josh helped me the entire time, as the nurses handed him some rags and a bedpan. I wanted to go to a restroom, but they would not allow me out of bed. When my stomach settled down, the doctor came in and rolled me to one side, pressed a little on my back, rolled me back on my back and told the nurse to give me a shot to settle down the pain. The doctor gave me more prescriptions and sent me home.

Josh got me home, but he was mad at the hospital staff. The shot they gave me was powerful, and I was able to sleep. It was about 3 a.m. when we got home. Josh needed to leave for work by 6 a.m., and he did. Around 7 a.m., the shot wore off. I was awake and in the same level of pain as I had been in previously. I yelled for my sons, Carl and Steven, to come help me. They called my parents and Josh again. Josh got home and called the ambulance again. Back to the hospital, with siren blaring, my body was shaking in pain, my mind was loopy, and I was trying to fight off the escalating anxiety.

When I arrived, Josh was not there yet. They rolled me into a hallway and I listened to the paramedic talk to the nurse. The paramedic said, "Claims she came here last night due to severe back pain. Was given a shot and sent home." "What? Is she out of her pain meds?" the nurse asked. "No, she was sent home with a new prescription last night."

I was hurting so bad; barely able to move, and could not believe that I was being accused of looking for drugs! The nurse thought I was faking my pain. I cried out for help and asked the nurse to help me. My husband showed up shortly after I arrived.

This is all I can remember because after Josh arrived, I was out of it. I recall being in a bed in the hallway for a long time. They gave me an IV, and the nurse administered pain meds every so often. Josh helped me to the restroom a few times. About 7 p.m., Josh got mad because I simply was not getting help that I needed. He got firm with the doctor and explained to him that I had an MRI set up for the following Tuesday, and I was not going to make it until then. He demanded that they give me one right then, and there. After they realized the insurance had approved an MRI already, things went smoothly. They conducted the MRI. Afterwards I was wheeled right back into the hallway.

A man who had taken one of his family members to the ER was just finishing up with the doctors. Apparently, he had been noticing the lack of care and attention I was getting. He told the nurse that the room he was leaving was to be for me. My husband thanked him for saying that. They put me in that very ER room.

It was not long before the results of my MRI came in. The same nurse that had accused me earlier of just wanting pre-scription drug medication was standing in the doorway. Before the doctor gave the results to my husband, I looked up at the nurse to make sure she would be listening. The doctor told my husband I would not be going home because the MRI showed a severe back injury. I laid my head back down and do not recall anything after that.

I woke up the next morning in my room on the third floor. I was extremely loopy from the drugs I had been given. When the nurse came in, I asked if a doctor would be seeing me today.

She said yes, that an orthopedic doctor would be seeing me later that day.

In walked Dr. J, an orthopedic surgeon, with my MRI films. He pointed out my injury, while explaining to me the course of action he would take. He had a sense of humor about him that made me feel at ease in light of everything going on. My parents were now in the room, and my mother had a ton of questions for him. She wanted to know why I had not received better care up to that point. He could not answer that, but explained my injury to all of us. All I wanted to know from him was if my back would ever be the same. His answer was not a surprise, but he said, no.

Okay the mission was on. When he said the word no, I let it bounce right off me. I refused to let it penetrate into my heart and get into my inner being. It was off limits. For the next five days, I was given IV drug medication every four hours and steroids. By the fifth day, they brought on a pain management doctor who thought a steroid injection might help. They took me to the surgical wing, and gave me two of the most painful shots I had ever endured. They did not help, even making my condition a little worse.

Dr. J no longer operated on backs, so he referred me to Dr. S, a doctor out of The Woodlands, Texas. I spent three more days in the hospital with Dr. J because they did not want me to go home before my surgery. He ended up releasing me a couple of days before, if I promised to take it easy. I laughed because I had no choice. My husband and parents were there, and he told them that he has seen this type of injury bring grown men to their knees. He was amazed that I could laugh and get along like I did. He did not realize that I had God on my side. Even though I was in pain and could barely use my left leg, my Creator was sustaining me. I had to place all I was going through in His hands, and I did.

They released me from the hospital on December 15, 2003. They admitted me to The Woodlands Hospital on December

17, 2003 for major back surgery. I met Dr. S on the same day of my surgery — never before. Talk about having trust and faith in God! I had to, as there was no other option. He was a nice man, and it appeared he knew his business. I knew I was safe as they took me into the operating room because I felt the Lord's presence with me. They were doing their best to put me at ease and trying to make me smile. Right before I went under, the anesthesiologist said, "Okay, the good stuff is going on board." I looked up and said, "Jesus, I am in your hands."

Next thing I knew I was waking up in the recovery area with a nurse by my side. I wanted to go back to sleep. The area on my back I had surgery on was hurting and I was very uncomfortable. I was so thirsty, my mouth felt like I had been licking the lint screen in my dryer. I tried to move, and the nurse stopped me, telling me to lie still. I asked about Josh, and she said she would get him in a little while. I asked for some water, but given only a wet rag to moisten my lips.

Around 9:30 p.m., Josh came back to see me and told me he had been praying for me the whole time. He grabbed my hand and told me everything would be okay. The doctor came by to see me. He said my back was in bad shape, so the surgery took longer than he expected. I asked him if there had been any treatment option besides surgery. He said, "No." A room finally opened up for me. My room seemed miles away from the recovery area. I wondered if we would ever get there.

I told Josh to go home and get some rest. We live a good drive away from The Woodlands, so I told him to call me every day, but he did not need to come see me. I knew he would be tired and I did not want him to have to drive all the way out there after work. If I needed him, I knew I could call him, and he would be there.

I woke up the next day with a breakfast waiting for me. I was super hungry. I tried to move around a bit, but I was in pain. The nurse came in to help me out and told me that a physical therapist would be coming by to see me. They also had a rack that ran the length of my bed that had a rectangular pull bar for me to help pull myself up. I asked if I could get out of bed, and she said I could, but to move very slowly. That is when I realized my left leg was not working with me. She helped me to the restroom, and then back to bed. I ate breakfast, then lunch and right before dinner, the physical therapist came in and explained what would take place the next day.

My doctor came in right after dinner and explained a little bit more about what he had found in my back. My L4/5 disc was herniated as well as my S1 disc, which was severely herniated, and had been compressing my spinal column along with the nerve roots. The opening in my lumbar spine was also very narrow so he had to open it up more by removing some bone. Overall, he said my back was a mess. (I later learned from a cousin, himself waiting for back surgery, that the narrow lumbar spine is a genetic thing in our family.)

When I filled out the paperwork prior to being admitted into The Woodlands Hospital, I placed a check mark by no, asking if I wanted a member of clergy to visit me. I chose no because I did not know who would be coming in. On my second day, I was eating breakfast when a member of the clergy came into my room. He was a Catholic priest. I was a bit surprised because I had checked, no.

I set my breakfast aside and we began to chat. He asked me if I needed prayer and I said, "I can always use prayer." Before he started to pray, I felt the Holy Spirit begin to move and my mouth began to speak, but it was not me speaking. I cannot recall all that I said, only that God had me here for a purpose, and Christ was walking me through it. My body is hurt and injured, but my spirit is not.

I cannot say how long I talked but I can remember what his reaction was. He stood there and listened to the Holy Spirit minister to him through me and he said, "I pray that I have faith like that one day." He prayed for me and left quietly. I knew from the past moves of the Holy Spirit that when He moves you can have a hard time recalling what came out of your mouth because it is not you speaking.

The Physical Therapist (PT) came in later that day to start physical therapy. It consisted of me trying to regain use of my left leg. I could barely put one foot in front of the other. I felt as if I was learning how to walk all over again. He placed a strap around my waist and held the other end so he could stop me if I began to fall. I spent 3 days in the hospital before being released to recover at home.

I thought part of my journey would be over and my life would be back to normal. I learned at my first check up after surgery that life would never go back to what my normal had been. God wants us moving forward in a constant learning phase. I was keenly aware of that, but I wanted my back, well, back. Dr. S checked my reflexes and said I would probably never get them back. I said, "Nope, my God is bigger than that." I went in for my next check up, and still no reflexes. I told my doc, "Nope just wait, God is not through." At my next check up, my reflexes were back, but weak and "backwards." I laughed at this, saying, "God's sense of humor." God was reminding me that He did not want me to go backwards.

At my next checkup and the appointment to get my staples out, my reflexes had turned around and though weak, they were back. With my staples out and my reflexes back, I walked out of there thinking, "Okay, what now?" We walked outside of the doctor's office and I said, "Okay, that's over, lets move on."

It took me a year to recover, and though my back is still a mess, I fully expect God will heal me when He gets ready to do that, if that is His choice to do so. I have gone through physical therapy many times through the years and have to manage pain with pain medication still to this day. I am slow in my movements, but I am moving forward.

I have a fantastic primary care doctor now, Dr. P. She genuinely cares for each of her patients, and takes the time to listen. I thank God for sending her into my life to care for my injured back, and to help me through my panic attacks and anxiety issues. Though driving even short distances is uncomfortable for me, I was able to go back to the Chiropractic Wellness Center. Though probably not as often as Dr. Watson would prefer.

I shared my story with you to get to this main point—If I had not been sustained by the Word of God and the revelations God had given in the two years leading up to this injury, I know full well, I would not have made it through. I want to share all that God shared with me through those two years and beyond. Since 2002 I have enjoyed many teachable moments that quenched the barren desert of lack, and grew within me, the understanding of "why?"

> **[34]And when he had called the people unto him with his disciples also, he said unto them, Whosoever will come after me, let him deny himself, and take up his cross, and follow me. [35]For whosoever will save his life shall lose it; but whosoever shall lose his life for my sake and the gospel's, the same shall save it. (Mark 8:34-35)**

Do I understand all that Scripture has to offer? No, we will never know all things Scripture offers until we are with Jesus in Heaven. We can know enough to qualify to share what He has done for us. I can say I am thankful for what I have gone through because through it all, He has never left my side and He has taught me so much more than I could have ever imagined.

I realize now, that yes, God answered many of my prayers through these experiences. One of my main prayers was, "Lord, I want You to talk to me in the same manner You spoke to Moses." As a little girl, I used to pray, "Lord I want to be on the front lines with You." For those who do not see the parallel, "I had to be removed before God could use me." I can no longer ask God, "God, why did you allow this to happen to me?" I know why now, and I love Him so much more for it. For this very reason, I understand now the full ramifications of what the power of prayer truly means. Praying constitutes movement in the heavens in a magnitude one could never imagine. Remember, God's thoughts are not our thoughts. This is one giant key to grasp!

As I write this part of my testimony, I admit that I still hold onto some residual anger. It is an honest admission and being able to admit it is the first step in walking into your healing. In the beginning, I directed my anger toward God because I lacked understanding of what God was doing with me. I questioned Him intensely on how He could allow such a terrible thing to enter my life. After all, I had immersed myself in His Word. Those understandings came slowly, but they came. I can praise God and thank Him for sending me through such a trial because without it, I would have missed what He called me to do. If I had done it, in my timing, it would not have been from Him.

My residual anger centers on my inability to move around freely as I used to do, and on having to endure days and nights of pain in my legs and back. At one time, I was so angry with God that the enemy had me believing that if I let this anger go, my injury would become permanent. The thing that really drove the anger nail in was the enemy sending people into my life who attempted to tie me up in grief and anger. I adopted this useful credo into my life, "You don't have to entertain every argument you're invited to."

Anger had blocked me from accomplishing God's call in my life. I came to believe that the lie of permanent injury was wrong, and I began to cover it with the truth of what God's Word says. My father says, "God is large and in charge!" He tells me, "All the way to the grave, Pamela, follow Jesus all the way to the grave!" Amen! I thank God for my parents and the prayers they have sent up on my behalf.

If you seek God, you will find Him. You cannot imagine the roads God will take you on to mold you to into readiness for His service. (Just ask Moses, Noah, or Abraham!) God works in the lives of all believers the same way, the trials and tribulations are just different.

Moses had a speech impediment. Did God heal Moses? No, he sent his brother Aaron to help him speak. Will God choose to heal me? Only He knows, but He has sent me an aide as well, the Holy Spirit, to help me on the path God has set for me. Praise God and all glory to Him, amen.

CHAPTER TWO
How Many Squares Do You See?

Proverbs 18:13 He that answereth a matter before he
heareth it, it is folly and shame unto him.

I prayed and asked the Lord to show me how He would have me teach a person who remains in a justified relationship with Him. I asked Him how I could spark others into realizing just how much more there is to Him if they were to move with Christ, into a sanctified relationship with God. God put in me a desire to share with others just how rich His Word truly is, and that when they seek it out and allow Him to reveal Himself to them, just how much there is waiting for them as a mature seeker. It was not long before God answered my prayer, because about two weeks later, He showed me. Not only did He show me, but He taught me something as well.

Count the squares and place the number you see in the blank _____.

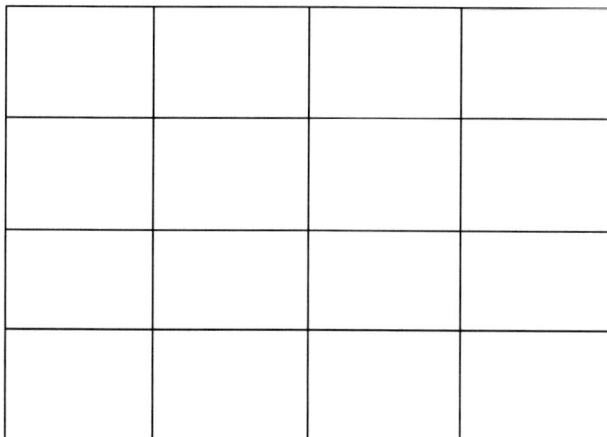

When I first took this test, I said, "There are 17 squares." I counted all the squares I could see on the *surface* but failed to dig deeper to see that there are actually thirty squares. If I would have taken the time to dig a little deeper I would have seen that, but I was quick to reply with what I thought was the correct answer.

This exercise illustrates what this book is all about—it is all about the dig. That is, digging and seeking for the real gems that is in God's Word. Digging is the key to developing one's relationship with Christ. We must go beneath the surface of what we read, to uncover not just what it says, but what it means. The Word tells us in **Isaiah 40:31, "But they that wait upon the LORD shall renew their strength; they shall mount up with wings as eagles; they shall run, and not be weary; and they shall walk, and not faint."**

The digging exercise gave me a renewed meaning to that scripture in Isaiah 40:31. There is so much more to find in God's Word than what we see on the surface. If we grab our shovel and keep digging in the text, studying it, seeking Him out in spirit and truth, and do not faint or grow weary, God will be faithful and reveal Himself to us through His Word. God will begin to open up the deeper truths to us as we allow ourselves to go through the sanctification process. Sanctification is the important next step in our relationship with Christ, after salvation.

There are so many people sitting in the pews who never grasp the importance of sanctification. Those who overcome and become part of the Bride of Christ receive their rewards. But the price of being part of the Bride requires us to take that walk of dying to ourselves and allowing Christ to mature us. Sanctification is God molding us into who He has planned us to be.

Before continuing, I want to pray for you. I know some readers are tempted to skip over prayers written in a book, but I ask that you take the time to read this prayer.

Father, I thank You for hearing my prayer as I lift up the reader in the name of Jesus. Father, You are a merciful God, a God of great glory, strength, and power. I ask you to prepare the reader for the journey that lies ahead of them. I ask that you show them mercy and grace as they begin to walk in this race to get to know more of You. Father, as they seek you in spirit and truth, I ask that as trials and tribulations come upon them, that they understand that this is part of the process of dying to self, meant to make them more mature in You. Remind them when they grow weary that these tribulations come about as a part of their walk. Remind them of those who walked in the wilderness. Remind them that You will not give them more than they can handle and that You will supply all their needs. Father I ask that as the reader begins on the path that the blessings and richness of Your Word will begin to fill their heart and their mind with Your presence. Saturate them in You Lord, in Jesus name I pray and ask, Amen.

How to Judge Truth from Error
Seven ways to judge truth: earthly wisdom versus heavenly wisdom.

Knowing how to dig is one thing, knowing how to judge truth from error correctly is another. Discerning truth from error is a vital weapon in your spiritual war chest. One could make the Bible say anything one wants it to say. Gaining an understanding of biblical symbolism, types and shadows in their respective contexts, and more can allay such false thinking. It is very helpful if one has a spiritual hunger as well as an intellectual quest to study God's Word effectively.

An intellectual quest alone will see apparent contradictions which spiritual hunger can resolve. Spiritual hunger implies that a person has a heart for God and His righteousness. The power of the Holy Spirit in one's life can enlighten the understanding, in a life-giving way that exceeds mere intellectual comprehension, however helpful that may be.

[17]But the wisdom that is from above is first pure, then peaceable, gentle, and easy to be intreated, full of mercy and good fruits, without partiality, and without hypocrisy. [18]And the fruit of righteousness is sown in peace of them that make peace. (James 3:17-18)

James 3:17-18 contains seven requirements for any concept or precept to be regarded as truth: "But the wisdom that is from above is first pure, then peaceable, gentle, and easy to be intreated, full of mercy and good fruits, without partiality, and without hypocrisy."

Wisdom that is from above is:

1) **PURE** When a concept is pure, it is completely consistent with all other truths and precepts. There will be no contradictions. The Holy Spirit can witness to one's own *spirit* when a symbolism, type or shadow illustrates a truth. (The *spirit* is the new creature or creation in Christ Jesus, 2 Corinthians 5:17.)

Romans 8:16 says, "The Spirit itself beareth witness with our spirit, that we are the children of God."

2) PEACEABLE The first thing we experience as a newborn Christian is peace. Romans 5:1 states, "Therefore being justified by faith, we have peace with God through our Lord Jesus Christ." Having peace about any truth is a normal characteristic of a precept. Any concept that leaves one out of rest, wondering how something is supposed to fit with other truths, or otherwise causes confusion, is incorrect most likely.

3) GENTLE God is a gentleman. He does not force Himself on anyone. He has given man freewill, which He will not violate. For example, if you pray for patience, do not be surprised if God causes a "circumstance" that will require you to be patient or practice patience. God is waiting for us to choose Him and His righteousness voluntarily. Consider the case of a person who is in rebellion against God. When a godly person is praying for them, God knows how to rearrange circumstances in such a way that the rebel will find it very helpful to call on God for help. We have preconceived ideas of how God answers prayer. We must forsake those and use the Bible as our guide to see how God worked in the lives of the men and women in its pages.

4) EASY TO BE INTREATED When questioned, truth is not offended. Truth makes no defense and brings peace and rest. One should not present concepts in a defensive manner. Truth is uncovered with interrogatives designed to either prove or expose it. A truth will not contradict other truths. If a person presenting a false concept becomes offended when questioned, that offensive mannerism exposes the bad spirit connected to the concept. Use wisdom and discernment to determine this.

5) FULL OF MERCY AND GOOD FRUITS God knows we are but dust and that we are born with a sinful nature. We are capable of sinning at any time, especially when we least expect to do so. When we do so, we need mercy. God desires that we build up His good fruits in our lives to guard against the wiles and schemes of the devil that will try to trip us up. The purpose of truth is to increase our faith and understanding of God and His righteousness. One list of good fruits is Galatians 5:22-23, "But the fruit of the Spirit is love, joy, peace, long-suffering, gentleness, goodness, faith, meekness, temperance: against such there is no law."

6) WITHOUT PARTIALITY Truth has no favorites. There is no favoritism toward any person or group at the expense of another person or group. Wisdom is fair to all and is for spiritual building up.

7) WITHOUT HYPOCRISY Truth does not say one thing and then do the opposite. This is a theatrical term. The hypocrites were the actors in theaters Bible, Greek and Roman times. An actor portrayed someone or something that he or she was not. When we look at the covers of magazines at the checkout counters of our supermarkets, we can certainly see photos of people who need to stop acting as if they are living, and start living for real. Jesus can and will help them do this if they submit themselves to Him and admit sin.

Concerning *actions* and *deeds*, we must always ask ourselves, will it draw us to the mercy of Christ or put us under someone's control? If anything is true, it will pass the seven principles in **James 3:17-18.** Weigh things out and measure them against James 3:17-18. Toss out those things that do not line up to it. As we do this, the character of Christ will begin to build in us, as will our ability to discern properly the truth contained within God's Word.

¹²Unto whom it was revealed, that not unto themselves, but unto us they did minister the things, which are now reported unto you by them that have preached the gospel unto you with the Holy Ghost sent down from heaven; which things the angels desire to look into. ¹³Wherefore gird up the loins of your mind, be

sober, and hope to the end for the grace that is to be brought unto you at the revelation of Jesus Christ. (1 Peter 1:12-13)

Reading about people in the Bible who went through difficult or tricky situations has given me tremendous understanding of spiritual truth. Witnessing their walk is a valuable key that unlocks powerful understanding. For the longest time, I could never grasp why Job went through such a terrible ordeal. Finally, I realized that he was locked in the "me, myself, and I" syndrome. Seeing God tumble Job because of it, gave me the most insight of all.

CHAPTER THREE

FOUNDATION

Proverbs 24:3, "Through wisdom is an house builded;
and by understanding it is established."

W hen a builder builds a home, he must first construct a solid foundation. If not, when the first strong storm *(trial and tribulation)* hits that house *(person),* that home will crumble and fall to the ground or show signs of great damage. Therefore, before the building can begin, that builder must first clear all the underbrush off the land, so he has a clean slate to build upon.

God's Word leads us into foundation building as well. It gives us the tools to build our home (our body, our vessel) into a living testimony of Christ Jesus. In turn, if we take the journey in building a relationship with Jesus Christ, our life will become a light to the lost world. By allowing Jesus to build us, we will become equipped to bring the gospel to the entire world. This great commission is no different from what Jesus Christ did while He was with us in the flesh, and He is our example to follow.

Some churches fail to teach the importance of building a solid foundation in Jesus Christ, or even the fact that Jesus Christ is our foundation. Yes, they preach that Jesus is our Lord and Savior, but when it comes to foundation, little to nothing. Because of this, there are many in the Body of Christ that believe one must be saved repeatedly, which is simply not true.

After we are saved, who is our foundation? The Scriptures show that Jesus is the foundation upon which we, as Christians, must build. A great start to building this foundation is by reading His Word and seeking Him. We choose to allow Jesus to build us by dying to our flesh daily and allowing more of Him to live through us. He will build us up if we allow Him to do so. Often we must get out of His way because He knows what we need more than we do.

The more we seek His Word in spirit and truth, the more we will begin to understand what to do for God and how to respond to Him. The scriptures offering the most evidence of Who our foundation is can be found in:

> **For other <u>foundation</u> can no man lay than that is laid, <u>which is Jesus Christ</u>. (1 Corinthians 3:11)**
>
> **From the end of the earth will I cry unto thee, when my heart is overwhelmed: lead me to the rock that is higher than I. (Psalm 61:2)**
>
> **He only is my rock and my salvation; he is my defense; I shall not be greatly moved. (Psalm 62:2)**
>
> **Except the LORD build the house, they labour in vain that build it: except the LORD keep the city, the watchman waketh but in vain. (Psalm 127:1)**
>
> **[47]Whosoever cometh to me, and heareth my sayings, and doeth them, I will shew you to whom he is like: [48]He is like a man which built an house, and digged deep, and laid the foundation on a rock: and when the flood arose, the stream beat vehemently upon that house, and could not shake it: for it was founded upon a rock. (Luke 6:47-48)**
>
> **And we know that the Son of God is come, and hath given us an understanding, that we may know**

him that is true, and we are in him that is true, even in his Son Jesus Christ. This is the true God, and eternal life. (1 John 5:20)

One can rest assured of these things because God knows all things. Psalm 147:5, "Great is our Lord, and of great power: his understanding is infinite."

Right from the beginning, a babe in Christ must grasp this building block. In the Scriptures, Jesus is referred to as the "Chief Corner Stone" as seen in this passage:

⁵Ye also, as lively stones, are built up a spiritual house, an holy priesthood, to offer up spiritual sacrifices, acceptable to God by Jesus Christ. ⁶Wherefore also it is contained in the scripture, Behold, I lay in Sion a chief corner stone, elect, precious: and he that believeth on him shall not be confounded. (1 Peter 2:5-6)

Who, What, When, and Where

What do we do? How do we build? What are our tools? Speaking to the believer I would say, "That's your choice." Speaking to a non-believer I would say, "That's your choice." Why the same answer for both? When God created us, He gave us a gift called **"freewill."** This simply means "free choice."

Even though God created us to have a relationship with Him, He designed this relationship based on choice and love, not force. He loves us so much that He allows us to choose whether we want to build a relationship with Him or not. For the believer, **Matthew 13:3-9,** quoted below is for you. It serves as your "growth chart," for building your relationship with Jesus, and is based entirely on what you choose to do. By, "what you choose to do," I am only speaking about building your relationship. Later on in the chapter I give five Greek words that show the growth progression for all those who go on to become mature in Christ.

> **³And he spake many things unto them in parables, saying, Behold, a sower went forth to sow; ⁴And when he sowed, some seeds fell by the way side, and the fowls came and devoured them up: ⁵Some fell upon stony places, where they had not much earth: and forthwith they sprung up, because they had no deepness of earth: ⁶And when the sun was up, they were scorched; and because they had no root, they withered away. ⁷And some fell among thorns; and the thorns sprung up, and choked them: ⁸But other fell into good ground, and brought forth fruit, some an hundredfold, some sixtyfold, some thirtyfold. ⁹Who hath ears to hear, let him hear. (Matthew 13:3-9)**

God's Word teaches us that there are three types of ground and each produces a different level of growth in the believer. You determine that level of growth by what you choose to do. The first ground spoken about, in verse four, is that upon which the seed fell "by the way side" and birds came and devoured the seed up. If one chooses to walk upon this ground, absolutely no growth will take place in that believer. Though they are justified before the Lord Jesus Christ, they will experience lack in heaven by not receiving their full rewards.

The second ground, spoken of in verses 5-7, states that some seed fell upon "stony places," where there was not much earth. They sprang up, but because of the believer's lack of foundation and understanding, the sun scorched them, and because they had no root, they withered. Some even fell amongst thorns, which choked them off. This type of believer knows some of what God's Word speaks, but lacks in understanding it. Due to the lack of understanding, they do not allow God's Word to penetrate their hearts leaving them unable to grow into a deeper relationship with Him. They are justified before the Lord but they will not receive their full reward in heaven.

The third ground spoken about in verse eight states that some seed fell onto good ground and brought forth fruit, "some an hundredfold, some sixtyfold, some thirtyfold." Good ground is perfect for a solid foundation. Now we are getting somewhere in building our relationship with Jesus Christ. Unfortunately, in too many churches, people learn that this ground means money, cars, homes and a luxury lifestyle.

Here is what the Word says about treasures:

[19]Lay not up for yourselves treasures upon earth, where moth and rust doth corrupt, and where thieves break through and steal: [20]But lay up for yourselves treasures in heaven, where neither moth nor rust doth corrupt, and where thieves do not break through nor steal. (Matthew 6:19-20)

Before proceeding, it is important to cite a few scriptures about "sustaining":

But seek ye first the kingdom of God, and his righteousness; and all these things shall be added unto you. (Matthew 6:33)

Cast thy burden upon the LORD, and he shall sustain thee: he shall never suffer the righteous to be moved. (Psalms 55:22)

Put all those Scriptures together to paint the bigger picture here and what will one see? How well does that picture fit with the idea of "prosperity preaching"—that God will give you a car, home, money? Did Jesus go around preaching that type of message? No, but these types of messages have infected some churches for far too long. This teaching led people to seek after God as if He was some type of lotto ticket and they were waiting in the pews for their jackpot to hit.

God is not a God who gives out worldly treasures to keep us focused on keeping up with the Jones' or chasing the American dream. I have spoken with many people who are turned off toward God because of the luxury car the pastor drives, or the luxury home he lives in, and by how dressed up and over the top some people get when going to church. These people look around at a community that is sick, poor, and hungry and it makes no sense to them. One important thing to grasp is that, as believers in Jesus Christ, we must never make our brother stumble.

> **[1]Then said he unto the disciples, It is impossible but that offences will come: but woe unto him, through whom they come! [2]It were better for him that a millstone were hanged about his neck, and he cast into the sea, than that he should offend one of these little ones. (Luke 17:1-2)**

I have an idea where this wrong thinking came from and how the enemy uses pastors to mix this belief system in with the real message the Lord intends the flock to hear. This account is of what Jesus experienced when he fasted forty days and nights.

> **[8]Again, the devil taketh him up into an exceeding high mountain, and sheweth him all the kingdoms of the world, and the glory of them; [9]And saith unto him, All these things will I give thee, if thou wilt fall down and worship me. [10]Then saith Jesus unto him, Get thee hence, Satan: for it is written, Thou shalt worship the Lord thy God, and him only shalt thou serve. [11]Then the devil leaveth him, and, behold,**

angels came and ministered unto him. (Matthew 4:8-11)

Jesus was in a vulnerable state. He had not eaten and he was weary. The devil tempted Him with food and tried to trick Him. By the third temptation, the devil tempted Jesus with the riches of this world, those things that rot, which are not eternal. Jesus rebuked the devil once again and spoke the key words here: *"Thou shalt worship the Lord thy God and him only shalt thou serve."*

Will God bless you? Yes. One must understand the proper context of what God's Word promises the believer. One must ask, "What are the treasures I am truly seeking?" The riches God promises are the knowledge and understanding of His Word and the treasures He has stored up for us in heaven.

While we are on earth, if we are seeking Him and casting all our cares upon Him, He will sustain us while we are here. A great example of God's sustenance is in the account of the Israelites in the wilderness as documented in the book of Exodus. There was a reason the tabernacle was erected in the wilderness *after* the Israelites were released from bondage, but not *before* they entered the Promised Land (Exodus 40).

Abundance comes with truth and maturity. **Before** Jesus began to preach, He fasted for forty days, during which, the devil tempted Him. Today we see the preacher as if he is the sole leader of the church. There is an important connection here between Jesus being tempted and passing the criteria **before** He went into His preaching ministry rather than man just appointing Him to preach. We hear far too often of preachers who have fallen due to the temptations that seem to surround their calling. Jesus was the example for all preachers and believers (Matthew 4).

What happened to those Israelites who did not trust in God while wandering in the wilderness? Complaints, murmuring and gossip caused sickness and even death upon those Israelites who participated in it. Due to this lack of trust in God, complaining, and murmuring, whole generations of Israelites did not reach the Promised Land. This is huge! Always give God all the thanks and praise Him for all things you receive because He is the one who allows you to have it.

And we know that all things work together for good to them that love God, to them who are the called according to his purpose. (Romans 8:28)

Be careful for nothing; but in every thing by prayer and supplication with thanksgiving let your requests be made known unto God. (Philippians 4:6)

Now back to the soils in Matthew 13:8, and those who "hear" God's voice. Those who grasp His Word and allow it to sanctify them will become mature in Christ. They allow God to use them as He tills the ground through them and He sends them out to co-labor with Christ. They spread the gospel of Jesus Christ and are concerned only with receiving God's truth. Amen.

Here is a list that will you show the progression of those who believe in Jesus Christ. Can you spot where you may be?

The Steps of Maturity in Jesus Christ

Growth Progression: The Greek Words of Growth

1. **NEPIOS**: Means "Babe in Christ," akin to birth through two years old.

¹²For when for the time ye ought to be teachers, ye have need that one teach you again which be the first principles of the oracles of God; and are become such as have need of milk, and not of strong meat. ¹³For

every one that useth milk is unskilful in the word of righteousness: for he is a babe. (Hebrews 5:12-13)

A *NEPIOS* will operate in his own intellectual understanding. He is focused on himself and his needs. A *NEPIOS* cannot be expected to perform as a mature person, though the Lord can quicken someone in the Spirit to do things beyond their maturity, if He so chooses. Most important: Once a *NEPIOS* recognizes that it's not through his own strength, then he begins to mature.

2. PAIDION: A *PAIDION* goes back and forth between the carnal mind and the spiritual mind.

> **Therefore leaving the principles of the doctrine of Christ, let us go on unto perfection; not laying again the foundation of repentance from dead works, and of faith toward God. (Hebrews 6:1)**
> **But if ye bite and devour one another, take heed that ye be not consumed one of another. 16 This I say then, Walk in the Spirit, and ye shall not fulfill the lust of the flesh. (Galatians 5:15,16)**

In this stage, one still lives in the flesh. Galatians 5:19-21 lists seventeen works of the flesh, while Galatians 5:22-23 lists nine fruits of the spirit. At the *PAIDION* stage, the person operates primarily in the realm of intellectual understanding (legalism), but is capable of some spiritual understanding. The flesh can run rampant in this stage if it is not recognized and countered with self-control. The person at this stage can recognize how to resist the enemy, which requires discipline.

3. TEKNON: In this stage, the flesh expresses itself and one must learn to crucify it. Do not think in terms of the flesh. Some things we do cannot be undone. Esau, even though he cried out with tears, gave his birthright to Jacob. We gain and lose in our sanctification, not our justification.

⁵And ye have forgotten the exhortation which speaketh unto you as unto children, My son, despise not thou the chastening of the Lord, nor faint when thou art rebuked of him: ⁶For whom the Lord loveth he chasteneth, and scourgeth every son whom he receiveth. ⁷If ye endure chastening, God dealeth with you as with sons; for what son is he whom the father chasteneth not? ⁸But if ye be without chastisement, whereof all are partakers, then are ye bastards, and not sons. ⁹Furthermore we have had fathers of our flesh which corrected us, and we gave them reverence: shall we not much rather be in subjection unto the Father of spirits, and live? ¹⁰For they verily for a few days chastened us after their own pleasure; but he for our profit, that we might be partakers of his holiness. ¹¹Now no chastening for the present seemeth to be joyous, but grievous: nevertheless afterward it yieldeth the peaceable fruit of righteousness unto them which are exercised thereby. ¹²Wherefore lift up the hands which hang down, and the feeble knees; ¹³And make straight paths for your feet, lest that which is lame be turned out of the way; but let it rather be healed. ¹⁴Follow peace with all men, and holiness, without which no man shall see the Lord: ¹⁵Looking diligently lest any man fail of the grace of God; lest any root of bitterness springing up trouble you, and thereby many be defiled; ¹⁶Lest there be any fornicator, or profane person, as Esau, who for one morsel of meat sold his birthright. ¹⁷For ye know how that afterward, when he would have inherited the blessing, he was rejected: for he found no place

of repentance, though he sought it carefully with tears. (Hebrews 12: 5-16, 17)
[14]That we henceforth be no more children, tossed to and fro, and carried about with every wind of doctrine, by the sleight of men, and cunning craftiness, whereby they lie in wait to deceive; [15]But speaking the truth in love, may grow up into him in all things, which is the head, even Christ. (Ephesians 4:14-15)

As long as one is like a child and immature spiritually, they will believe every doctrine that comes along. You seek out the truth; do not just take man's word for it. It is your relationship so you must build it. You build this relationship by maintaining a solid prayer life, seeking God daily, reading, studying, and "rightly dividing" God's Word. If you were married, would you trust someone else to build your marriage? Of course not! Your marriage is between you and your spouse and you both must nurture it together. Most often, we draw our examples from our parents but we are to draw our example from Jesus Christ.

[1]Be ye therefore followers of God, as dear children; [2]And walk in love, as Christ also hath loved us, and hath given himself for us an offering and a sacrifice to God for a sweet smelling savour. (Ephesians 5:1-2)

We are to be childlike but not childish. Being "childlike" is being humble, able to receive, and teachable. Being childish is being all about me, me, me, concerned only about oneself. The childish person thinks he knows it all already and tends to be legalistic. A person with childish behavior cannot admit faults, mistakes and are prone to blame others. They fail to see their own fault and do not typically take responsibility for their attitudes and actions.

4. HUIOS (pronounced "WE'OSS"): We ask the Lord what we are to do and He leads us. We have to come to a place of leaning on the Lord and His revelation and not of our own understanding. The whole Bible brings us into this maturity where we are able to study the more complicated things of the Word.

[14]But strong meat belongeth to them that are of full age, even those who by reason of use have their senses exercised to discern both good and evil. (Hebrews 5:14)
[14]For as many as are led by the Spirit of God, they are the sons of God. [15]For ye have not received the spirit of bondage again to fear; but ye have received the Spirit of adoption, whereby we cry, Abba, Father. (Romans 8:14-15)

5. PATER (pronounced "pot-T-air"): *PATER* is the most wonderful of the five words reviewed in this section. The *PATER* is the person who reveals spiritual understanding, AMEN! A spiritual father is only concerned about the spiritual needs of those around them. A spiritual father is about others and not about "me, me, and me." A *PATER* is **selfless** not selfish.

The Bible says, "For though ye have ten thousand instructers in Christ, yet have ye not many fathers: for in Christ Jesus I have begotten you through the gospel." (1 Corinthians 4:15)

Reach for Matthew 13:8 and be the good ground that enjoys multilevel harvests of understanding and growth! AMEN!

CHAPTER FOUR
Justification

It is not a process that needs to be done repeatedly!

⟨⟩

The focus of this chapter is *justification*. How can one receive it? Can one lose it once one has received it? Are we "once saved, always saved"? What does it mean to be justified?

The Bible says the Lord, **"is become my salvation"** (Exodus 15:2) This is the simple key to unlocking what justification is and gives merit to the OSAS view (**Once Saved Always Saved**). Salvation is a one-step, done deal. Most of our churches end the relationship growth right here, unfortunately. They never go on to the next step, which is teaching and leading people into sanctification. (Sanctification is the focus of another chapter.) This is where Matthew 13:4 comes in, as once the altar call is over, most people just end up sitting in the pew, service after service, never applying Scripture to their lives.

In Exodus 15:2, the Bible says, "The LORD is my strength and song, and he is become my salvation: he is my God, and I will prepare him an habitation; my father's God, and I will exalt him." When we are saved, the LORD becomes our salvation. Not only is He our salvation, but He is also your strength.

If you are a believer, you are already justified. If you are not a believer, justification is the proper way of saying, "I am saved." How am I justified? There is only one way you may receive salvation. If you are not a believer, this scripture is for you:

For God so loved the world, that he gave his only begotten Son, that whosoever believeth in him should not perish, but have everlasting life. (John 3:16)

That is it! God so loved the world that He gave his only begotten Son, that whosoever believeth in Him should not perish, but have everlasting life. The key is what you choose to believe, by faith, and if you choose, in your heart, with all sincerity, that Jesus died on the cross for you so that you would be forgiven of all your sins. By accepting Him into your heart, you are saved. You are justified.

You must receive the Word by faith. If you do not, you will not understand it correctly, if at all. The Bible is not a cafeteria line; one does not get to select some parts to live by and ignore others. We must "eat" the whole Word, not just the parts we want to live by. If you chose to accept the Lord as your Savior, your salvation is assured, and you are now justified before the Lord.

God has given everyone a "mustard seed" of faith. If you can believe in John 3:16, and accept that as truth, you are now saved. Though, you must activate that belief with faith. **Luke 17:6 says, "And the Lord said, If ye had faith as a grain of mustard seed, ye might say unto this sycamine tree, Be thou plucked up by the root, and be thou planted in the sea; and it should obey you."** Your relationship with God grows, by what you choose to do.

Your foundation is now set into place and your dwelling place (your body) is now ready to serve Christ. In First Corinthians 3:11, the Bible says, "For other <u>foundation</u> can no man lay than that is laid, <u>which is Jesus Christ.</u>"

If you are an unbeliever and you still need clarity on what you must do to become a Christian, here is a simple action plan:

1.) **Admit you are a sinner.** All you need to do is truly recognize this fact and tell Jesus, "I am a sinner." When you truly feel this in your heart, you will begin to feel emotions rising up which is okay. You may even feel ashamed of some of the things you may have done. Later chapters are going to be important for you to know and understand. Do not allow the devil to get you caught up in condemnation. What you are feeling when you truly do this is conviction. Conviction is the proper response to the realization that one is a sinner, but the devil will try to trick you into feeling condemned. You are no longer condemned because your life now belongs to the Lord.

2.) **Be willing to turn from your sins and truly repent when you sin.** Remember, no sin is too big. Jesus died on the cross for all our sin.

3.) **Believe Jesus Christ died for you on the cross and rose from the grave.**

4.) **Through prayer, invite Jesus Christ to come into your heart and invite the Holy Spirit to guide you through the lifelong process of sanctification.**

5.) **Be prepared for tribulations, tests, and trials to come along because they will.** These tests will come to purify you, and to remove the "sediment" of the flesh out of the way. This is our "wilderness" walk.

Pray this prayer if you are ready: "Dear Lord, I know that I am sinful and I need your forgiveness. I believe that You died to pay the penalty for my sin. I want to turn from my sinful nature and develop a relationship with You instead. I invite you to come into my heart and my life, in Jesus' name. Amen."

If you prayed this prayer sincerely, and asked Jesus Christ to come into your life do you know what He has given you? When you receive Christ, the Holy Spirit comes to reside in you in your human spirit.

Here are some Scriptures to encourage you:

For whosoever shall call upon the name of the Lord shall be saved. (Romans 10:13)

Neither height nor depth, nor any other creature, shall be able to separate us from the love of God, which is in Christ Jesus our Lord. (Romans 8:39)

He that hath the Son hath life; *and* he that hath not the Son of God hath not life. These things I have written unto you that believe on the name of the Son of God; that ye may know that ye have eternal life, and that ye may believe on the name of the Son of God. (1 John 5:12-13)

Now receive them by the faith that Christ has given you!

What does it mean to be justified before the Lord? It means that you can now approach the throne of God boldly and have direct communication with Him. It means we can know we are *saved* by grace through faith.

It is important to recognize that I am referring to salvation and not heavenly rewards yet. Salvation is concerned with how we get into heaven. Rewards are given once we are in heaven. Failing to make the distinction between salvation and rewards can cause all kinds of confusion and wrong application of biblical truth. After we have been spiritually reborn, we can lose some of our eternal rewards by our sinful actions, but we cannot lose our salvation. Once again, we cannot lose our salvation because Jesus Christ has become our foundation, once we receive Him.

The Spirit of Christ has been joined with our human spirit to form a "new creature." In **Second Corinthians 5:17, the**

Bible says, "Therefore if any man be in Christ, *he* is a new creature: old things are passed away; behold, all things are become new." No person and no sin can remove our salvation foundation.

In Psalms 89:29-33, the Bible says, "His seed also will I make to endure for ever, and his throne as the days of heaven. If his children forsake my law, and walk not in my judgments; If they break my statutes, and keep not my commandments; Then will I visit their transgression with the rod, and their iniquity with stripes. Nevertheless my lovingkindness will I not utterly take from him, nor suffer my faithfulness to fail. Remember, Jesus died on the cross for the forgiveness of our sins. Yet we still need to repent of and turn away from our sin daily.

Let me touch on works for a moment. Many people believe that only "good" people go to heaven, due to their good works. One might say, "I'm basically a good person, so I'll go to heaven, right? I do more good things than I do bad things. God will not send me to hell just because I do not live by His word or by His will. Only really bad people like robbers, child molesters, and murderers go to hell, right?"

What does the Bible say about this? Before we look at that, it is very important to understand that **ALL** things done by us is considered a "work"—even faith. That is why the Bible says:

> [8]For <u>by grace are ye saved through faith</u>; and that <u>not of yourselves</u>: it is the gift of God: [9] <u>Not of works</u>, lest any man should boast. (Ephesians 2:8-9)
> [17]Even so faith, if it hath not works, is dead, being alone.[26] For as the body without the spirit is dead, so faith without works is dead also. (James 2:17,26)

A question to ask yourself is "what type of **work** am I doing and what is it producing?" I am not referring to your job or vocation.

I am going to touch on some things now that we will go deeper into in later chapters.

We should mirror the work Jesus did and become a disciple. A disciple will be like His master. What was Jesus' work? It was to bring the testimony of His Father. Jesus said, **"But I have greater witness than that of John:(The Baptist); for the works which the Father hath given me to finish, <u>the same works that I do, bear witness of me, that the Father hath sent me</u>" (John 5:36).**

Through the works that Jesus did, the Father was giving testimony. The Bible says, "Jesus answered them, I told you, and ye believed not: <u>the works that I do in my Father's name, they bear witness of me</u>" (John 10: 25).

No matter what it is, all things done by each and every one of us is considered a work—even faith. Ponder that thought and place it in the context of the verses I have quoted above, especially the underlined parts. It will be important to recall this information in the following chapters.

Our relationship with God is a step-by-step process. It is a relationship that takes nurturing and attention. It is growing from a babe in Christ, a *nepios*, into a spiritually mature believer, a *huios* and eventually a *pater*.

In Genesis 17:1, God asked Abraham to walk before Him and promises him that he would be made perfect, "And when Abram was ninety years old and nine, the Lord appeared to Abram, and said unto him, I am the Almighty God; walk before me, and be thou perfect" (Genesis 17:1). In the minds of most people, reading this in English may lead the reader to believe that God wants us to be perfect before Him, as in, "to never sin." Recall the squares in Chapter 2. Dig a little deeper and the real meaning of the statement, "be thou perfect," comes into understanding.

The word "perfect" in the King James Version of the Bible, comes from the Hebrew word *Tamiym* (Strong's # 8549), which actually means "spiritual maturity." God wants us to be spiritually mature before Him. It is important to understand that our Bible was not written in the English language originally. You have to go to the sources of the original context to draw out a better understanding of what His word tells us. When you do, it opens up a correct understanding.

Those who do not have the Holy Spirit—listen to their conversation and observe what they are producing. For example, a person who believes in evolution will deny that God created this universe. An atheist or liberal cannot proclaim Jesus as their Lord and Savior. Their desires differ from the desires of the Lord. They also cannot stand to hear the truth of God's Word. Those who walk after the flesh and the things of this world do not understand the spiritual things. If it were completely up to them, they would remove God's Word and all things of God from the United States and other places. We see further evidence of this through certain "unions" that commit every waking moment bringing lawsuits to remove any trace of God from our country. This is my question for church leaders: "Where have you been and where is your voice as the precious things of God are being removed from our Nation systematically?"

How do you know for sure that you are saved? The spirit testifies of itself. The following verses do not speak of salvation. In them, Jesus speaks about those who are already saved and how they should live their lives. Jesus is making it very clear that those who follow Him will live their lives and will not walk in darkness.

Then spake Jesus again unto them, saying, I am the light of the world: <u>he that followeth me shall</u>

not walk in darkness, but shall have the light of life. (John 8:12)

I am come a light into the world, that whosoever believeth on me should not abide in darkness. (John 12:46)

He that loveth his life shall lose it; and he that hateth his life in this world shall keep it unto life eternal. (John 12:25)

We are to lay down our lives for our brothers and sisters in the Lord in service to God.

Yet I supposed it necessary to send to you Epaphroditus, my brother, and companion in labour, and fellowsoldier, but your messenger, and he that ministered to my wants. (Philippians 2:25)

[29]Receive him therefore in the Lord with all gladness; and hold such in reputation: [30]Because for the work of Christ he was nigh unto death, not regarding his life, to supply your lack of service toward me. (Philippians 2:29-30)

Therefore doth my Father love me, because I lay down my life, that I might take it again. (John 10:17)

It is important to remember that the Word of God is the key to our witness. That is why it is vital that we are in the Word, seeking revelation of His Word and seeking Him daily. His Word must be in us so we can witness as Jesus has done and be a testimony of God the Father. This is where the next step comes in, sanctification and rewards. This next step is your journey to take if you so choose to do so.

The OSAS Argument

The OSAS (Once Saved Always Saved) discussion can be a hotly debated topic among churches. This subject can cause confusion. The Lord is not the author of confusion, so I sought the Lord earnestly about this because I wanted final rest about it. The answers are always in His Word.

OSAS is a **condition of the heart**, as the Lord looks at the heart of a person, because in it resides the truth concerning that person.

But the LORD said unto Samuel, Look not on his countenance, or on the height of his stature; because I have refused him: for the LORD seeth not as man seeth; for man looketh on the outward appearance, but the LORD looketh on the heart. (1 Samuel 16:7)

Lip service is a condition born out of the flesh. Phoniness before God is unacceptable. Whether we are happy, sad, or mad, honesty is essential. God does not want false expressions of worship any more than He wants false statements about people or circumstances. One thing I have witnessed is that when one tries to build on a lie, it leads one into a degree of devastation in their lives. The Word states:

He answered and said unto them, Well hath Esaias prophesied of you hypocrites, as it is written, This people honoureth me with their lips, but their heart is far from me. (Mark 7:6)

FOUNDATION

For any house to be strong, it must start out with a strong, solid foundation. Our foundation is found in His Word.

The Bible says, **"For other foundation can no man lay than that is laid, which is Jesus Christ"** (1 Corinthians 3:11).

Our foundation must be sure and true. When we are genuinely following Christ, our foundation is established. The materials in the foundation within us are the characteristics of Christ Jesus. He is transforming our soul's life.

WORKS

Works are where exposure happens. What one does and what one produces in their life exposes where their heart truly is. Our foundation is laid bare in the extreme when tribulation comes upon us. It exposes what currently occupies the heart.

> **[47]Whosoever cometh to me, and heareth my sayings, and doeth them, I will shew you to whom he is like.**

> **[48]He is like a man which built an house, and digged deep, and laid the foundation on a rock: and when the flood arose, the stream beat vehemently upon that house, and could not shake it: for it was founded upon a rock. (Luke 6:47-48)**

Verse 47 explains that we must do what the Lord instructs because this is the evidence of Him in us. Verse 48 explains that when a trial comes to a believer whose foundation is true, they will not move, but will stand firm. They may express emotion, but their faith will remain unshaken. Trials offer us the opportunity to explode in growth. Trials and tribulations will come and the purpose for them is to expose a little more of our flesh that needs to die to allow the Lord to do works through us. What works? Here are some:

[19]**Go ye therefore, and teach all nations, baptizing them in the name of the Father, and of the Son, and of the Holy Ghost.** [20]**Teaching them to observe all things whatsoever I have commanded you: and, lo, I am with you always, even unto the end of the world. Amen. (Matthew 28:19-20)**

I truly believe that one must know that what they preach or teach is true, according to the Word of God, and not simply their own belief. One must not teach what one thinks the Word of God says. Truth according to God's Word is the utmost thing we can share, but it is the responsibility of the hearer to seek the Lord on what they hear. Only the Lord can produce the "life to the bones" revelation that exposes truth to you!

WALK and RELATIONSHIP
God does not forsake those who He has saved; they are *preserved forever*.

For the LORD loveth judgment, and forsaketh not his saints; they are preserved for ever: but the seed of the wicked shall be cut off. (Psalms 37:28)

And because ye are sons, God hath sent forth the Spirit of his Son into your hearts, crying, Abba, Father. (Galatians 4:6)

I know that, whatsoever God doeth, it shall be for ever: nothing can be put to it, nor any thing taken from it: and God doeth it, that men should fear before him. (Ecclesiastes 3:14)

Jesus saith to him, He that is washed needeth not save to wash his feet, but is clean every whit: and ye are clean, but not all. (John 13:10)

In regard to John 13:10, the bath, which represents salvation, is only needed once. Foot washing symbolizes confession of sins daily.

Who shall separate us from the love of Christ? shall tribulation, or distress, or persecution, or famine, or nakedness, or peril, or sword? As it is written, For thy sake we are killed all the day long; we are accounted as sheep for the slaughter. Nay, in all these things we are more than conquerors through him that loved us. For I am persuaded, that neither death, nor life, nor angels, nor principalities, nor powers, nor things present, nor things to come, Nor height, nor depth, nor any other creature, shall be able to separate us from the love of God, which is in Christ Jesus our Lord. (Romans 8:35-39)

Who shall also confirm you unto the end, that ye may be blameless in the day of our Lord Jesus Christ. (1 Corinthians 1:8)

Which is the earnest of our inheritance until the redemption of the purchased possession, unto the praise of his glory. (Ephesians 1:14)

God gives us the Holy Spirit as a "pledge." The word for pledge used here is, *arrhabon* (Strong's # 728) which means "a pledge of future blessings." A pledge is a solemn, binding promise to do something. God gives the Christian the Holy Spirit as His promise for the future blessings of heaven that awaits them. Once given, it is irrevocable, though through sinful actions of men, it can be made less evident.

In Ephesians 4:30, the Bible says, "And grieve not the holy Spirit of God, whereby ye are sealed unto the day of

redemption." The Holy Spirit seals Christians for the day of redemption.

> **"For the which cause I also suffer these things: nevertheless I am not ashamed: for I know whom I have believed, and am persuaded that he is able to keep that which I have committed unto him against that day" (2 Timothy 1:12).** Paul is convinced that God is able to guard what He has entrusted to him until the Day of Judgment.

In 2 John 1:2, the Bible says, "For the truth's sake, which dwelleth in us, and shall be with us for ever." The truth now abides in Christians and will be with them forever.

Finally, Ephesians 1:4 says, "According as he hath chosen us in him before the foundation of the world, that we should be holy and without blame before him in love."

A. Jesus is your foundation.

> **"For other foundation can no man lay than that is laid, which is Jesus Christ" (1 Corinthians 3:11).**

B. Seek the Kingdom of God and his righteousness first!

> **"But seek ye first the kingdom of God, and his righteousness; and all these things shall be added unto you" (Matthew 6:33).**

C. Cast your burdens upon the Lord and He will sustain you! Do not make it your life goal to achieve those things that rot. Develop your relationship with Jesus first and He will sustain you.

"Cast thy burden upon the LORD, and he shall sustain thee: he shall never suffer the righteous to be moved" (Psalms 55:22).

Part Two

Recognizing Justification and Sanctification and Meeting the Bride of Christ and the General Church Through Parables

The Bride is spotless and wearing a robe of white raiment. Reading Scripture you read about those who wear white raiment and those who wear white robes. Have you ever wondered why the Bible speaks about two types of robes? Could it be that we have been tripping over something so simplistic, but yet it could cost us some rewards?

"He that overcometh, the same shall be clothed in white raiment; and I will not blot out his name out of the book of life, but I will confess his name before my Father, and before his angels" (Revelation 3:5).

The Bible tells us that God wants to transform us and sanctify us by the renewing of our minds. He wants to transform us into the express image of His Son, Christ Jesus. For Him to transform us, we must apply the Scripture to our everyday lives. We must wake up! Sitting in the pew each Sunday, doing time, does not transform a person.

"And some of them of understanding shall fall, to try them, and to purge, and to make them white, even to the time of the end: because it is yet for a time appointed" (Daniel 11:35).

"But now, O LORD, thou art our father; we are the clay, and thou our potter; and we all are the work of thy hand" (Isaiah 64:8).

CHAPTER FIVE
The Fig Tree and Recognizing the Times

As the end of this age draws closer what rewards are you storing up the most while you are still here on earth? Are you collecting more gold, silver and precious stones or wood, hay and stubble? (1Corinthians 3:12-15)

A Christian must learn the difference between justification and sanctification. Justification is what happens in the transference of the soul upon our salvation. Sanctification is the process that we choose to go through so that Christ can live through us daily as we die to our flesh daily.

The next few chapters will explore the Bride of Christ, according to the Bible. The Bride of Christ is representative of the sanctification process. We will also cover who belongs to the general church. (The general church is representative of those who never go beyond justification, in other words, the "pew warmer.")

Jesus wants us to learn a parable from the fig tree. To understand the symbolic truth of it requires spiritual discernment. Once you understand this parable, you will know that you need to be ready, you will begin to feel the need to be ready, and you will begin to understand what you need to do to get ready. The "getting ready" is the sanctification process. Understanding the differences between verses that describe justification and those that describe the sanctification process is the key to opening up deeper understanding in your spiritual walk.

The Fig Tree Parable

32Now learn a parable of the fig tree; When his branch is yet tender, and putteth forth leaves, ye know that summer is nigh: 33So likewise ye, when ye shall see all these things, know that it is near, even at the doors. 34Verily I say unto you, This generation shall not pass, till all these things be fulfilled. (Matthew 24:32-34)

This parable is perfect for showing us why we must seek God for His revelation. The point is not to simply watch for the blossoms of the fig tree to know when the end of the age will come. So what is Jesus teaching us? The passage says to *learn* from the fig tree. The first thing we must understand is that the fig tree is a picture of Israel. It is symbolic for Israel in the New Testament.

12And on the morrow, when they were come from Bethany, he was hungry: 13And seeing a fig tree afar off having leaves, he came, if haply he might find any thing thereon: and when he came to it, he found nothing but leaves; for the time of figs was not yet. 14And Jesus answered and said unto it, No man eat fruit of thee hereafter for ever. And his disciples heard it. 15And they come to Jerusalem: and Jesus went into the temple, and began to cast out them that sold and bought in the temple, and overthrew the tables of the moneychangers, and the seats of them that sold doves; 16And would not suffer that any man should carry any vessel through the temple. 17And he taught, saying unto them, Is it not written, My house shall be called of all nations the house of

prayer? but ye have made it a den of thieves. [18]And the scribes and chief priests heard it, and sought how they might destroy him: for they feared him, because all the people was astonished at his doctrine. [19]And when even was come, he went out of the city. [20]And in the morning, as they passed by, they saw the fig tree dried up from the roots. [21]And Peter calling to remembrance saith unto him, Master, behold, the fig tree which thou cursedst is withered away. [22]And Jesus answering saith unto them, Have faith in God. [23]For verily I say unto you, That whosoever shall say unto this mountain, Be thou removed, and be thou cast into the sea; and shall not doubt in his heart, but shall believe that those things which he saith shall come to pass; he shall have whatsoever he saith. [24]Therefore I say unto you, What things soever ye desire, when ye pray, believe that ye receive them, and ye shall have them. [25]And when ye stand praying, forgive, if ye have ought against any: that your Father also which is in heaven may forgive you your trespasses. (Mark 11:12-25)

Christ is hungry and from a distance, He spots a fig tree but when He comes upon this tree, it is void of fruit, so he cursed it. He cursed it because it was not yet time for the figs. This does not seem fair, so what in the world is the lesson from this parable? One thing about the fig tree is that it will first bring forth its blossoms with the **potential** of bringing forth fruit, before it brings forth leaves. The fruit and the leaves develop together so if there is not fruit with the leaves, there will not be fruit on it for that season.

In our lives, God wants us to bring forth fruit, but most of the time we just want the leaves. Bringing forth fruit and leaves together takes molding by the Lord's hand. What He requires of us is that we have the desire to go through the molding process. It requires action from us. Sometimes our desire is there but we do not want to go through the molding process because it brings us to a place where we must be emptied of all that keeps us from growing spiritually. We are clay vessels crafted by Him for His works, not ours. He wants to bring forth fruit with leaves so we can become spiritually mature.

In the beginning, it may be small, immature fruit, but at least there is fruit. Recall when the stages of growth were presented in an earlier chapter, the beginning stage is called being a "babe in Christ," the Greek word nepios. Spiritual begins with milk and then proceeds to meat.

Jesus was hungry for the fruit on the tree and the Word said it was not yet time for the fruit. You could also say that the tree was not yet ready to produce. The principle of the parable searches out what the problem with Israel is:

⁴¹And when he was come near, he beheld the city, and wept over it, ⁴²Saying, If thou hadst known, even thou, at least in this thy day, the things which belong unto thy peace! but now they are hid from thine eyes. ⁴³For the days shall come upon thee, that thine enemies shall cast a trench about thee, and compass thee round, and keep thee in on every side, ⁴⁴And shall lay thee even with the ground, and thy children within thee; and they shall not leave in thee one stone upon another; because thou knewest not the time of thy visitation. ⁴⁵And he went into the temple, and began to cast out them that sold therein, and them that bought; ⁴⁶Saying unto them, It is written, My house is the house of prayer: but ye have made it a den of thieves. (Luke 19:41-46)

Before He goes into the temple, Jesus states that peace belongs to you. Christ came to save the Jewish people and to save the nation of Israel. They did not recognize the time of their visitation and Christ wept. He did not say this with vengeance because it is His heart's desire to save men, not to destroy them. Because they were not ready to receive, they were out of season and not in tune with God's timing.

One thing about God's time is that we are in the grace age. That is, we are under grace, not under the law. No matter how many times we miss it, it is always God's time. In grace, Jesus never leaves us nor forsakes us. Faith is not faith in faith, meaning it is more than a matter of simply believing enough. Our faith is in God and He will fulfill our faith so we can believe that He will do what He said He would do.

A Quick Story: Trusting That God Will Do What He Has Promised

As you read this, ask yourself, could this be me? A young man who had only been a believer for two years attended one of those huge convention services. This young man wanted to be baptized, or filled with the Spirit, so badly. Everyone around him was falling down "under the power of the Spirit" (slain in the Spirit) while others were being healed, yet he felt as dry as a bag of crackers. He was reaching up saying, "I believe, I believe." This man was looking at himself and going on a feeling based on others around him. What he did not recognize is that he was not trying to believe in God, he was trying to "stir up enough faith" so he could operate like those around him.

Being able to recognize and operate in true faith is important. Some Christians walk in emotion-fueled "faith" which is when one gets all excited; convinced they have found faith or the way to get faith. Others walk in intellectual "faith," telling themselves they believe, but continually asking what they believe.

True faith, which is the faith in Christ Jesus in us, comes forth and says "Yes, my God is faithful!" It is the only faith we should have. Sadly, too many Christians are walking around with emotional or intellectual faith that is really unbelief. Then they question why God's power does not operate in their life to produce fruit and provide the evidence He truly operates through them.

Within ten minutes of each other two men rushed up to this young man and gave him the same word, "God's favor is upon you; whatever you ask for tonight, God will grant." This man got so excited he prayed, "I want to be used by you Lord, totally sold out for you God. I just want to live for you, and I want to walk in your presence." Something happened that night. He cried tears of bitterness and disappointment. Why, because God did not move on this man's timing and heaven and earth did not move for him that night. He left that convention the same way he entered.

Two years later, while in a Bible study, the Lord brought back to the young man's memory the prayer he prayed at that convention. The Lord spoke to him, "I am answering that prayer right now." This person had a lot of zeal, but not enough of Christ in his soul at the time he first uttered that prayer. If the Lord had answered that prayer to fulfill his desire before he was ready to receive it, he could have become a legalistic tyrant. Maturity causes the characteristics of Christ to move within our soul.

Do you know why there is an inconsistency in the Church today? It is due to impatience within the Body of Christ. To do the work of God requires patience and stillness before Him before He moves us forward for His work. However, we mill about doing our works in the name of Jesus. There is a huge difference between the two.

I am sure that John, while imprisoned on the Island of Patmos, could teach us a thing or two about patience and maturity. We tend to overlook all the "trial by fire" parts of the Bible and run right into the great works of God. We fail to see the wilderness walks men and women of the Bible went through before they obtained victory. So much of our preaching focuses on the victory but fails to teach us how to overcome the fiery trials and tribulations.

If anything of our self is involved when we are attempting to produce fruit, we will taint the work. For example, have you seen someone giving a prophecy, but as he gives it, he adds a good performance to it as well? It is as if they feel we need to be entertained to keep our attention. When confronted, such a person typically responds with an excuse or a cold shoulder, thus revealing their character. Defense of our faulty character can never be placed above or hinder the truths that Christ wants to come forth. Performance must never distract from the prophecy.

The soul is a vessel we must allow God to empty of all sediment of the flesh. If fleshly sediment remains, it mixes in with the revelation. It does not mean that none of the revelation shared is from God; it just means that it was not all from God. When a person is not mature, one must be careful about the words that come forth. This is why the Word tells us to judge everything and test every spirit. We must take every word to the Lord and ask if it bears witness and lines up to the Word. If it does, it will develop maturity.

Good character reveals itself by a focus on Jesus and praying with no preconceived or judgmental thoughts. Those with good character allow the spirit of God to speak through them in a clear, precise manner, with an anointing of the Holy Spirit which brings forth healing and not confusion or pain.

All of what the young man had prayed at that convention required God to empty him first. His immaturity and lack of understanding at the time blocked him from understanding that the "emptying" process was not finished and what he was asking God for in prayer was out of season.

When we pray in spirit and truth, we do not really realize what takes place in the heavens. If we do not die voluntarily to ourselves daily, God is going to allow circumstances to do it for us. At the time of the young man's prayer, he did not realize the scope of what he sought.

God does not normally baptize you in the Holy Spirit until He has emptied those things in your soul that are not from Him. God can quicken the process but it is His choice to do so. He deals with the heart first. Christ comes in to dwell within your heart when you are reborn. Then He starts cleaning house in your heart so He can flow through you with His words and His ways.

We must learn to say, "***it's not me, it's Christ in me' and 'by the power of the Holy Spirit.***" We need to know that every day is our day of visitation, not saying "well one day," God will move through me. If we miss it today, that is okay because God is always there to meet us. We need to start drinking spiritual milk and begin understanding that before we can move on to the spiritual meat. God gives us a certain number of days in this life so we must allow God to fill those days with His purpose and plan for our lives.

Back to the Fig Tree

Israel was not under grace and the Israelites did not realize the time of visitation was upon them but it is now for us. Learn from the fig tree; it was not ready, so Jesus cursed it. It withered and never bore fruit again. When we read Mark 11, we see Jesus went in and cleansed the temple, showing that it was unfruitful. When he came out and Peter saw the fig tree dried up, he was astounded. He said, 'How can this be?' Jesus answered, "If you believe in God you will be able to do the same things."

Some people have faith in the Word of God, but not in God Himself, and they never really get to know Jesus. The Word is the message but God is the producer (author) of the message. When we "eat" and activate the word with faith, Christ is then evident, and fruit will appear. There He instructs us that whatever we ask for in prayer He will do, if we believe in Him. If we have the heart of God, we will desire what He desires as well. He answers our prayers when they line up with His ways. Though we must understand that His time is not our time and it may not happen right away.

Most of us have misconceptions of God's love. If we truly understood God's love perfectly we would never be fearful or anxious again. Not only is He perfect love but He is completely sovereign. His Word says, not even a hair on our head will perish. God wants us to understand this so He restores and renews our understanding when we seek Him out. The purpose of everything is to know His love spoken of in Ephesians. It is not to know doctrine, Scripture, and to have a bunch of head knowledge, but to know Him and His love. The Lord wants us to know that the time of visitation is today. Today is the day you begin to know Jesus better.

This is where so many people get confused. Many say, "The Word tells us that He will give us the desire of our hearts." This is so true, but if you do not line up to Him, your desires may not be according to His desires. If your life is in turmoil or just seems to continually take left turns, ask yourself what is in your heart.

If your heart is anxious over money all the time, so shall you be. God will ordain trials in your life where things seem crazy and all He wants from you is to practice trust and faith. He will sustain you all the way through it if you face it with trust and faith and seek God for what role you might have played in the trial coming about. With that recognition, we can begin to learn from our "fig tree." This is part of the preparation (sanctification) process.

The withered fig tree was also a prophetic word for Israel. For almost 2000 years, Israel was withered and dry. In 70 AD, Israel withered because the people failed to recognize the season. The Bible says, **"I say then, Hath God cast away his people? God forbid. For I also am an Israelite, of the seed of Abraham, of the tribe of Benjamin" (Romans 11: 1).**

The great thing is, even though the Israelites missed their time of visitation, God did not cast them away because they are His people. We, as Christians, have Christ in us and we sometimes blow it with God. We can wither up and withdraw from Him but He will not cast us away. Romans says, **"I say then, Have they stumbled that they should fall? God forbid: but rather through their fall salvation is come unto the Gentiles, for to provoke them to jealousy" (Romans 11:11).** They have stumbled not unto destruction, but unto restoration by God. The Gentiles (Christians) have the opportunity to be that vessel of restoration.

Romans 11:29 says, "For the gifts and calling of God are without repentance." Salvation is the gift God gave Israel and is without repentance. No matter how much they rejected, reviled or crucified Christ, God did not reject them. They are still His people. The Gentiles are a heavenly nation chosen by God and Israel is an earthly nation chosen by God.

> **For as ye in times past have not believed God, yet have now obtained mercy through their unbelief: ³¹Even so have these also now not believed, that through your mercy they also may obtain mercy. ³²For God hath concluded them all in unbelief, that he might have mercy upon all. ³³O the depth of the riches both of the wisdom and knowledge of God! how unsearchable are his judgments, and his ways past finding out! ³⁴For who hath known the mind of the Lord? or who hath been his counsellor? (Romans 11:30-34)**

Paul is overwhelmed because he understood the love of God in His perfection.

When we go through trials, we must not allow ourselves to get into, "OH NO! WHY ME?" Paul saw his nation rejecting Christ and the persecution against Christians. He knew the difficulty the Church would go through over the next 2000 years. He also knew the end and was overwhelmed at God's love toward such a rebellious nation. This is why the Word tells us to give thanks in all things for all things. We cannot see the big picture but God's ways are perfect. When we go through a trial and God brings us through it, we must say, "WOW! God brought me through to the end." We want to see the glory without the suffering that is required to bring forth the glory.

More Points Found in the Fig Tree

Eve took from the tree of knowledge. There were three types of trees in the Garden of Eden, one for the spirit, one for the body, and one for food. Adam and Eve chose the tree of knowledge and fleshly things over Christ. As soon as they ate it, they realized their nakedness and grabbed some fig leaves to cover themselves. We all know the difference between good and evil but until we are born again we will not know what to do with the knowledge.

You can know a lot of intellectual knowledge about God but until you allow God to reveal Himself to you, your knowledge is just that, yours. The Bible says, **"And when the woman saw that the tree was good for food, and that it was pleasant to the eyes, and a tree to be desired to make one wise, she took of the fruit thereof, and did eat, and gave also unto her husband with her; and he did eat. And the eyes of them both were opened, and they knew that they were naked; and they sewed fig leaves together, and made themselves aprons" (Genesis 3:6-7).**

Another point on this is found in John's gospel, "Philip findeth Nathanael, and saith unto him, We have found him, of whom Moses in the law, and the prophets, did write, Jesus of Nazareth, the son of Joseph. And Nathanael said unto him, Can there any good thing come out of Nazareth? Philip saith unto him, Come and see. Jesus saw Nathanael coming to him, and saith of him, Behold an Israelite indeed,

in whom is no guile! Nathanael saith unto him, Whence knowest thou me? Jesus answered and said unto him, Before that Philip called thee, when thou wast under the fig tree, I saw thee. Nathanael answered and saith unto him, Rabbi, thou art the Son of God; thou art the King of Israel. Jesus answered and said unto him, Because I said unto thee, I saw thee under the fig tree, believest thou? thou shalt see greater things than these. And he saith unto him, Verily, verily, I say unto you, Hereafter ye shall see heaven open, and the angels of God ascending and descending upon the Son of man" (John 1:45-51).

Nathanael was sitting under a fig tree before he found Christ and Philip tells him he found Christ. He states, "can there any good thing come out of Nazareth?" The fig tree was shading him and he could not receive revelation. He could not see his wrongs. The fig tree of wrong understanding shaded the people of Israel. It is only after Philip, an evangelist, called him out from under the fig tree that he then received revelation.

Our own fig tree prevents us from receiving what God has for us. We get a word of encouragement and we wonder if God could really want that for us. Doubt kicks into overdrive. When we begin to rationalize everything, whatever faith we had is now covered up by our "fig tree." We must say, "I know my God is faithful," in spite of everything.

"And be not conformed to this world: but be ye transformed by the renewing of your mind, that ye may prove what is that good, and acceptable, and perfect, will of God" (Romans 12:2). We need a transformation of our understanding. Transformation comes from meditating on the Word and allowing Christ to come forth in us to transform us. Far too often, we allow man to transform us. When we pray, we must focus on His love and get into a place where God can reveal Himself to us so we can move away from that shaded fig tree of "past experiences."

This is what the Bride of Christ does. She gets up and away from the wrong understandings that have robbed her for far too long. She moves in the revealed Word of God and produces fruit. She fully understands that it is all God and that she is only the vessel.

What about Israel? Romans says, "Brethren, my heart's desire and prayer to God for Israel is, that they might be saved. For I bear them record that they have a zeal of God, but not according to knowledge. For they being ignorant of God's righteousness, and going about to establish their own righteousness, have not submitted themselves unto the righteousness of God. For Christ is the end of the law for righteousness to every one that believeth" (Romans 10:1-4). The Jews had a zeal for God, so why were they not saved? They were establishing their own self-righteousness, not submitting to God's righteousness, so they were dwelling under that shaded fig tree.

Adam and Eve took the fig leaves and tried to cover their nakedness. That is what legalism is and what the laws accomplish. In their own self-effort to be righteous, they did this. They will suffer until they allow God to remove those leaves, exposing their nakedness (sin), so they can repent and be clothed in the blood of Jesus.

We sometimes have this same problem because of our lack of understanding; we seek to establish our own righteousness. When you do something wrong and start to feel the conviction rising up, yet you tell yourself, "Okay, I will feel bad for two or three days over this sin before I seek forgiveness." This is not something we need to do because we only need to seek forgiveness, repent for our sins truthfully, and move on, without returning. It is that simple but the devil tries to complicate it into something more through condemnation.

When we accept Jesus Christ as our Lord and Savior, there are two types of repentance. When we first accept Him as Lord, we confess our sinfulness; our sinful state, our sinful nature, but we do not confess our individual sins. We confess our need for a Savior and we are justified immediately. The Holy Spirit comes into us, and we are born again children of God.

We are free from the penalty of sin because we confessed our sinfulness.

The other type of repentance is the confession of particular or individual sins that sets us free from the power of sin. Many sin, but do not realize that they are sinners and do not recognize their need for a Savior yet. The Bible says, **"That was the true Light, which lighteth every man that cometh into the world" (John 1:9).**

If we feel that we need to beg God for forgiveness, we are expressing unbelief. He loves it when we confess our sins because it starts to give His hands (His Spirit) freedom to move in our lives, and bring forth more of the redemption of Christ to be manifested in our lives. This is what we should be praying: "Lord I recognize now that I have a critical thought. In fact my feelings like that critical thought, but I choose to say this is sin, and I choose to confess it to you and I thank you right now for your forgiveness and your cleansing." All we need to do is confess our sin, and God washes us, so do not pick it back up.

We have confidence in Christ's redemption when we say, "LORD, I have sinned and this is sin and I confess it. I even confess that I was happy about doing it, but it is sinful and my attitude was sinful, my feelings were sinful and I thank you for forgiving me. Thank you for cleansing me through the atonement of Jesus." At that moment, Christ forgave you and cleansed you.

Do not meditate on your forgiven sins; meditate on God's love. Believe in the redemption of Christ. Wailing and yelling about it is establishing your own self-righteousness and when you stop moaning and groaning, and start confessing, God will begin to set you free.

You can tell when someone is hungry for the Lord and when someone is not. When a person is hungry, they will go into a group or listen to a speaker and it makes no difference if they understand everything taught or not, they will not care because they just want more of Jesus. They just want to be around people who saturate themselves with Jesus, hoping it rubs off on them. They will seek out the truth by studying the Word. This is what the Bride of Christ does!

When a person is not hungry, they will leave complaining about this or that, with thoughts of criticism about what they just heard. They will nitpick about the service or song. Can you imagine Jesus going into the garden to pray to His Father and complaining the whole time instead? Picture this, "Father, I'm not going to die on the cross for them. They are rude, they talk about me behind my back, spit on me, and want to put me in jail! Look at my disciples; they cannot even stay awake for one hour to pray for me. While they are sleeping, Father I think I will just sneak out of this town let them hang themselves. Thank you Father amen." Then Jesus sneaks out of town. This is what the general church does.

OH, BUT THANK GOD! Jesus stood strong, silent, and on His Word in the face of adversity. "**But God commendeth his love toward us, in that, while we were yet sinners, Christ died for us" (Romans 5:8).** His feet stood firmly on that rock. He was unshakeable. Victory belongs to Him so we need to drop our untimely figs and those things we have been holding on to. When we become desperate, all we want to know is Jesus, and all those out of season figs no longer matter. When we are in despair, we will begin to receive the ministry of the Body of Christ around us without complaint. When we drop those untimely figs, we do not pick them back up, or they will hinder us and keep us in bondage. Christ will begin to move in our lives once we drop those figs for good.

And the heaven departed as a scroll when it is rolled together; and every mountain and island were moved out of their places. (Revelation 6:14)

The heavens declare the glory of God; and the firmament sheweth his handywork. (Psalms 19:1)

Thy mercy, O LORD, is in the heavens; and thy faithfulness reacheth unto the clouds. (Psalms 36:5)
For thy mercy is great unto the heavens, and thy truth unto the clouds. (Psalms 57:10)

We can see that the heavens are a testimony to His mercy, grace and faithfulness. When the general church is "taken up," in the middle of the seven-year tribulation, the wrath of God will pour out on the earth. God's mercy will be "rolled up" and the book closed. There will be no time for mercy, for seeing His righteousness manifest among us, or for a spoken language. God will fulfill His words and bring them back together.

The Lord is now saying, "Be ready!" That is a sign the fig tree is bringing back her shoots again after 2000 years. The Bride of Christ, which will be "caught up" at the beginning of the seven-year tribulation is being made ready in season—right now. BE READY, HE IS COMING. HE WILL SET UP HIS ONE THOUSAND YEAR REIGN FROM JERUSALEM AND THE BRIDE (MATURE, SANCTIFIED CHRISTIANS) WILL RULE AND REIGN WITH HIM. AMEN!

CHAPTER SIX
Parallels of the Bride of Christ and the General Church

To understand what Scripture teaches, we must understand three aspects. First, we must understand the church aspect. There are two parts to the Church, the Bride of Christ, and the Body of Christ. When we are first born again, we are part of the Bride, but if we do not nurture our understanding, our love grows cold. If we allow the Holy Spirit to operate through us, He will continually keep us in that "first love" state that allows us to walk in fruitfulness. Walking in first love means everything in life is secondary to knowing Christ and being with Him. Second, we will see that, in the middle of the seven-year tribulation, the general church is taken up. Third, we will see how Israel and the world (unbelievers) see Christ's return.

Here is how the Bride and Body of Christ will see Christ' return:

And be found in him, not having mine own righteousness, which is of the law, but that which is through the faith of Christ, the righteousness which is of God by faith: That I may know him, and the power of his resurrection, and the fellowship of his sufferings, being made conformable unto his death; If by any means I might attain unto the resurrection of the

dead. Not as though I had already attained, either were already perfect: but I follow after, if that I may apprehend that for which also I am apprehended of Christ Jesus. (Philippians 3:9-12)

Paul is seeking to attain unto the resurrection of the dead. This is speaking about attaining a walk that makes him part of the Bride because he was already saved and justified. The evidence for this is in what he was seeking to do. He was saying that he was going on to press in and continue so he will not lose sight of the high calling of Christ, (characteristic of the Bride.) He did not stop at just being saved (justified).

There is the "better" resurrection that is only going to be for those who allow the Holy Spirit to conform them into the image of Christ and those that remain in their first love. Too many men and women allow themselves to be conformed to man. Their eyes are on man's ways and traditions. The main reason for this is that we tend to follow what we can see, feel, and touch. Jesus is in our midst, though we cannot literally see Him, so the danger is that we will ignore Him.

Most do not hear the words preached or taught because they do not get past their emotions. People get worked up during a church service, flying high with emotion, and mistake it for a move of the Holy Spirit. There are too many "Christians" in trouble because they were made to "feel good" during the service, but leave with no spiritual substance or training. The follow through of "seeking" is aborted.

My guess is that 98% of the time when people dismiss from the service their mind veers off the message and immediately goes onto, "What's for lunch?" Alternatively, the cliques band together, maybe even for lunch, to recite the latest gossip. Do such people really need to inquire of God as to why they are still so spiritually weak and beggarly?

Look at what the Pharisees were doing, as recorded in Luke:

[20]And when he was demanded of the Pharisees, when the kingdom of God should come, he answered them and said, The kingdom of God cometh not with observation: Neither shall they say, Lo here! or, lo there! for, behold, the kingdom of God is within you. (Luke 17:20-21)

The Pharisees were defending when the kingdom of God was coming because their concept of how He was going to establish His kingdom was backwards. Jesus said to them, essentially, "Do not look over here or over there," because the kingdom of God is within them and He was standing right there among them. Jesus is within you constantly, even if it sometimes does not feel that way. Do not depend on what you are feeling to determine your service to Him. Follow what the Word of God is instructing you to do regardless of your feelings.

So many times, we will run around trying to find the kingdom of God, yet He is right there with us all along. Sometimes we think we need a special preacher to get a blessing, but the Word says not to go here or there, for the Kingdom is there inside you. If you want to have a relationship with the Lord, it starts with you. It starts when you close the door and spend time with Him. It develops in personal prayer time and in studying His Word.

You could be in the midst of an outpouring of the Holy Spirit, perhaps in a conference, but as soon as you leave, you begin to feel as though you are drying up. If you JUST go to church services and do nothing else, you will most likely go through this. You are solely depending on that service to feed you, yet wonder why you feel choked off and spiritually dry. You are not eating from the whole spiritual "meat plate." You placate yourself with nibbles off someone else's plate, from their knowledge and revelation. When tribulations hit or something does not go your way, you wonder, "God, what's going on here?" When God does not seem to answer, you begin to dry up and get into your own self-effort and self works.

There is a warning found in Luke, "And he said unto the disciples, The days will come, when ye shall desire to see one of the days of the Son of man, and ye shall not see it. And they shall say to you, See here; or, see there: go not after them, nor follow them" (Luke 17:22-23).

There is going to be a time when believers are going to be dry and desire more of God, though that dryness will lead them to follow man more so than they do today. The warning in these verse are, when you have a person of God with God's anointing, but you look at them as if there is something special about the man, in his flesh, instead of the ministry of God in them, you are deceived.

Every time we think we are better than the next person, we are "knowing ourselves after the flesh," and this is one way to miss being part of the Bride. You become a person chaser instead of a God chaser. Paul said in Second Corinthians, **"Wherefore henceforth know we no man after the flesh: yea, though we have known Christ after the flesh, yet now henceforth know we him no more. Therefore if any man be in Christ, he is a new creature: old things are passed away; behold, all things are become new" (2 Corinthians 5: 16-17).**

You must understand that it is Christ in that person and the anointing on that person and not the person. Paul said be a follower of me as I am in Christ. Paul did not say follow me no matter what. He said, as I follow Christ, you follow me, because Christ was in Paul.

To be part of the Bride is to be totally in love with Christ and one another. A great way to tell if Christ resides in you or others is discerning if the power of Christ is evident. Man cannot fake

Christ's power. Ask yourself, "Where is the evidence of the power of Christ in the part of the Body of Christ I am fellow-shipping with?" However, be sure to ask yourself that question along with this one, "Am I about to answer that question while having looked at the outward characteristic of the person or the power of Christ working through them?" Do you truly see God moving or are you actually just participating in a church that meets in a building on Sundays and Wednesday?

Ephesians 4 makes the point that every joint supports the body. Too many churches are built around personalities or characters, which is unstable ground. Christ will tumble those stones (people) and re-lay them. When we start to value one another in Christ, it becomes a true body ministry. When we start to elevate one over another, we begin to do the work and not the Holy Spirit.

God is no respecter of persons and there is no favoritism. Imagine Christ praying for you when a God-focused person prays for you. Some people are shy about praying because they believe that they cannot put together a nice sounding prayer. Pray anyway because prayer comes from your heart and does not need to sound like a poetry entry. If you are concerned about the words, you are caring what others will think, and that is of the flesh (you are, "knowing yourself after your own flesh"). It is Christ in us that brings divine order to the church, which is the purpose of the fivefold ministry.

"For as the lightning, that lighteneth out of the one part under heaven, shineth unto the other part under heaven; so shall also the Son of man be in his day. But first must he suffer many things, and be rejected of this generation" (Luke 17:24-25). Why did he describe suffering?

The Body of Christ is a beautiful picture of Christ's redemption, but the Bride of Christ is the perfection of Christ's redemption. Everyone who accepts Christ is justified but those who allow the sanctification and the love of Christ to come forth are the perfect example of perfect giving in a perfecting of Christ suffering for us. If you want to appreciate the suffering of Christ the most, allow Christ to sanctify you, because that is why He died. He did not only die to justify and sanctify you, but He died so you could be one with Him in every way. Doing good works does not qualify you.

Noah and Lot: A Picture of Justification and Sanctification

And as it was in the days of Noe, so shall it be also in the days of the Son of man. They did eat, they drank, they married wives, they were given in marriage, until the day that Noah entered into the ark, and the flood came, and destroyed them all. Likewise also as it was in the days of Lot; they did eat, they drank, they bought, they sold, they planted, they builded; But the same day that Lot went out of Sodom it rained fire and brimstone from heaven, and destroyed them all. Even thus shall it be in the day when the Son of man is revealed. (Luke 17: 26-30)

Important: Keep this in mind as you read the following section. We will look at **A)** the Bride of Christ as seen through Noah, the overcomer, and; **B)** The general church as pictured through Lot. Seeing the symbolic pictures of these two men will give you a better understanding of these two aspects concerning the Body of Christ.

1. The name Noah means *rest*. Noah was at rest with God. (Strong's #5146)

The name Lot means *veiled*. Lot veiled the life of God within him by his flesh. That is what happens when you walk in carnality. (Strong's #3875)

2. After Noah entered the ark, the judgment did not fall right away. It was seven days before judgment fell, "For yet seven days, and I will cause it to rain upon the earth forty days and forty nights; and every living substance that I have made will I destroy from off the face of the earth" (Genesis 7:4).

God's judgment fell on Sodom a short time after Lot was removed from the city. Lot and his family had to be removed far enough away as to not be affected by God's judgment upon the city (Gen. 19:22-24). The reason Lot had to be taken out of the city is found in First Thessalonians, **"For God hath not appointed us to wrath, but to obtain salvation by our Lord Jesus Christ" (1 Thessalonians 5:9).**

Take note of the two time differences concerning these two judgments. One took seven days before it fell. The other judgment took a shorter time and fell on the same day. The comparison here is that, when the Bride of Christ is caught up, God's wrath does not fall, though it marks the beginning of the seven years of tribulation. There will still be time for repentance for the world and a time of preparation for the general church for the first half of the seven years of tribulation.

In the middle of the seven years, Christ will come on the clouds to gather His church out of the cities and nations and thus the last half of the tribulation begins. Those will be extremely difficult times, though people will still be able to choose God. (Revelation 20:4 speaks of those who make a "late" decision during the latter of the tribulation period.)

Lot is symbolic of the general church. Once Lot was removed far away from Sodom, God's wrath fell upon it. When the general church has been taken up (removed), God's wrath will fall upon the earth. Just as the sins of Sodom were wiped in a single day, along with the city, so will this world's sin be wiped out as God's wrath rains upon it.

Who are those who judge themselves?

"For if we would judge ourselves, we should not be judged. But when we are judged, we are chastened of the Lord, that we should not be condemned with the world" (1 Corinthians 11:31-32).

Those who can admit they have sinned judge themselves. Just as those who can recognize their steps are off the path of righteousness and those who allow the Holy Spirit to show them the way.

In the first part of the seven years of tribulation, God chastises the general church so they can be made ready for Him. Why does He do this? In layman terms: He is trying to get our attention. If He has to do that by causing us to go through the first part of the tribulation, He will, because He loves us that much!

These shall make war with the Lamb, and the Lamb shall overcome them: for he is Lord of lords, and King of kings: and they that are with him are called, and chosen, and faithful. (Revelation 17:14)

And the armies which were in heaven followed him upon white horses, clothed in fine linen, white and clean. (Revelation 19:14)

We can choose right now to allow the Lord to make us ready for His service or we can endure the last terrible times of testing in the first half of the tribulation years. Look back at Revelation 19:14 to see what He wants for us. We are coming back with Him at the end of the tribulation period!

We will also receive some of the rewards He has waiting for us in heaven. If we judge our self, the Lord will not chasten us. Mature people do not make excuses for their sins—they confess them and move on. Those who are not caught up (raptured) before the tribulation will remain to be purified. In addition, after the rapture occurs it becomes the last chance for unbelievers to recognize the season so that they can turn to God and be saved. Time will eventually run out and the door to salvation will shut forever. Do not miss it!

3. In the days of Noah they were still marrying and being given in marriage. Presently, the Lord is preparing His Bride yet some believers are not hearing His voice. They are "marrying" false things, immature leadership, and establishing their own self-righteousness. They marry these things instead of being married to Christ. Therefore, when the Lord comes, they will be left behind for their heart is not totally "married" to the Lord Jesus Christ.

If you are reading this, you must ask yourself if "worldly prestige" and "recognition of men" are really worth losing your eternal rewards. After you have dressed, but before you leave to go to church this Sunday, really look in the mirror. Ask yourself, "What is the purpose of going to church today? For whom did I dress up today? How is Christ's light shining through me?" When you return home, ask yourself, "What difference did I make today in the lives of those around me?"

The Bible says, **"Now I praise you, brethren, that ye remember me in all things, and keep the ordinances, as I delivered them to you. But I would have you know, that the head of every man is Christ; and the head of the woman is the man; and the head of Christ is God. Every man praying or prophesying, having his head covered, dishonoureth his head" (1 Corinthians 11:2-4).** Paul has promised them (the ten virgins) to one husband, Christ. His fear was they would be led astray before he presented them as pure virgins (spiritually mature).

Paul's desire was that they be part of the Bride and that he would present them to the Bridegroom as pure virgins. He was saying that there is a possibility that they will not be pure enough to be ready to go, so catch the readiness warning here. It is not speaking about coming into salvation, it is essentially saying, "if you don't follow after the flesh and are not one who receives another spirit other than the one Paul preached, which is Christ, you will be part of the Bride." Spiritual maturity took place!

In the day of Sodom's judgment, they talked about business; they were eating and drinking. His identity was with those in the city, though the Lord had him removed before judgment fell. This describes the general church after the Bride has been caught up. This is an encouragement in the Bible for those who will be left behind. They will still be able to get a reward but will not take part in the better resurrection, which is being part of the Bride. They can still allow Christ to build them and upon their death will receive some rewards. However, the Scripture records that once Lot walked out of the city far enough removed, God's wrath was poured out and it was finished.

4. Noah's faith is written about in Hebrews 11:7, "By faith Noah, being warned of God of things not seen as yet, moved with fear, prepared an ark to the saving of his house; by the which he condemned the world, and became heir of the righteousness which is by faith."

Noah was motivated by his faith in things that he did not see. Noah built an ark out of his faith.

Lot was motivated by his eyes, as recorded in Genesis 13:10, "And Lot lifted up his eyes, and beheld all the plain of Jordan, that it was well watered every where, before the LORD destroyed Sodom and Gomorrah, even as the garden of the LORD, like the land of Egypt, as thou comest unto Zoar." He looked at Sodom and Gomorrah and said it was a beautiful place. He was attracted by the physical appeal of the world. Too many preachers build their church so beautifully that for some, it is the only reason they attend it.

5. Noah was a man moved by fear. The word for *fear* in Hebrews 11:7 means, *"to be circumspect; apprehensive; to reverence* (Strong's #2125). Noah was a man who acted circumspectly; he looked around and understood what God was saying and doing in his life, so he acted accordingly. Be vigilant and do not slumber concerning the times and seasons.

"Wherefore he saith, Awake thou that sleepest, and arise from the dead, and Christ shall give thee light. See then that ye walk circumspectly, not as fools, but as wise, Redeeming the time, because the days are evil. Wherefore be ye not unwise, but understanding what the will of the Lord is" **(Ephesians 5:14-17).** When you are in your own self-effort you are actually sound asleep to the things of the Lord. Prayer will be a chore and reading the Bible will be hard. No matter how hard you try, you just will not get it. When times call for a rebuke or correction toward you, your reaction will be anger or becoming upset. You will not be able to see your error due to your blindness.

Noah learned to trust in God and this is what you have to do. Many people are motivated by their own works, but not by the faith they have been given. The Lord says rest and look to the finished works of Christ. When you start lifting your eyes in faith to God, all those blinders begin to fall to the ground and you are set free. Lot disregarded God's warnings and accepted what was going on around him.

6. Noah prepared an ark, thus saving his house. His whole family was saved because he reached out to them. He tried to reach out to others around him but they mocked him.

Another characteristic of those who are part of the Bride is that they reach out to all those around them. They are always pouring out because it is Christ in them reaching out. They are feeling what God feels. Their heart is committed to saving their family, friends, and the world. Noah did all this and it gives us a perfect picture of sanctification.

Lot did little, if anything, of what the Lord commanded him. He was living in a city of sin and he may have even been an elder. An example of an elder going with the flow instead of doing what is right in the eyes of the Lord. He became complacent with the world around him and just went with it. Today we see some churches turning tide and going with the politically correct wave. That wave will soon turn into a tsunami and tumble every stone (person) in those churches. If your church is preaching a social justice doctrine, run far away from it and do not look back!

7. Noah condemned the world. The word condemned means: *"blame; find guilty; doom; find, declare unfit for use."* Due to a lack of understanding the proper way to "judge according to the Word," many have a tendency to condemn and bring judgment down because of what they **feel** a person may be doing wrong. The discernment is missing. When we judge according to the Word, it should be through our lifestyle that allows Jesus to live through us. When we allow ourselves to be that "light" to the world, they see Jesus living through us, which exposes the sin around us—and we need not say a word.

The true fruit of the Spirit comes forth when we do not give in to self-effort, and focus totally on Jesus and His love. The fruit comes forth and changes the people around us. This way Christ lives through us and brings about the judgment. If people come up and tell us, "You have to act more like Jesus," "You have to act like this or that," (act, act, act!) that would be false fruit because your consciousness will be on your actions instead of on Jesus.

The Flood Came

Before the flood came, the door of the ark was ALREADY closed. When the flood came and the end was near, do you think some of the people left behind repented? Yes, according to this passage from First Peter, "**For Christ also hath once suffered for sins, the just for the unjust, that he might bring us to God, being put to death in the flesh, but quickened by the Spirit: By which also he went and preached unto the spirits in prison; Which sometime were disobedient, when once the longsuffering of God waited in the days of Noah, while the ark was a preparing, wherein few, that is, eight souls were saved by water" (1 Peter 3:18-20).**

Because Noah had reached out to them, some remembered what he had been saying; they reached out to God in repentance and were saved. If only they would have listened before the judgment fell. Is your ear hearing what I am saying? When Jesus went into the city of refuge (paradise) to preach to the spirits in prison, some of them were from the days of Noah. Even though the doors closed and they lost their physical lives in the flood, those that repented were saved.

Lot did not have a witness, according to Genesis, "And Lot went out, and spake unto his sons in law, which married his daughters, and said, Up, get you out of this place; for the LORD will destroy this city. But he seemed as one that mocked unto his sons in law" (Genesis 19:14).

They thought he was joking and this speaks hugely about his lifestyle. His witness was worthless and parts of his family were not believers. Lot did nothing to prepare his house (family) and it is evident he did not reach out to those around him.

Noah became an heir of righteousness and received what God had for him. Lot escaped a fiery death at the last minute, but was saved.

Those are the differences of being part of the Bride and the general church as shown in the lives of Noah and Lot. It also gives us a picture of the first half verses the middle event of the seven years of tribulation.

Looking Back Once You're Removed

Don't become a pillar of salt and be damned!

There is a warning about looking back written in Luke, **"In that day, he which shall be upon the housetop, and his stuff in the house, let him not come down to take it away: and he that is in the field, let him likewise not return back. Remember Lot's wife" (Luke 17:31-32).** Lot's wife was not destroyed in the city, though we can see she was unbelieving and disobedient. At some point, she desired to be saved because she left with her husband. God commanded them not to look back, but she did. She heard the judgment falling upon the city and her heart disobeyed God. She turned toward the sinful people that remained in the city. This is where choice comes in. She chose the city instead of God and He judged her accordingly. At least Lot received some reward because at the end he obeyed God.

Compare this now with the general church and the world. It is possible for the general church to receive rewards. There will be some, like Lot's wife, whose hearts remain in the world and they will be destroyed. **"Wash you, make you clean; put away the evil of your doings from before mine eyes; cease to do evil" (Isaiah 1:16).**

One Taken One Left Behind

Whosoever shall seek to save his life shall lose it; and whosoever shall lose his life shall preserve it. [34]I tell you, in that night there shall be two men in one bed; the one shall be taken, and the other shall be left. [35]Two women shall be grinding together; the one shall be taken, and the other left. [36]Two men shall be in the field; the one shall be taken, and the other left.[37]And they answered and said unto him, Where,

Lord? And he said unto them, Wheresoever the body is, thither will the eagles be gathered together. (Luke 17:33-37)

In verse 37, they asked where they were going and The Lord replied, "where the eagles will be." Eagles are symbolic of an overcomer. The Bible says, **"And the first beast was like a lion, and the second beast like a calf, and the third beast had a face as a man, and the fourth beast <u>was like a flying eagle</u>" (Revelation 4:7).** Out of the four faces, one is like an eagle.

And I saw in the right hand of him that sat on the throne a book written within and on the backside, sealed with seven seals. ²And I saw a strong angel proclaiming with a loud voice, Who is worthy to open the book, and to loose the seals thereof? ³And no man in heaven, nor in earth, neither under the earth, was able to open the book, neither to look thereon. ⁴And I wept much, because no man was found worthy to open and to read the book, neither to look thereon. ⁵And one of the elders saith unto me, Weep not: behold, the Lion of the tribe of Judah, the Root of David, hath prevailed to open the book, and to loose the seven seals thereof. ⁶And I beheld, and, lo, in the midst of the throne and of the four beasts, and in the midst of the elders, stood a Lamb as it had been slain, having seven horns and seven eyes, which are the seven Spirits of God sent forth into all the earth. (Revelation 5:1-6)

Christ is worthy! AMEN! The Spirit of Christ is the High Priest and He offered Himself up by His eternal spirit; the two goats, one slain, represented His physical body.

Who and What are We Trusting In?

Trusting in your wealth is not going to save you nor give you the better resurrection. We see this written in Luke:

> **And one of the company said unto him, Master, speak to my brother, that he divide the inheritance with me. ¹⁴And he said unto him, Man, who made me a judge or a divider over you? ¹⁵And he said unto them, Take heed, and beware of covetousness: for a man's life consisteth not in the abundance of the things which he possesseth. ¹⁶And he spake a parable unto them, saying, The ground of a certain rich man brought forth plentifully: ¹⁷And he thought within himself, saying, What shall I do, because I have no room where to bestow my fruits? ¹⁸And he said, This will I do: I will pull down my barns, and build greater; and there will I bestow all my fruits and my goods. ¹⁹And I will say to my soul, Soul, thou hast much goods laid up for many years; take thine ease, eat, drink, and be merry. ²⁰But God said unto him, Thou fool, this night thy soul shall be required of thee: then whose shall those things be, which thou hast provided? ²¹So is he that layeth up treasure for himself, and is not rich toward God. (Luke 12:13-21)**

How can one person be rich and poor? He places his trust in his wealth and not in God. God provides for you, He may even allow you monetary wealth, but everything depends on where your heart is.

> **Sell that ye have, and give alms; provide yourselves bags which wax not old, a treasure in the heavens that faileth not, where no thief approacheth, neither moth corrupteth. ³⁴For where your treasure is, there**

will your heart be also. [35]Let your loins be girded about, and your lights burning; [36]And ye yourselves like unto men that wait for their lord, when he will return from the wedding; that when he cometh and knocketh, they may open unto him immediately. [37]Blessed are those servants, whom the lord when he cometh shall find watching: verily I say unto you, that he shall gird himself, and make them to sit down to meat, and will come forth and serve them. [38]And if he shall come in the second watch, or come in the third watch, and find them so, blessed are those servants.[39]And this know, that if the goodman of the house had known what hour the thief would come, he would have watched, and not have suffered his house to be broken through. [40]Be ye therefore ready also: for the Son of man cometh at an hour when ye think not. (Luke 12:33-40)

This is an expectation meant to purify us. Be ready no matter what "time" of the season you find yourself caught up in.

Luke 12:41 says, "Then Peter said unto him, Lord, speakest thou this parable unto us, or even to all?" This is where Peter is starting to catch on by way of the Holy Spirit.

Luke 12:42 says, "And the Lord said, Who then is that faithful and wise steward, whom his lord shall make ruler over his household, to give them their portion of meat in due season?" This verse is talking about the believers who are part of the Bride of Christ. The ones who chose to be part of the Bride will be made rulers over their household. Those who are part of the general church will remain for the first part of the tribulation, and will be served their own portion.

Luke 12:43-44 says, "Blessed is that servant, whom his lord when he cometh shall find so doing. Of a truth I say unto you, that he will make him ruler over all that he hath. The overcomer will inherit all things.

Luke 12:45-46 says, "But and if that servant say in his heart, My lord delayeth his coming; and shall begin to beat the menservants and maidens, and to eat and drink, and to be drunken; The lord of that servant will come in a day when he looketh not for him, and at an hour when he is not aware, and will cut him in sunder, and will appoint him his portion with the unbelievers." This is a warning for those who backslide and do not repent. These will be like the unbeliever who receives nothing. A saying my teacher uses is, "You had better have your funeral insurance paid up because it is going to get used sooner than later."

When we anticipate the coming of the Lord, it purifies us and we become simple. Today we hold grudges against people and do not show compassion to others, though we should. If we knew the Lord was returning tomorrow, we would run around like crazy asking for forgiveness and making things right in our lives. So what is stopping us from doing that now? It is God's desire that we have forgiveness always on our lips and compassion always in our heart. There is too much emphasis on worldly wealth today—even in churches. Trust in the Lord is diminishing and we can see lawlessness beginning to rise.

Luke 12:47-48 says, "And that servant, which knew his lord's will, and prepared not himself, neither did according to his will, shall be beaten with many stripes. But he that knew not, and did commit things worthy of stripes, shall be beaten with few stripes. For unto whomsoever much is given, of him shall be much required: and to whom men have committed much, of him they will ask the more. This is speaking about the levels of walking with God. Believers that are left behind will have a certain amount of relationship built with Jesus, but not much. Because they have a certain amount of relationship left at this time, it will help them grow again, just as when they first came to the Lord.

Remember when you first came to the Lord; how excited and in love with Him you were? It is that first love, that pure love that He desires from you. In the years of tribulation, life for believers who were carnal will be very difficult. For those who were openly rebellious, it will be extremely difficult, because their relationship with God is so distant that it will be harder to receive God's forgiveness. Whether carnal or rebellious, both types of believer will be left here with the knowledge that they could have been part of the Bride.

The carnal and rebellious believers can overcome their coldness and distance from God by repenting and receiving God's forgiveness, but it will be difficult. It is not that God does not want to forgive them; it is because they will feel so condemned that they will feel they cannot ask for forgiveness. The blows they feel will be their own emotions, as their feelings will overtake them in waves. Condemnation will attempt to set up house within their souls. They must fight against this and allow conviction to take over so they are able to repent.

When the warnings are speaking about the Bride, it speaks about something happening very quickly. It speaks about great rewards for those who are ready, and consequences for those who are not ready. The general church will observe Christ's visible return (in the clouds). Those who are not taken up (raptured) at the beginning of the tribulation will remain. Over the first half of the seven years of tribulation, they will have the opportunity to be purified by Christ and made ready for Him.

CHAPTER SEVEN

Overcomers: The City of Refuge and the Better Resurrection

A dam is also a picture/shadow of Christ before he fell with Eve. Eve was formed from Adam, not from his whole body, but from a hidden part, a rib bone. This can be seen as a warning for believers to enter into the holy place and be hidden in Christ now.

In the previous chapter, "overcomers" were touched on. This chapter will present a clearer picture of these overcomers. This chapter will be particularly useful in challenging you to think about walking the road of overcoming power and victory so you might be part of the Bride. That road is the sanctification process!

Revelation says, "And hast borne, and hast patience, and for my name's sake hast laboured, and hast not fainted" (Revelation 2:3). This is speaking about the seven churches and the overcomers. The term "overcomers" is another name for the Bride of Christ. Not every believer will choose to have Christ mold him or her as is required to be part of the Bride of Christ. Some want to live their own way, while others lack understanding of what it means to be clay vessels in the hands of the Master Potter (God).

The Bible says, **"Behold, I stand at the door, and knock: if any man hear my voice, and open the door, I will come** in to him, and will sup with him, and he with me. To him that overcometh will I grant to sit with me in my throne, even as I also overcame, and am set down with my Father in his throne. He that hath an ear, let him hear what the Spirit saith unto the churches" (Revelation 3: 20-22). This is describing the Bride; those who heard the voice of the Lord while on earth, who will sit with the King on the throne. They lived as Noah, overcoming the obstacles of life by hearing His voice.

Our salvation (justification) is not a reward or an inheritance because the Bible is clear that it is a gift. "For by grace are ye saved through faith; and that not of yourselves: it is the gift of God: Not of works, lest any man should boast" (Ephesians 2: 8-9).

The Bible says, "And, behold, I come quickly; and my reward is with me, to give every man according as his work shall be" (Revelation 22:12). He will have His reward with Him at an event that will happen quickly. This quick event is the catching up, the rapture. Following the example of biblical overcomers is how we learn how to become part of the Bride of Christ. The Old Testament and the New Testament contain so many types/pictures and shadows that teach us how to prepare.

This passage is helpful for gaining a better understanding of both Old and New Testament overcomers:

And what shall I more say? for the time would fail me to tell of Gedeon, and of Barak, and of Samson, and of Jephthae; of David also, and Samuel, and of the prophets: ³³Who through faith subdued kingdoms, wrought righteousness, obtained promises, stopped the mouths of lions.³⁴Quenched the violence of fire, escaped the edge of the sword, out of weakness were made strong, waxed valiant in fight, turned

to flight the armies of the aliens. ³⁵Women received their dead raised to life again: and others were tortured, not accepting deliverance; <u>that they might obtain a better resurrection</u>: ³⁶And others had trial of cruel mockings and scourgings, yea, moreover of bonds and imprisonment: ³⁷They were stoned, they were sawn asunder, were tempted, were slain with the sword: they wandered about in sheepskins and goatskins; being destitute, afflicted, tormented; ³⁸(Of whom the world was not worthy:) they wandered in deserts, and in mountains, and in dens and caves of the earth. ³⁹And these all, having obtained a good report through faith, received not the promise: ⁴⁰God having provided some better thing for us, that they without us should not be made perfect. (Hebrews 11:32-40)

We are the ones to complete what they started so we need to understand the better resurrection. A great example of understanding this is seen in the Bible account of Samson.

Samson made the better resurrection. He misused the anointing of God for his own lusts but after doing so, he became an overcomer, and received his full reward.

¹⁷That he told her all his heart, and said unto her, There hath not come a razor upon mine head; for I have been a Nazarite unto God from my mother's womb: if I be shaven, then my strength will go from me, and I shall become weak, and be like any other man. [Here we see Samson choosing the lust of the flesh and betraying God.] ¹⁸And when Delilah saw that he had told her all his heart, she sent and called for the lords of the Philistines, saying, Come up this once, for he hath shewed me all his heart. Then the lords of the Philistines came up unto her, and brought

money in their hand. [19]And she made him sleep upon her knees; and she called for a man, and she caused him to shave off the seven locks of his head; and she began to afflict him, and his strength went from him. [20]And she said, The Philistines be upon thee, Samson. And he awoke out of his sleep, and said, I will go out as at other times before, and shake myself. And he wist not that the LORD was departed from him. [21]But the Philistines took him, and put out his eyes, and brought him down to Gaza, and bound him with fetters of brass; and he did grind in the prison house. [22]Howbeit the hair of his head began to grow again after he was shaven. [23]Then the lords of the Philistines gathered them together for to offer a great sacrifice unto Dagon their god, and to rejoice: for they said, Our god hath delivered Samson our enemy into our hand. [24]And when the people saw him, they praised their god: for they said, Our god hath delivered into our hands our enemy, and the destroyer of our country, which slew many of us. (Judges 16: 17-24)

Delilah seduced Samson and the spirit of seduction that gripped Delilah got him to give up his secret. In his deception, he fell asleep, and when he was not aware, the Philistines came for him. When he awakened (physically), he realized the enemy surrounded him. He thought to himself that his strength, his spiritual relationship in the Lord, was going to be the same, but it was not. The Lord departed from him because of his sin. He was delivered into the hands of the enemy through his own sinful desire. They took him to prison and, while there, he was broken. While in this bondage, his hair started to grow back.

When we are first born again, we immediately look to Jesus when tribulation comes about in our lives. However, as time passes and our situation appears to remain the same, we have the tendency to slid back into our works. Many of us, while in the wilderness forget that Jesus is supposed to be building us because our flesh does not like to be pressed.

> **²⁵And it came to pass, when their hearts were merry, that they said, Call for Samson, that he may make us sport. And they called for Samson out of the prison house; and he made them sport: and they set him between the pillars. ²⁶And Samson said unto the lad that held him by the hand, Suffer me that I may feel the pillars whereupon the house standeth, that I may lean upon them. ²⁷Now the house was full of men and women; and all the lords of the Philistines were there; and there were upon the roof about three thousand men and women, that beheld while Samson made sport. ²⁸And Samson called unto the LORD, and said, O Lord God, remember me, I pray thee, and strengthen me, I pray thee, only this once, O God, that I may be at once avenged of the Philistines for my two eyes. ²⁹And Samson took hold of the two middle pillars upon which the house stood, and on which it was borne up, of the one with his right hand, and of the other with his left. ³⁰And Samson said, Let me die with the Philistines. And he bowed himself with all his might; and the house fell upon the lords, and upon all the people that were therein. So the dead which he slew at his death were more than they which he slew in his life. (Judges 16:25-30)**

The Philistines made sport of Samson and mocked him. When he asked to be put between the pillars, the Philistines placed him there. Samson then called out to God, he said, "Let me die with the Philistines!" What happened? Samson was finally willing to die to himself to do God's business. He was ready to die physically as well.

The Word says that we must identify ourselves with the cross. It was in Samson's death, that victory came over the Philistines. Victory was not won in his lifetime or through the works he did. His victory was not for the glory of man but solely for the glory of God.

So many times in our lives, we are trying to fight the Philistines. In the Greek lexicon, the word *Philistine* comes from the Hebrew word *Philistia*, which means *"wanderer."* A wanderer, sojourner spirit never gives us rest. That spirit keeps us worried, full of anxiety, and fearful. We must be willing to die to ourselves to overcome this sojourner spirit.

In Judges 16, the Bible says, "Then his brethren and all the house of his father came down, and took him, and brought him up, and buried him between Zorah and Eshtaol in the burying place of Manoah his father. And he judged Israel twenty years" (Judges 16:31). The word *Manoah* means *rest* (Strong's # 4495). Samson died and entered into his rest. Samson realized in his tribulation what he had to do to bring glory to God and he did it!

Samson went through a terrible thing. In a moment of despair, at the end of his life, he chose to die to himself. It was not God's choice for Samson to suffer as he did. God sent Samson through all that "stone tumbling" so He could restore him to the calling God had placed on his life. His choice to be an overcomer in the end allowed God to give Samson his reward. When Samson finally realized what he needed to do to bring God glory, he did it.

We have the same choice Samson did, to choose the easier road and recognize now the things that are not right in our lives—our sin and disobedience. We can go to the Lord right now, repent in our hearts, and be cleansed. However, if we choose not to do this now, God will ordain trials in our lives to purify us. Once we confess our sins, with a truthful heart, we will be back on the correct path, walking where we should walk. We do not need to suffer the shackles, getting our eyes plucked out, or being made to grind in the prison as Samson did. Our confession frees us from bondage to sin and sets our sight on where we need to go.

Lot was an Old Testament saint who did not receive the full reward, for he did not overcome.

> **⁷And delivered just Lot, vexed with the filthy conversation of the wicked: ⁸(For that righteous man dwelling among them, in seeing and hearing, vexed his righteous soul from day to day with their unlawful deeds;) ⁹The Lord knoweth how to deliver the godly out of temptations, and to reserve the unjust unto the day of judgment to be punished. (2 Peter 2:7-9)**

It says that Lot is a righteous man and he is justified by his faith in God, but his soul is vexed. The word *vex* means to *oppress* or *suppress* in the Greek translation, (Strong's # 2669). Lot allowed his soul to be oppressed and afflicted.

In Genesis, the Bible records, **"And there came two angels to Sodom at even; and Lot sat in the gate of Sodom: and Lot seeing them rose up to meet them; and he bowed himself with his face toward the ground" (Genesis 19:1).** When Lot saw the angels approaching, he bowed his face to the ground due to conviction in his heart. He also knew to be reverent toward God and His messengers.

Genesis 19:24 says, "Then the LORD rained upon Sodom and upon Gomorrah brimstone and fire from the LORD out of heaven." When Lot left the city, fire came down. Everything he owned burned up, leaving him impoverished. (Material goods are as wood, hay and stubble and easily burned up.)

At the judgment seat of Christ, there will be a fire to purify us as well.

According to the grace of God which is given unto me, as a wise masterbuilder, I have laid the foundation, and another buildeth thereon. But let every man take heed how he buildeth thereupon. ¹¹For other foundation can no man lay than that is laid, which is Jesus Christ. ¹²Now if any man build upon this foundation gold, silver, precious stones, wood, hay, stubble; ¹³Every man's work shall be made manifest: for the day shall declare it, because it shall be revealed by fire; and the fire shall try every man's work of what sort it is. ¹⁴If any man's work abide which he hath built thereupon, he shall receive a reward. ¹⁵If any man's work shall be burned, he shall suffer loss: but he himself shall be saved; yet so as by fire. (1 Corinthians 3:10-15)

This fire will burn up anything that does not glorify God. Whatever passes through that fire and survives will determine the rewards we will receive.

Lot lost everything when Sodom burned up. That is, he lost worldly riches, but gained some heavenly reward. God tumbled him because of what he chose. God showed his love and mercy to Lot by saving him from Sodom's destruction. Lot is the perfect example of a "satisfied pew warmer," intent on doing nothing for God beyond just sitting.

King Saul

Another Old Testament saint who did not get his full reward was King Saul. God chastised Saul because Saul refused to submit to Him. When Saul went against God's Word and visited a medium, she called up Samuel. Samuel came forth through God's power, not due to the power of the medium. God spoke to Saul one more time and still he did not repent.

¹³And the king said unto her, Be not afraid: for what sawest thou? And the woman said unto Saul, I saw gods ascending out of the earth. ¹⁴And he said unto her, What form is he of? And she said, An old man cometh up; and he is covered with a mantle. And Saul perceived that it was Samuel, and he stooped with his face to the ground, and bowed himself. ¹⁵And Samuel said to Saul, Why hast thou disquieted me, to bring me up? And Saul answered, I am sore distressed; for the Philistines make war against me, and God is departed from me, and answereth me no more, neither by prophets, nor by dreams: therefore I have called thee, that thou mayest make known unto me what I shall do" (1 Samuel 28: 13-15).

Take note that Samuel was at a place of peace and rest, yet he was called up from below.

"Moreover the LORD will also deliver Israel with thee into the hand of the Philistines: and tomorrow shalt thou and thy sons be with me: the LORD also shall deliver the host of Israel into the hand of the Philistines" (1 Samuel 28:19). The Lord was going to deliver Israel into the hands of the Philistines and he and his sons would go to God. Though Saul was not an overcomer but he was a saint, so in the end, he was saved.

What is the secret to becoming an overcomer? "And they overcame him by the blood of the Lamb, and by the word of their testimony; and they loved not their lives unto the death" (Revelation 12:11). We overcome when we are willing to die to our selfish ambition, personal agendas and sinful desires. We do not need a person to help us figure ourselves out in Christ. Having a mentor is fine but we must work out our own walk. Every time we are in despair, under pressure, stressed, anxious, or discouraged it is that philistine, sojourning spirit trying to overcome us.

That is why it is so important to get into our correct identity with the death, burial, and resurrection of Jesus Christ, so we will overcome the enemy!

The Better Resurrection

Understanding what the Word says about the better resurrection and what it means, can really blow open one's understanding. First, we must understand the better resurrection for Old Testament saints. A place of paradise existed before the time of Jesus' resurrection. Some mistakenly believe this to be purgatory.

We see the picture of paradise and a picture of hell in Luke:

And it came to pass, that the beggar died, and was carried by the angels into Abraham's bosom: the rich man also died, and was buried; ²³And in hell he lift up his eyes, being in torments, and seeth Abraham afar off, and Lazarus in his bosom. ²⁴And he cried and said, Father Abraham, have mercy on me, and send Lazarus, that he may dip the tip of his finger in water, and cool my tongue; for I am tormented in this flame. ²⁵But Abraham said, Son, remember that thou in thy lifetime receivedst thy good things, and likewise Lazarus evil things: but now he is comforted, and thou art tormented. ²⁶And beside all this, between us and you there is a great gulf fixed: so that they which would pass from hence to you cannot; neither can they pass to us, that would come from thence. (Luke 16:22-26)

Paradise is located above hell yet also in the earth with a great chasm separating them. Those in hell are in great agony and they can see across the great chasm. Before Christ was raised from the dead, paradise was under the earth and hell, though a separate place, was also located there.

Here is a picture of paradise as recorded in Numbers:

Then ye shall appoint you cities to be cities of refuge for you; that the slayer may flee thither, which killeth any person at unawares. [12]And they shall be unto you cities for refuge from the avenger; that the manslayer die not, until he stand before the congregation in judgment. [13]And of these cities which ye shall give six cities shall ye have for refuge. [14]Ye shall give three cities on this side Jordan, and three cities shall ye give in the land of Canaan, which shall be cities of refuge. [15]These six cities shall be a refuge, both for the children of Israel, and for the stranger, and for the sojourner among them: that every one that killeth any person unawares may flee thither. [16]And if he smite him with an instrument of iron, so that he die, he is a murderer: the murderer shall surely be put to death. [17]And if he smite him with throwing a stone, wherewith he may die, and he die, he is a murderer: the murderer shall surely be put to death. [18]Or if he smite him with an hand weapon of wood, wherewith he may die, and he die, he is a murderer: the murderer shall surely be put to death. [19]The revenger of blood himself shall slay the murderer: when he meeteth him, he shall slay him. [20]But if he thrust him of hatred, or hurl at him by laying of wait, that he die; [21]Or in enmity smite him with his hand, that he die: he that smote him shall surely be put to death; for he is a murderer: the revenger of blood shall slay the murderer, when he meeteth him. [22]But if he thrust him suddenly without enmity, or have cast upon him any thing without laying of wait, [23]Or with any stone, wherewith a man may die,

seeing him not, and cast it upon him, that he die, and was not his enemy, neither sought his harm: ²⁴Then the congregation shall judge between the slayer and the revenger of blood according to these judgments: ²⁵And the congregation shall deliver the slayer out of the hand of the revenger of blood, and the congregation shall restore him to the city of his refuge, whither he was fled: and he shall abide in it unto the death of the high priest, which was anointed with the holy oil. (Numbers 35:11-25)

If you killed someone by accident, you are to go to a city of refuge. If they judged it was an accident, you would not be sentenced to death at the hand of the avenger of blood. Though you would have to stay in the city, you could not leave. The penalty for leaving would be death.

The city of refuge was a place you could go if you committed a crime unintentionally to avoid having revenge taken against you. All the Old Testament saints had sinned, but they were not considered guilty because of the coming justification. They looked forward to the crucifixion and resurrection of Christ. When the Old Testament saints died, they went to the city of refuge (paradise). It was a place of protection, yet also a place of captivity.

When were they set free? How were they justified? At the death and resurrection of Jesus, the great High Priest, they were justified and set free! Not one person before the death and resurrection of Jesus Christ was justified before Him until then. He had to complete His work first, and in that completion, His Spirit went into paradise to preach to the Old Testament Saints who had to make a choice. A passage from Luke explains this more clearly:

And one of the malefactors which were hanged railed on him, saying, If thou be Christ, save thy-

**self and us. ⁴⁰But the other answering rebuked him, saying, Dost not thou fear God, seeing thou art in the same condemnation? ⁴¹And we indeed justly; for we receive the due reward of our deeds: but this man hath done nothing amiss. ⁴²And he said unto Jesus, Lord, remember me when thou comest into thy kingdom. ⁴³And Jesus said unto him, Verily I say unto thee, Today shalt thou be with me in paradise"
(Luke 23:39-43).**

The thief recognizes who is hanging next to Him. This thief was not born again because he could not be until after Christ's resurrection. The thief's salvation was the same as the Old Testament saints. Look at what verse 43 says again: "Today shalt thou be with me in paradise."

The Word also speaks about Christ going into hell, which should have been our punishment (Acts 2:22-27). Our redemption was not only about Christ hanging on the cross, receiving the curses, but also about us deserving to suffer in hell for eternity. Acts 2:22-27 quotes from the book of Psalms.

This Psalm was prophetic, speaking of Christ suffering in hell. **"Thou hast laid me in the lowest pit, in darkness, in the deeps" (Psalm 88:6).** Psalm 88 speaks of Christ's soul in hell and the wrath of God coming down upon him for what each one of us should be receiving for eternity. Christ absorbed all of it for 3 days and 3 nights.

₇ Thy wrath lieth hard upon me, and thou hast afflicted me with all thy waves. Selah. ⁸Thou hast put away mine acquaintance far from me; thou hast made me an abomination unto them: I am shut up, and I cannot come forth. ⁹Mine eye mourneth by reason of affliction: LORD, I have called daily upon thee, I have stretched out my hands unto thee. ¹⁰Wilt thou shew wonders to the dead? shall the dead arise

and praise thee? Selah. ¹¹Shall thy lovingkindness be declared in the grave? or thy faithfulness in destruction? ¹²Shall thy wonders be known in the dark? and thy righteousness in the land of forgetfulness? ¹³But unto thee have I cried, O LORD; and in the morning shall my prayer prevent thee. ¹⁴LORD, why castest thou off my soul? why hidest thou thy face from me? ¹⁵I am afflicted and ready to die from my youth up: while I suffer thy terrors I am distracted. ¹⁶Thy fierce wrath goeth over me; thy terrors have cut me off. ¹⁷They came round about me daily like water; they compassed me about together. ¹⁸Lover and friend hast thou put far from me, and mine acquaintance into darkness. (Psalm 88:7-18)

Christ's soul would soon be suffering in hell, but he said to the thief, "Verily I say unto thee, today shalt thou be with me in paradise." It is important to note that it was the Passover, a Jewish festival. Jesus also fulfilled the Day of Atonement, the middle of the three fall festivals. Knowing the festivals of the Old Testament and discerning the shadows and pictures from them is important. (I recommend reading, *The Seven Festivals of the Messiah,* by Rabbi Eddie Chumney.) In Leviticus, we find this:

⁷And he shall take the two goats, and present them before the LORD at the door of the tabernacle of the congregation. ⁸And Aaron shall cast lots upon the two goats; one lot for the LORD, and the other lot for the scapegoat. ⁹And Aaron shall bring the goat upon which the LORD's lot fell, and offer him for a sin offering. ¹⁰But the goat, on which the lot fell to be the scapegoat, shall be presented alive before the LORD, to make an atonement with him, and to let him go for a scapegoat into the wilderness. (Leviticus 16:7-10)

This is what the high priest did for the atonement of sins and Christ literally fulfilled on Calvary for the spirit, soul, and body. Christ is the High Priest and He offered Himself as the sacrifice. He bore our sins and for 3 days and 3 nights, He endured the wilderness. The word *wilderness* (Strong's #8414) means, *an uninhabitable place,* which is hell. He went there so we would not have to. His soul went down into the depths of hell for three days and three nights (Matthew 12:38-40). His soul was sacrificed for us, but not His spirit; it is our soul that sins.

If His soul went into hell for 3 days and 3 nights, where did His spirit go? **"For Christ also hath once suffered for sins, the just for the unjust, that he might bring us to God, being put to death in the flesh, but quickened by the Spirit" (1 Peter 3:18).** Christ died for our sins once and for all, for the righteous and the unrighteous, to bring us all unto Him.

Christ was put to death in the body but made alive by the Spirit, **"By which also he went and preached unto the spirits in prison; which sometime were disobedient, when once the longsuffering of God waited in the days of Noah, while the ark was a preparing, wherein few, that is, eight souls were saved by water" (1 Peter 3:19-20).** Verse 19 says that Jesus went into the city of refuge (paradise) to preach in Spirit to the spirits already there. The spirits of all the Old Testament dead who died in the Lord were in Paradise. His soul was not preaching in hell because His soul was the sacrifice. His Spirit as High Priest went into the city of refuge, paradise, and set the captives free.

When a person dies as an unbeliever, the spirit of that man goes back to God; his soul is sent to hell, and his body returns to the dust of the earth. If the rich man in hell was talking, feeling torment, and thirsty, why was he considered dead? He was alone in the wilderness in an uninhabitable place. He could still know things but no longer had a consciousness of God, because when one is in hell, God is no longer conscious of him.

Where there is a spirit, there is a consciousness of God. Where there is no spirit, there is no consciousness of God. The unbeliever, when alive but not born again, has an awareness of God. There is a potential for him to be born again, but if that person does not accept Christ as their Lord and Savior at death, the spirit leaves and the soul goes to hell. It is absolutely correct to call that state in hell "death" because one is without spirit and it is ABSOLUTE SECLUSION! This means no communication with God. The rich man is still there! He is being tormented as his sins wash over him forever.

Why did Jesus say He just preached to the spirits? They were not in the agony of being without a spirit or being without a consciousness of God. They were sent into a place of protection to wait for Him because while alive their actions concerning God, met the right criteria.

Where is the better resurrection?

The bible tells us about the better resurrection in Matthew:

[50]Jesus, when he had cried again with a loud voice, yielded up the ghost. [51]And, behold, the veil of the temple was rent in twain from the top to the bottom; and the earth did quake, and the rocks rent; [52]And the graves were opened; and many bodies of the saints which slept arose, [53]And came out of the graves after his resurrection, and went into the holy city, and appeared unto many. (Matthew 27: 50-53)

Where was the better resurrection when Christ rose from the dead? When Christ died many of the saint's tombs opened up. When He rose from the dead, they also rose. The saints that rose were the ones who overcame. The overcomers received their new bodies because while they were alive, they went the distance seeking Christ, which is the better resurrection. All the spirits that were in the city of refuge, even the ones that were not overcomers, were taken up. **"Wherefore he saith, When he ascended up on high, he led captivity captive, and gave gifts unto men" (Ephesians 4:8).**

Paul talks about *all* of the dead in Christ being changed at the resurrection (1Corinthians 15: 51-54). He also talks about attaining *unto the resurrection of the dead* (Philippians 3:11). What is the difference?

The Greek word for resurrection in Philippians 3:11 is *exanatello* (Strong's #1816). This is the only time it is used anywhere. It means, *springing up abundantly above*. The Greek word for resurrection everywhere else is *anastasis* and means *a rising up*. This is the difference between the rapture of the Bride at the beginning of the tribulation and the rapture of the general church in the middle of it. The level of maturity makes the difference. The Bride of Christ is mature, while the general church is immature.

The Two Judgment Seats

The first seat is the Great White Throne judgment, which is for all the Old Testament believers who did not rise when Jesus did, and for all the unbelievers. Here they will be judged and sent to heaven or cast into the lake of fire. This happens at the end of the one thousand year reign of Christ on earth.

The Judgment Seat of Christ is for all born again believers who are part of the church. This judgment is a place for receiving rewards where our works will be tried by fire. Anything that is not of Christ will burn. This happens at the first part of the Second Coming of Christ (Revelation 22:12). Amen.

A Few Points to Ponder

Adam	The Bride & The General Church
The body of Adam	The Body of Christ
A hidden part, a rib, was used to form Adams bride, Eve.	Those who hide themselves in Christ will be made into His Bride.
The rest of his body remained, in tack, to be formed.	The general church will remain for the first 3 ½ years of the 7 year tribulation to be purified.
Adam suffered after he sinned.	They will suffer because of their sin.

CHAPTER EIGHT

The Ten Virgins and the Five Characteristics

God's desire is for everyone to be part of the Bride of Christ. Whether or not we will be a part of the Bride of Christ or not depends on our sanctification and how much we lovingly yield to the Lord.

The parable of the 10 virgins in Matthew 25:1-13 is well known, but many interpret it incorrectly. As you read this chapter, remember the whole parable is about the end times and about being ready. It is not speaking about justification. If it was about justification it would not contain the word *watch* because all you have to do is receive the Lord and you are saved, or justified. *Watchfulness* is part of any growing relationship.

"Then shall the kingdom of heaven be likened unto ten virgins, which took their lamps, and went forth to meet the bridegroom" (Matthew 25:1). Christ is speaking here of a future event, His return. The Kingdom of God will be like the ten virgins and all ten of them are representative of the Kingdom of Heaven. They took their lamps and went forward to meet the bridegroom. This means ALL ten virgins had a desire to be part of the Bride, at least at the beginning.

Remember, not all believers desire to be part of the Bride. They are saved, happy and they are going to do what they want, but they are still children of God. (Remember Lot. Though his soul was vexed, he just sat in his situation. Nothing changed nor improved for him.)

First, the ten virgins are not representing people invited to a wedding as guests. Second, if they were bridesmaids they would be waiting for the bride. They are waiting for the Bridegroom who is Jesus Christ because they want to be the Bride.

The parable goes on to say the virgins took out their lamps. What do lamps represent? The Bible tells us that believers are the light of the world. Our witness, our testimony is a lamp unto the world. This is our confession before the world. **"Ye are the salt of the earth: but if the salt have lost his savour, wherewith shall it be salted? it is thenceforth good for nothing, but to be cast out, and to be trodden under foot of men. Ye are the light of the world. A city that is set on an hill cannot be hid" (Matthew 5:13-14).**

Just because we have a lamp does not mean it is burning bright or even lit. Some believers allow their lamp light to flicker or burn out. A flicker glows bright, then dims, which is representative of an emotional spirit. Once the "high" of the emotion is spent, we will dim.

Ten is also the number of testing to see if we fit the right criteria. "And he declared unto you his covenant, which he commanded you to perform, even ten commandments; and he wrote them upon two tables of stone" (Dueteronomy 4:13). Ten is the number of "right criteria." So do we fit the right criteria?

Here is an example of ten fitting the right criteria:

²And Abraham said unto his eldest servant of his house, that ruled over all that he had, Put, I pray thee, thy hand under my thigh: ³And I will make thee swear by the LORD, the God of heaven, and the God of the earth, that thou shalt not take a wife unto my son of the daughters of the Canaanites, among whom I dwell: ⁴But thou shalt go unto my country,

and to my kindred, and take a wife unto my son Isaac. (Genesis 24:2-4)

Take note of these comparisons:

1. Abraham sent his chief servant out to find a bride for his son Isaac.
2. God the Father sent the Holy Spirit out to prepare a bride for His Son. The Holy Spirit is the one entrusted with preparing the Bride.
1. The chief servant was entrusted with all that Abraham had when he set out to find and prepare a bride for his son. In verse 4, it says he went into Abraham's own country to get a wife for his son.
2. Through the Father, believers are related in Christ. Since we all have the same Father, the Holy Spirit goes out among God's people to find His Bride.

"And the servant took ten camels of the camels of his master, and departed; for all the goods of his master were in his hand: and he arose, and went to Mesopotamia, unto the city of Nahor" (Genesis 24:10).

1. He took all the goods of his master.
2. God has devoted everything to prepare His Bride. He gave His own Son so He could bring forth a Bride.

[11]And he made his camels to kneel down without the city by a well of water at the time of the evening, even the time that women go out to draw water. [12]And he said O LORD God of my master Abraham, I pray thee, send me good speed this day, and shew kindness unto my master Abraham. [13]Behold, I stand here by the well of water; and the daughters of the men of the

city come out to draw water: (Now listen to the criteria for the Bride.) **¹⁴And let it come to pass, that the damsel to whom I shall say, Let down thy pitcher, I pray thee, that I may drink; and she shall say, Drink, and I will give thy camels drink also: let the same be she that thou hast appointed for thy servant Isaac; and thereby shall I know that thou hast shewed kindness unto my master. (Genesis 24:11-14)**

The servant would know the woman who was to be Isaac's bride by these criteria: she would provide water for the chief servant and all ten of his camels. Those who are part of the Bride of Christ love to go the extra mile. They are obedient and give service to others without complaint. Going the extra mile requires pressing forward with God even when it hurts our flesh. When God is working in our hearts, we are willing to do what He requires. Even when it hurts or causes us to deny ourselves some pleasure or ambition, we must still press forward.

Rebekah not only gave the chief servant water, but the camels as well. She did not complain or ask questions. Hers was the desire to serve. Servanthood allows us to be a part of the Bride of Christ. (Do you realize how much water a camel drinks? A lot! Yet she gave them water without complaining.)

If one cannot be a servant to his fellow man, without complaint, how can one be a servant to God? Rebekah served as needed. God provides for our needs. He provides for you and me and all we have to do is have the desire for Him and then allow the Holy Spirit to manifest it through us. Rebekah fit the right criteria.

The Virgins

The Bible records, **"And five of them were wise, and five were foolish" (Matthew 25:2).** They were all virgins. Why?

Because when we receive the Lord as our Savior we are born again and Christ enters our spirit. We become justified before God the Father. Judicially we are made perfect and in our spirit we are made perfect. Have you seen a fellow believer being unwise? Five are foolish and five are wise.

Before I go further, allow me to point something out here. Many believers understand this parable to be speaking about five saved (wise) and five unsaved (foolish) people. The Bible, when it speaks of the unsaved, the words used are different. We see words such as, fornicators, whores, and harlots. One must realize that the word "virgin" denotes purity. Ask yourself, "Would the Lord use that word to describe the lost world?" No.

"They that were foolish took their lamps, and took no oil with them" (Matthew 25:3). Why did they take their lamps and leave their oil behind? If you have a flashlight with you in the daytime, would you be worrying about batteries at that given moment? No, because the day lights your path and all seems well.

They thought it was foolish to carry around the lamps, perhaps thinking, "Yeah, we got a real good witness here, and as long as it doesn't get dark, we will be just fine." They probably didn't know that it was going to get dark and they would have no need to see where they were going. It was not because their lamps were shining because it was still light outside.

This is how it is with us when we think we have a closer walk with God than we actually do. We begin to see just how much of a relationship we have when it gets dark. Trials and tribulations come upon us suddenly, so we must keep our lamps burning bright. God allows us to go through trials to wake us up to check what is truly in our heart. Trials help us see if we are holding onto our lamp and how much oil we have with us. **"But the wise took oil in their vessels with their lamps" (Matthew 25:4).** The wise ones had their oil in their jars. They grew spiritually.

Have you ever pondered the word *vessel* in this parable, and what it signifies? What contains the anointing in our lives? The character of Christ in us contains the anointing. When we pray for others, they are healed because God is faithful.

People often blame God for not healing them or for removing them from their circumstances. They will say "God doesn't work in my life," or "God doesn't heal me." God always does his part, though we often fail or have a hard time doing our part. Many of us find it is easier to complain and murmur than to press in and walk through a wilderness experience. We do not want to admit our faults or that we are wrong. What takes tremendous character is to respond with love and faith when people hurt us. It also takes tremendous character for us to admit when we've hurt others.

The five wise virgins had vessels and these vessels contained oil.

[19]Nevertheless the foundation of God standeth sure, having this seal, The Lord knoweth them that are his. And, let every one that nameth the name of Christ depart from iniquity. [20]But in a great house there are not only vessels of gold and of silver, but also of wood and of earth; and some to honour, and some to dishonour. [21]If a man therefore purge himself from these, he shall be a vessel unto honour, sanctified, and meet for the master's use, and prepared unto every good work. (2 Timothy 2: 19-21)

The foundations of God stand sure, amen! He does the preparation in us if we are willing to submit to His ways. How is your vessel? Is it refined and purified as gold and silver or is it merely wood and stubble? Which one is your character compared to?

When we are born again we have the nature of Christ within our spirit. The fullness of God is within our spirit. As we allow

Christ to live through us, His character becomes evident in our soul, and is outwardly evident. As our character grows and matures, that influence of God touches the people around us. It also brings judgment to those in sin without us even speaking a word at times. That is the oil burning in us as the light shines through us.

Some people have the nature of Christ, but they do not allow the development of the character of Christ in their souls. For such requires a process of denial, intimacy with God and seeing who we really are.

What are the characteristics the Lord is looking for? From Hosea we glean five characteristics of the of the Bride: **"And I will betroth thee unto me for ever; yea, I will betroth thee unto me in (1)righteousness, and in (2)judgment, and in (3)lovingkindness, and in (4)mercies. ²⁰I will even betroth thee unto me in (5)faithfulness: and thou shalt know the LORD" (Hosea 2:19-20).** (Numbers added.) The five wise virgins had these characteristics and the five foolish ones did not. Once you begin to recognize these characteristics developing, it does not mean the process is over, it just means you now have the right criteria for the process to begin.

Love goes beyond words. We can say to God, "I love you! I love you!" but how do we respond when someone hurts us? Whatever love we express in that instance is the amount of love that has grown in our character. Through trials, the Lord shows us where our love and character still need work. When we are in love with Jesus beyond mere words, He starts moving us forward.

"And because iniquity shall abound, the love of many shall wax cold" (Matthew 24:12). The true love of God will carry us through when everything around us grows dark, cold, and wicked. When we read of injustices in our society, of the failures of our government, of people getting away with hideous crimes—what happens to our hearts? What begins to grow in our hearts? Does the light of Christ begin to burn the oil and shine brightly through us, or do our wicks dry out as hate begins to dim our light?

Most of us do not realize that iniquity around us must not to quench the love of Christ in our heart, but is meant to enhance and purify it. When we have the love of Christ in us and we become hurt or offended, that love will continue to strengthen us if you allow it to and it will keep us close to the Lord.

The process of having our character molded into the character of Christ is difficult. But if we try to buck the process, it only makes it more difficult. There is only one way to experience the full process. In Ephesians, we find this: **"From whom the whole body fitly joined together and compacted by that which every joint supplieth, according to the effectual working in the measure of every part, maketh increase of the body unto the edifying of itself in love" (Ephesians 4:16).**

The only way a believer can come to the place of full reward (the hundredfold reward), is with the rest of the Body of Christ. If you say you are going to serve Christ on your own or restrict any ministry of Christ from any brother or sister in the Lord, you have just said no to the Holy Spirit and rejected what Christ has planned for you.

When you have a hard time and you do not want to see people—you do not want to pray, or think you do not need Jesus—that is when you need Him the most. Deception can creep in very easily when you are hurting or vulnerable.

Sometimes we need to be carried to Jesus. The Bible recounts the story of a paralyzed man who wanted to receive healing from Jesus. To get to Him, the man had to be carried by his friends. His friends lowered him down through the ceiling of the place where Jesus was speaking and placed him right before Jesus.

There will be times in our lives when we will be so weak or "paralyzed" that we will need our brothers and sisters to carry us in prayer to the Lord Jesus, so we can be touched and healed. We are united and we need each other. Every one of us is important to God and must be important to one another. We must lift one another up so we can receive blessing.

Your walk is tied to my walk and my walk is tied to your walk. If we are not pulling each other up, we are both missing the boat. Salvation is a singular event but "iron sharpening iron" is a collective event. There seems to be a "new" way of thinking creeping into the church, that salvation is somehow a collective event! The Word of God refutes that and those that know the truth know to rebuke it. (2 Cor.11:3-4).

"While the bridegroom tarried, they all slumbered and slept" (Matthew 25:5). What's going on here? Why did the bridegroom tarry or take long in coming? If he had not taken long, would that have been better? **"The Lord is not slack concerning his promise, as some men count slackness; but is longsuffering to us-ward, not willing that any should perish, but that all should come to repentance" (2 Peter 3:9).** It is God's will for all to become part of the Bride so He gave them a greater chance to prepare by taking a long time in coming. He is not saying that He is going to take a long time so that more will fall away. He is waiting for us to catch the vision and be part of the Bride and for more to come into salvation.

Matthew 25:5 says they became drowsy and slept. When Adam was in a state of slumber, God formed his bride Eve. There are two ways of looking at how they slept. One is a matter of entering into God's rest, which is a place where we stop striving and struggling. We rest in what God is doing in us and through us.

The other way of looking at sleep is that of not being watchful. When Jesus went into the garden to pray He asked His disciples to watch and pray, but they fell asleep. When you see two Christians side by side, you cannot tell who is sleeping in rest or in turmoil until you see their lives. It is not until someone upsets them or a trial comes along, that you will be able to tell the truth in them.

The five virgins who were ready and prepared with the oil were at rest. The five foolish virgins were sitting around with the five wise ones thinking they must be okay because the wise ones were still there and it was still light outside. They just slacked off and didn't realize it was getting dark, so they didn't prepare for the coming darkness, (tribulation).

The five wise ones were prepared because they were entering in and maintaining that readiness in their relationship. The five foolish ones were fooled because they thought, "well, we've got lamps too and were right here too." They were not ready and they took for granted the time that was passing. They did not realize that God was giving them the opportunity to get the oil and prepare—to get vessels that had character and receive the anointing that they needed.

"And at midnight there was a cry made, Behold, the bridegroom cometh; go ye out to meet him" (Matthew 25:6). When did the bridegroom come? At midnight, like a thief in the night. Why did He do that? Because one needs a lamp at midnight. Also, it was a Jewish custom for the bridegroom to *abduct* his bride in the middle of the night with a shout and the sound of a ram's horn!

In the end times, darkness grows more and more abundant. The children of God who allow Christ to shine forth will be brilliant and shine brighter and brighter. A hundred years ago, you could tell a Christian apart from someone who was not. Now there is a vast array of churches, a wide assortment of lifestyles, and so many voices that they drown each other out. A follower of Christ Jesus should be standing out from the rest, their light penetrating all those worldly voices.

"Then all those virgins arose, and trimmed their lamps" (Matthew 25:7). They all woke up, trimmed their lamps, and tried to light them. "And the foolish said unto the wise, Give us of your oil; for our lamps are gone out" (Matthew 25:8). The foolish said to the wise, 'give us some of your oil.' They thought they could live off someone else's sanctification and anointing.

You cannot do this. You have to allow Christ to develop the anointing and sanctification in your own heart.

The Bible says there will be two men sleeping and one will go while the other will stay. Two people will be in the field and one will go while the other will stay. It will not matter how close you are to the anointed people—you have to be one. You must grab the shovel and dig for the deeper things of God. It's a process of relationship, character, and love.

Verse 7 is the key evidence that all ten virgins were saved. If the five foolish were a reference speaking about the "lost," then the word "arose" would not have been applied to all ten. The world, out of their ignorance, remains asleep to the things of God.

Noah represents the overcomers. When they got into the ark and the door closed, the people outside could still repent and be saved, but they could no longer enter in and be part of God's better work. It did not matter how close they came or snuggled up to the ark. If they were not inside the ark, they were in trouble.

The same thing is going on here with the five foolish ones asking the wise ones for oil. They did **not** understand what it means to be sanctified. They thought, "Well, let's go to service, have a good time, pray and say 'Lord, sanctify me now,' and then we're done 'til next Sunday."

The second thing is, their lamps were going out and they failed to realize it. What happens to a wick when it doesn't have oil for fuel? It burns the wick only and for a very short time. The foolish were burning only their wicks. What happens when we try to pretend we have the light of God in us and we are just playing a game? For instance, when someone walks around trying to appear holy, proclaiming their love for you in Christ, yet if you hurt them, look out! The lines are drawn and the truth is exposed in the hearts of those involved. We try to pretend we have oil in our character when we are really just burning our wicks. That is what the five foolish virgins were doing. They were burning their wicks and they were burning out quickly. If only we could grasp the understanding that God allows difficulties in our lives to wake us up. Then when midnight comes we will be ready and the oil in us will shine forever.

Recognition of our faults is powerful thing! Sadly, some do not see this and their time on this earth is cut short and all the plans God had bestowed in their life withers up and dies.

"But the wise answered, saying, Not so; lest there be not enough for us and you: but go ye rather to them that sell, and buy for yourselves" (Matthew 25:9). You cannot live off someone else's anointing, you have to get it yourself. The wise told the foolish to go buy it for themselves. How do you suppose they buy it? Justification is free; it is the gift of God, not by works so that any man should boast. Therefore, it costs us nothing to be saved. It also speaks of rewards concerning our inheritance and working out our own salvation with fear and trembling. This is where the cost comes in because it costs us everything (our desires) to be a disciple.

"And he said to them all, If any man will come after me, let him deny himself, and take up his cross daily, and follow me. [24]For whosoever will save his life shall lose it: but whosoever will lose his life for my sake, the same shall save it" (Luke 9:23-24). The word *deny* means not only to deny but to affirm that you have no acquaintance or connection with yourself.

Why do we become offended or discouraged? Often it is because we, "Have a reputation to uphold!" or "I've got feelings!" or "I've got an agenda!" and "I'm not denying myself anything!" When someone tells us about a bad thing happening to someone else, our first response is most likely, "Oh, that's too bad." We do not get disgruntled, angry, or upset—we even pray for them. BUT if it happens to us, we get upset, angry— forget it if we have self-interest involved. The whole world must stop and pray for us!

And whosoever doth not bear his cross, and come after me, cannot be my disciple. [28]For which of you, intending to build a tower, sitteth not down first, and counteth the cost, whether he have sufficient to finish it? [29]Lest haply, after he hath laid the foundation, and is not able to finish it, all that behold it begin to mock him" (Luke 14:27-29). That's what happens to believers when we start walking with the Lord. After the newness wears off, some will begin to walk backwards. Unbelievers mock them if they backslide. They do this because they see the person walking in their old nature. The world is a place where "mockery" dwells. It waits to devour a backslidden Christian.

The Word says if we lay a foundation and are unable to finish it, everyone who sees it will ridicule us. Have you heard unbeliever's say, "Look at that guy; he was a Christian but look at him now!" He is in that state because he did not want to deny himself. He is saved but he is not going to get what God wants him to have.

"Saying, This man began to build, and was not able to finish. [31]Or what king, going to make war against another king, sitteth not down first, and consulteth whether he be able with ten thousand to meet him that cometh against him with twenty thousand? [32]Or else, while the other is yet a great way off, he sendeth an ambassage, and desireth conditions of peace. [33]So likewise, whosoever he be of you that forsaketh not all that he hath, he cannot be my disciple" (Luke 14:30-33). That is the key; it costs us everything.

"Again, the kingdom of heaven is like unto treasure hid in a field; the which when a man hath found, he hideth, and for joy thereof goeth and selleth all that he hath, and buyeth that field. [45]Again, the kingdom of heaven is like unto a merchant man, seeking goodly pearls: [46]Who, when

he had found one pearl of great price, went and sold all that he had, and bought it" (Matthew 13:44-46). You know what Christ did? He found that pearl of great price in us and He died and gave everything up for us.

If you want to know what it is going to cost you, read Isaiah 53. That is how we "buy" sanctification (the justification is free). The sanctification is a process of laying down our lives and it is going to cost us everything we are; everything our flesh desires and wants so we can allow Christ to live through us. This takes time and is a process of yielding. It is not like one day I decide to love the Lord and the next day I do what I want.

"And while they went to buy, the bridegroom came; and they that were ready went in with him to the marriage: and the door was shut" (Matthew 25:10).

"Let us be glad and rejoice, and give honour to him: for the marriage of the Lamb is come, and his wife hath made herself ready" (Revelation 19:7). The ones that can come in were the ones who were ready.

"Afterward came also the other virgins, saying, Lord, Lord, open to us. 12But he answered and said, Verily I say unto you, I know you not" (Matthew 25:11-12). Does this mean they were not saved? No, because remember He comes for the Bride first because He knows them and they know Him. The five foolish were not ready, because they did not get to know Him. (Take note, to *know* here means *intimately*; to develop a relationship.)

The door is shut just like the door on Noah's ark. It did not mean other people could not be saved, it means they did not choose to enter in and were not ready. The door was shut and the wedding of Christ and His Bride was taking place.

"Watch therefore, for ye know neither the day nor the hour wherein the Son of man cometh" (Matthew 25:13).

The key word here is *watch*. Remember there are five principles that God wants to develop in believers. We must allow Him (not men) to develop and form us.

The Five Characteristics and How They Apply to the Fivefold Ministry

There are five major principles we can glean from five major victories over the Philistines. In the same order, God develops these principles in us.

Remember that the word *Philistine* means *wander* and suggests an unsettled spirit. It is the spirit that takes us from the realm of faith into the realm of the five senses. For example, when we realize the scope of a challenge we are facing, and we stop having faith (faith realm), relying instead on our own understanding (five senses), we have just wandered off the lit path. As we allow God to build these characteristics in us, we will not do that as much, eventually stopping altogether.

"And I will betroth thee unto me for ever; yea, I will betroth thee unto me in righteousness, and in judgment, and in loving-kindness, and in mercies" (Hosea 2:19). The fivefold ministry, directed by God, is designed to develop these qualities in each one of us, even in the order they appear in this verse.

The Apostle: This is the one who is given the anointing to bring forth doctrine, unity of faith and a picture of God's blueprint. They have grasped the true understanding of ***righteousness***; which means right relationships.

Christ moves the apostle to guide righteousness within the church and in us as individuals. When it develops, we see one another as Christ sees us as God sees the world— in right relationships. The blueprint of the church is manifest through the apostolic ministry. The apostle deals with our hearing. If you want right relationships, it doesn't matter how much you see, it all depends on how you hear things.

The Prophet: Is the one who brings forth judgment and justice for us so we can judge ourselves correctly. **_Justice/judgment_**; Christ moves a prophet to give vision. We see things in our lives that are not right. We begin to judge ourselves and start to repent for those things, bringing forth the work of God. Many times, we do not want to judge ourselves. God did not call us to judge others according to what we feel someone is doing wrong. He wants His Word used as the standard by which a person is judged. He called us to judge ourselves so we can confess our sins and be set free.

The Evangelist: Is anointed to reach out with love to all. That means we love believers who are a mess and the world that is in sin. This calling is not about screaming messages that evoke fear in believers. God is not a God of scary fear, nor is an emotional, loud, screaming sermon a message from God. **_Loving-kindness_** is when we reach out and touch someone in love, which sets forth ministry in our own souls that ignites the souls it touches. When we hear an evangelist speaking about God's love, God uses the words to get us to reach out to others for Him. They stir our heart into loving-kindness that enables us to reach out to everyone.

The Pastor: Is the one God uses to lead His people (and is not voted in). Moses was not voted into leadership, he was anointed and called by God. The pastor has the calling of God on him to be a leader, a Shepard. **_Compassion or mercy:_** is one that touches the hearts of people; the shepherd; one who watches over the flock with careful attention, not allowing wolves to devour his sheep. The Pastor has God's agenda on his tablet and not his own self-interests. God gives him the words to preach to and guide his flock.

The Teacher: Is called to explain that God is sovereign and in control of our lives. They are allowed to teach His holy words not just by words, but also by their own actions. **_Faithfulness:_** is one who teaches faithfulness in God. When we understand that it is God, our trust and faith begin to increase. If we cannot trust God, we will not allow the faithfulness of Christ to be manifest in our souls. As we begin to realize how faithful He truly is we begin to rest in Him. This faithfulness brings forth Christ in us and allows us to be faithful to God and to those around us.

"Paul called *to be* an apostle of Jesus Christ through the will of God, and Sosthenes *our* brother, Unto the church of God which is at Corinth, to them that are sanctified in Christ Jesus, called *to be* saints, with all that in every place call upon the name of Jesus Christ our Lord, both theirs and ours:" (1 Corinthians 1:1-2). Notice the underlined parts of the passage above. What you see underlined above captures the essence of the message of this book. First, evidence is given to show we are CALLED to spiritual offices through the WILL of God. Men do not appoint us (period!). Second, one can clearly see two distinct addresses in verse 2:

1. The church of God which is at Corinth, and
2. Those who are sanctified in Christ Jesus.

(There are further evidences in this chapter speaking on being called, and how God wants His body of believers to work together.)

All of the offices require something from you; they require you to deny your flesh and pick up your cross. The five characteristics were missing in the five foolish virgins. Denying these characteristics is the first thing that takes us from a realm of faith and pulls us down to the realm of the five physical senses of sight, touch, smell, taste, and hearing. A very important door closes to those who choose to walk after the flesh instead of walking toward Jesus!

Remember, God appoints us, not men. Amen.

Part Three

Building Blocks of God's Divine Order Church

Not knowing how to tie it all together can hinder the seeker's walk because the task ahead "may seem" so utterly large and overwhelming. Though, our walk is our own, we must seek Him out; first as an individual to gain an assurance in Him and secondly by being consecrated unto Him so we can hear His voice speak the plan and purpose He has for us. Thus, so we can find our fit in the Body of Christ so He can operate through us, working in the five-fold ministry, to bring a lost world unto Jesus.

CHAPTER NINE

Reconstructing God's Church
Construction 101

O ne of the signs of the end times is God's restoration of His church to divine order. We find reference of the Lord preparing the Bride in these two powerful verses:

> ¹**And Jesus went out, and departed from the temple: and his disciples came to him for to shew him the buildings of the temple. ²And Jesus said unto them, See ye not all these things? verily I say unto you, There shall not be left here one stone upon another, that shall not be thrown down" (Matthew 24:1-2).**

Jesus was leaving the temple when his disciples are pointing out how magnificent it was. The disciples were amazed at its beauty. To paraphrase Jesus, *"Can't you see them for what they are, how they are being built, and for whom they are built?"* The disciples just saw beautiful buildings, perhaps worthy of God. They were missing the big picture, blinded by the physical beauty of the buildings.

What were they missing? What were they seeing? They were admiring Herod's temple, the temple, reconstructed after the restoration of Israel. It was repaired, but not according to God's plan, and out of His order. Herod, working through the flesh, added to it. Because of this, it was no longer totally God's temple.

When Jesus entered the temple, construction had been ongoing for fifty years yet the temple was still incomplete. Herod had big structures added to the temple. Builders used all kinds of beautiful stones and marble to adorn it. Herod's massive building project impressed the people. Jesus told his disciples that not one stone of the great structure would remain upon another.

"And he charged them, saying, Take heed, beware of the leaven of the Pharisees, and of the leaven of Herod. And they reasoned among themselves, saying, It is because we have no bread" (Mark 8:15-16). Jesus was warning them about the puffed up, boasting ways of the Pharisees and Herod. The disciples thought it was only a warning concerning forgotten bread. Jesus was giving them a simple warning, but the disciples did not understand it because they had lost sight of truth, and of Jesus momentarily.

The Pharisees were a sect of Judaism that considered themselves holy and they set themselves apart in their own mind and in traditions. The Pharisees represented self-righteousness and held strictly to the laws of Moses. The rule of law eventually caused their love to grow cold and legalism set in among them.

What was the leaven of Herod? Herod wanted to be a hero and he wanted to build magnificent structures for his glory, but in the name of God.

There were two elements being incorporated into the temple building; the glory of a man and self-righteousness.

Many churches struggle with this today. Too many people in the modern church have dimmed walks and a selfish agenda behind what they do in the church. People in need of ministry are ignored in churches that are distracted from their God-given purpose by beautiful things, like big buildings. Jesus was trying to show the disciples that they were looking at the beauty of the building and he was warning them to what was truly inside.

Our outward beauty is not what God looks at. It is what lives inside the heart. Herod built the temple for the glory of man, not for the glory of God. This is why Jesus said that not one stone would remain upon another.

"I indeed baptize you with water unto repentance. but he that cometh after me is mightier than I, whose shoes I am not worthy to bear: he shall baptize you with the Holy Ghost, and with fire" (Matthew 3:11).

It is in our attitudes that we protect ourselves from this wrong thinking—making certain we do not fall into false humility. John the Baptist understood the grace of God on his life, to be called the greatest of the Old Testament prophets. He said he was not worthy and he meant it from the depth of his being. He was ushering in the church, the Son of Man, the Messiah. He understood that he was not worthy because all that he accomplished was because of the anointing of God upon him, not he himself.

Too often, Christians build up ministries because of God's anointing in their lives, but fail to remain humble. They lose sight of God's purpose for the ministry. When one studies the spirit, soul, and body, one realizes it is not us at work, but Christ in us.

Oftentimes, when we see people with the anointing of God on them, we praise that person. We build up that person by saying things like, "When you were praying I saw this glow about you; you have something special." If the anointed person begins to believe it is them, the anointing will lessen. If the person thinks he has some special attribute and that is why God is using him, he has just limited the glory of God in his life. We must understand what "you are just the vessel" really means. All the glory must go to God, not to man or his actions.

We are to allow the Lord to build up the Body of Christ together making certain that emphasis is not on one person. Each of us is a vessel made for the Lord's use and we must submit willingly to Him. By his grace, God has poured His glory through each of us. If we would take on the same attitude that John the Baptist did, God's glory would flow through us. God has ordained a fivefold ministry, not a one-man pastoral show that we see too often in modern churches.

It is through a humble spirit that God can work. The best way to remain humble is to keep one's eyes on Jesus and off ourselves. John the Baptist spoke truth and showed humbleness when he said, "I am not worthy to loose His sandals." He could say this and mean it because he truly understood it.

Why do you think Paul said, "I am the chief of sinners?" He was an overcomer and he walked with God every moment of every day. However, when he compared his life with how Christ lived, he was the chief of sinners. Christ had His mind on His Father all day and all night, as he prayed and sought His wisdom, so mighty and glorious things poured out on mankind through Him every moment of His life.

God has anointed each of us to equip us for His ministry. We have to understand that it is not us, but God working through us. When we understand this and truly walk in it, God's glory will begin to manifest through us. If we think that God has chosen us because we think we are something special, we will limit the anointing. Christ gives us an illustration of this in Luke:

7But which of you, having a servant plowing or feeding cattle, will say unto him by and by, when he is come from the field, Go and sit down to meat? 8And will not rather say unto him, Make ready wherewith I may sup, and gird thyself, and serve me, till I have eaten and drunken; and afterward thou shalt eat and drink? 9Doth he thank that servant because he did the things that were commanded him? I trow

not. [10]So likewise ye, when ye shall have done all those things which are commanded you, say, We are unprofitable servants: we have done that which was our duty to do. (Luke 17:7-10)

This is not condemnation because there will be a day when God will take them and grant them to sit with Him on His throne. This attitude will protect us from building up empires and institutions that do not glorify Him.

God called us to serve the Body of Christ and if we do this, it keeps us Christ-centered. We need to remain mindful to the things of God while Christ builds our temples (vessels) with God's plan and purpose for our lives. Jesus said that not one stone will be left on another, and that the temple would be destroyed because it was no longer serving God's purpose. That also applies to governments and institutions. In the last days God says He will dismantle the religious system man has put together. God never said those stones, those people, were not worthy of something, but the way they were put together had to be taken apart.

A Slight Awakening

Today, the hearts of some people are beginning to inquire about the fivefold ministry. People are starting to talk about apostles, prophets, evangelist, pastors and teachers working together. After 2000 years, people around the world are beginning to wonder where the apostles, prophets, evangelists, pastors and teachers are. Some religions are attempting to overtake the Body of Christ and replace it with a social justice agenda. People are beginning to stir, recognizing this is not from God. We can see the mix of man's political institutions attempting to mix with God's established Word, for their own political gain.

The Body of Christ has been slumbering, but is awakening. God is restoring His order because people of God are hungering for God's way. The scriptures that follow should help you understand the true temple; one not built by man's hands. Spiritual hunger also comes with spiritual awakening and that is why we see a move of people slowly beginning to move away from large mega churches and opting for smaller home fellowships.

[19]What? know ye not that your body is the temple of the Holy Ghost which is in you, which ye have of God, and ye are not your own? [20]For ye are bought with a price: therefore glorify God in your body, and in your spirit, which are God's. (1 Corinthians 6:19-20)

[24]God that made the world and all things therein, seeing that he is Lord of heaven and earth, dwelleth not in temples made with hands; [25]Neither is worshipped with men's hands, as though he needed any thing, seeing he giveth to all life, and breath, and all things; [26]And hath made of one blood all nations of men for to dwell on all the face of the earth, and hath determined the times before appointed, and the bounds of their habitation; [27]That they should seek the Lord, if haply they might feel after him, and find him, though he be not far from every one of us: [28]For in him we live, and move, and have our being; as certain also of your own poets have said, For we are also his offspring. (Acts 17:24-28)

And I say also unto thee, That thou art Peter, and upon this rock I will build my church; and the gates of hell shall not prevail against it. (Matthew 16:18)

Christ said He would build His Church. He did not say Peter would build it. When Christ builds His church, not even the gates of hell will overcome it. God's Church is built to last. If man builds it, it will fall apart. Churches taken over by the political social justice agenda are not part of true body ministry. God will tumble them!

Men who love the Lord but who do not understand the Word of the Lord have built many churches. That is why, for the last 1500 to 1800 years, the church has been unable to overcome the works of darkness. Looking inside churches today, one can see they are full of sick, trembling, weak, and confused people. Men's vision has changed the message. It has veered off course severely. Just what in the world have the churches been doing for the past 1800 years? Where is the victory, freedom, and healing Christ died for on the cross? We can sing about it all day long, but if we don't produce it, it's nothing more than another temple built by Herod for the glory of men.

God has been tossing the stones. He is in the process of rebuilding His church His way with those who hear His voice and recognize the times. We are all part of the "mistake" and God is starting to restore the Church. Many home church groups, small in number, are forming all over the world. The mass exodus from the "mistake" akin to Moses leading the Israelites out of Egypt, is taking place. People are leaving "secular" churches in search of "true" church bodies. One important note to take heed of is that in between Egypt and the Promised Land is a wilderness walk. The wrong religion must be removed from us in order to establish in us, right relationship with God and others.

God's church is not a building; it is the body of believer's fellowshipping together. This is why we have to stop looking at this brother's church or that brother's church—it is not "their" church. God is bringing forth a prepared people who have His heart, who will minister to every believer. These will be people willing to minister to broken, angry, and bitter vessels. Amen.

How to Handle a Church "Situation" Properly

In Acts, a very interesting thing happens in the church. Though this church is set up in divine order, still they run into a problem. Here is the problem and how God settled it:

> **¹And certain men which came down from Judaea taught the brethren, and said, Except ye be circumcised after the manner of Moses, ye cannot be saved. ²When therefore Paul and Barnabas had no small dissension and disputation with them, they determined that Paul and Barnabas, and certain other of them, should go up to Jerusalem unto the apostles and elders about this question. (Acts 15:1-20)**

The problem is that some of the Jews who have become believers are saying that all the church, including the Gentiles, must be circumcised and live under the law. It was a problem so large that the church could have splintered into many factions had a solution had not found.

You have seen and heard churches split over the smallest of issues (for example, the color of carpet or the location of a parking lot). After a split, invariably one side or the other uses an expression like, "God was weeding out the 'bad seed' people." What such a person forgets is that the church is God's and Christ died for those so-called "bad seed" people too. Those who do not agree with a manmade agenda are suddenly "bad seeds." A true bad seed is one who comes in to destroy God's church, not man's agenda, and not simply someone who does not agree with us.

> **"Having your conversation honest among the Gentiles: that, whereas they speak against you as evildoers, they may by your good works, which they shall behold, glorify God in the day of visitation" (1 Peter 2:12)**

Now there are those the enemy will send in to try the stones, but God's Word tells us that not even the gates of hell will overthrow His temple.

This circumcision and living by the law issue facing the church was huge and it easily could have split the church. This went deep into the hearts of the Pharisees who had become believers because it was the Law of Moses concerning the circumcision. A legalistic Christian would say, "Get rid of them!" By doing so, they would avoid dissension and an uncomfortable confrontation.

Both sides needed grace to operate properly but all of them were in legalism to their own self-righteousness. So why did the church not split? First of all, they sent Paul and Barnabas to the apostles and elders, the authority structure God set up to get questions answered. Keep in mind that this was not a small problem, and all kinds of chaos could have resulted from a misstep here.

> **³And being brought on their way by the church, they passed through Phenice and Samaria, declaring the conversion of the Gentiles: and they caused great joy unto all the brethren. ⁴And when they were come to Jerusalem, they were received of the church, and of the apostles and elders, and they declared all things that God had done with them. ⁵But there rose up certain of the sect of the Pharisees which believed, saying, That it was needful to circumcise them, and to command them to keep the law of Moses. (Acts 15:3-5)**

The Pharisees were not there to bring division intentionally. They didn't want to cause trouble in the church. Their passion was with what they believed and how they believed was important to them.

One cannot simply tell someone not to believe something. That would be legalism because you are trying to force them to believe something God has not revealed to them yet. This is why the Pharisees were not to be excommunicated, disciplined, or anything else. We are not to wound a weak conscience. Allow them to believe in whatever tradition to which they are accustomed. Why? Because if they believe that they have to walk in those ways and feel forced to change, it could crush their spirits. God will show them otherwise at some point in time. Keep in mind as well, a persons understanding only goes as far as the revelation God has given them.

A person with a weak conscience will not do immoral things. It will restrict them from doing the things of God because of the rules and limitations they place upon themselves. They feel it is a spiritual thing to do by placing rules and limitations upon themselves but they actually hold no spiritual value.

⁶And the apostles and elders came together for to consider of this matter. ⁷And when there had been much disputing, Peter rose up, and said unto them, Men and brethren, ye know how that a good while ago God made choice among us, that the Gentiles by my mouth should hear the word of the gospel, and believe. ⁸And God, which knoweth the hearts, bare them witness, giving them the Holy Ghost, even as he did unto us; ⁹And put no difference between us and them, purifying their hearts by faith. ¹⁰Now therefore why tempt ye God, to put a yoke upon the neck of the disciples, which neither our fathers nor we were able to bear? ¹¹But we believe that through the grace of the LORD Jesus Christ we shall be saved, even as they. (Acts 15: 6-11)

Peter gets up and puts things in perspective. No matter what they had to say about the Gentiles, the Lord saved them and baptized them in the Holy Spirit. The Lord saved them even though they were uncircumcised and did not keep the Law of Moses. **"Then all the multitude kept silence, and gave audience to Barnabas and Paul, declaring what miracles and wonders God had wrought among the Gentiles by them" (Acts 15:12).** They started to listen and suddenly realized that God was doing miracles among the Gentiles and, no matter what the Pharisees traditions were, the Gentiles were okay.

> **"And after they had held their peace, James answered, saying, Men and brethren, hearken unto me: ¹⁴Simeon hath declared how God at the first did visit the Gentiles, to take out of them a people for his name. ¹⁵And to this agree the words of the prophets; as it is written, ¹⁶After this I will return, and will build again the tabernacle of David, which is fallen down; and I will build again the ruins thereof, and I will set it up" (Acts 15:13-16).**
>
> **Don't trouble these people and try to put more burdens on them. "That the residue of men might seek after the Lord, and all the Gentiles, upon whom my name is called, saith the Lord, who doeth all these things. Known unto God are all his works from the beginning of the world. Wherefore my sentence is, that we trouble not them, which from among the Gentiles are turned to God" (Acts 15:17-19).**

The verdict is, "But that we write unto them, that they abstain from pollutions of idols, and from fornication, and from things strangled, and from blood" (Acts 15:20). This is the verdict from the apostles given by the Holy Ghost. How many people knew to stay away from blood, food polluted from idols, and strangled animals? What is this saying?

The two groups involved here were the Jews and Gentiles. Jews were rooted in Judaism with the Levitical laws and restrictions ingrained in their souls. Gentiles did not have any of that. Ultimately, God said there are neither Jews nor Gentiles in His church.

In the same situation, many men might have decided to form two churches. God would have nothing to do with that, there was only to be one Church. (We have to ask of ourselves, "Is this the plan we have stuck to today?").

The solution was one the Pharisees could accept, one that set the Gentiles free. They did not say they could not have certain types of meat, they said to abstain. The word *abstain* here is a spiritual reference meaning they should stay away from the things that defile their soul and conscience. The Holy Spirit worked it in such a way that those who still held on to the Law of Moses were not pushed out, so they could receive grace and be set free afterwards. Those who were not under the law, the Gentiles, would not live under those laws and remained free. All this wisdom came by way of the Holy Spirit through men who knew the times, and understood God's plan and will for their lives.

The spirit of division did not work this time because God's grace prevailed through men who were humble and dedicated to the truth. If a church does not have the fivefold ministry in operation with Christ leading, it will not work and division will always ensue. It will never work without Christ being the head of the church. The Holy Ghost used the word "abstain" so that both sides would dwell together in unity until they matured. Everyone needs to reach maturity so they can love one another no matter what, without sacrificing truth in exchange for carnal fellowship.

It was very interesting that God used Paul and Barnabas to deliver the decision letter to the churches. Who was it that wrote about the revelation of grace? Paul did in First Timothy, **"Forbidding to marry, and commanding to abstain from meats, which God hath created to be received with thanksgiving of them which believe and know the truth. For every**

creature of God is good, and nothing to be refused, if it be received with thanksgiving: For it is sanctified by the word of God and prayer" (1 Timothy 4:3-5). Paul is saying that it is all okay to eat whatever meat placed before you <u>when it is received with thanksgiving.</u> What you are to abstain from are sinful desires and fleshly lust that war against your soul. **"Dearly beloved, I beseech you as strangers and pilgrims, abstain from fleshly lusts, which war against the soul" (1 Peter 2:11).** Meat cannot defile a person's conscience, only sinful desires can. (Later on in this book, the conscience will be explored in more depth.)

Judging one another incorrectly but "in the name of Jesus" appears holy, right? **"Let no man therefore judge you in meat, or in drink, or in respect of an holyday, or of the new moon, or of the sabbath days:" (Col. 2:16). Which things have indeed a shew of wisdom in will worship, and humility, and neglecting of the body: not in any honour to the satisfying of the flesh" (Colossians 2:23).** There are people who love to pick people apart and point out their faults. When this person appoints themselves judge over others, it is all in a guise, recognized or not, to give an appearance of godliness, but this is not true godliness. When a person is truly godly, they will not do these things. These types of situation require discernment and God moving upon the hearts and minds of men, to move in faith, into the correct place God wants them to be.

"Then pleased it the apostles and elders with the whole church, to send chosen men of their own company to Antioch with Paul and Barnabas; namely, Judas surnamed Barnabas and Silas, chief men among the brethren" (Acts 15:22). The whole church was pleased and it brought forth unity in Christ. They sent men of their own company back with Paul and Barnabas to show and give support of the letter.

The reason we do not have unity in the Church is we are solving things in our own strength. We saw in these scriptures how they overcame the enemy. Once we see we are overcoming the enemy, we see that God is starting to build within our soul. Christ builds the church and we need to stay out of His way so He can. We are too impatient because we live in a now, now, now society. If we see that the church is not overcoming the gates of hell, we need to recognize that there are stones (people) that are not in the place they are called to be.

The illustration of the general church and the Bride of Christ, along with the differences between the body of Christ and the way God wants to construct things in our hearts is found in Ephesians 5:20-32. It is important to look closely at this passage.

"Giving thanks always for all things unto God and the Father in the name of our Lord Jesus Christ" (Ephesians 5:20). The first thing we must do to get into divine order is to maintain a thankful heart. For a body of believers to come into divine order it must share a thankful heart. This is part of the foundation building. Complaining and murmuring about the past will hinder the thankful heart and disrupt foundation building. It will only bring about more flesh.

"Submitting yourselves one to another in the fear of God" (Ephesians 5:21). The second thing is to submit to one another, not just to the pastor, but foremost to the Body of Christ.

"Wives, submit yourselves unto your own husbands, as unto the Lord. [23]For the husband is the head of the wife, even as Christ is the head of the church: and he is the saviour of the body" (Ephesians 5:22-23). This uses the relationship between husbands and wives to illustrate the relationship between Christ and the Church. The distinction is Christ is the head of the church but He is the Savior of the body. Not every believer has allowed Christ to be head of their life. When we receive the Lord we are saved, yet many walk in their own way, believing it's okay to do so as long as they harm no one.

A glorious church is one in which Christ is the head of the church. When the pastor is doing one thing, the people are doing another thing, and the elders are doing yet another, what is going to happen? The church is going to tumble because we have so many people wanting to be the head, or pushing their own agendas that it messes everything up.

Christ has to be the head of the church and we have to learn to let go and let Christ lead. Everyone is worried about church problems and wants to solve them in their own strength. If Christ is truly the head of the church then He will build it. Is there something in the church that needs removal? Let God tear it down. Is there something in our local body that is not right? Let God take care of it.

Christ must be in control of the Church. When He is in control, there will be calmness and an assurance that He is going to restore things in His divine order. If Christ is not in the place of Headship over the Church, man will impose his will, his ambitions, and his thoughts upon the people, and Christ will dismantle it.

Not everyone is going to be the pastor. Some days everyone wants to be the pastor and some days no one wants to be the pastor.

THE MINISTRY GIFTS ARE NOT A CAREER! They are an anointing of the life of Christ flowing through different people. You have to know where God has placed you in ministry and stay there until God calls you out, to move you up as you mature in Him.

"Therefore as the church is subject unto Christ, so let the wives be to their own husbands in every thing" (Ephesians 5:24). The glorious Church the Lord is putting together is submitted to Him in everything.

"Husbands, love your wives, even as Christ also loved the church, and gave himself for it; That he might sanctify and cleanse it with the washing of water by the word, That he might present it to himself a glorious church, not having spot, or wrinkle, or any such thing; but that it should be holy and without blemish" (Ephesians 5:25-27). Not every believer will choose to walk in this type of submission before the Lord. For those who walk in their calling, God will work in us, so that we will pour out, so others can enter into the same body—it is that simple. We do what God has called us to do and become His witness—a work that will produce fruit and testify to the glory of the Lord. This is what pouring out means. It is being a light to those around us.

It is not our job to set other people straight. Our job is to love people into a deeper relationship with Christ. Christ gave Himself not only to save us but also to sanctify and cleanse us with the washing of the Word, so that He might present us as a glorious church, without spot or wrinkle, or any such blemish.

God will put you with people who are obnoxious in just the same manner as you may be. It can only be a work of the grace of God to put you in fellowship with someone just like you. Then He says, "Now allow the life of Christ to come through you to bring forth right relationships." Those who can look beyond themselves, and allow difficult relationships to grow their love, will mature and be more qualified to become part of the Bride of Christ.

"So ought men to love their wives as their own bodies. He that loveth his wife loveth himself. For no man ever yet hated his own flesh; but nourisheth and cherisheth it, even as the Lord the church" (Ephesians 5:28-29). You know what God is doing? He is taking every member in the body of Christ, loving and maturing us, so we can mature enough to become part of the Bride, so we can enter in before the door closes. When we submit to this, we put ourselves in a position to mature, so that we can be part of the "chosen and faithful" who are the Bride of Christ.

[30]For we are members of his body, of his flesh, and of his bones. [31]For this cause shall a man leave his father and mother, and shall be joined unto his wife, and they two shall be one flesh. [32]This is a great mystery: but I speak con-

cerning Christ and the church" (Ephesians 5:30-32). What is this great mystery?

"To whom God would make known what is the riches of the glory of this mystery among the Gentiles; which is Christ in you, the hope of glory" (Colossians 1:27). The mystery is the revelation of Christ is in your soul. The mystery is the body of Christ completely unified with God. The mystery is where He takes clay vessels and fills them with the exact image of His Son, Jesus Christ. This is the incomprehensible mystery for man. This is the mystery of the Bride of Christ being manifest, joined with the Son for all eternity. This is God's perfect will for the body of Christ though not everyone will choose it.

Just as we chose salvation, we now have to choose to be molded in His image and that is the sanctification process. Some will settle and stop maturing by choosing only the good or the acceptable will of God.

Christ's Coming Depicted as a Thief

"But know this, that if the goodman of the house had known in what watch the thief would come, he would have watched, and would not have suffered his house to be broken up" (Matthew 24:43).

"And this know, that if the goodman of the house had known what hour the thief would come, he would have watched, and not have suffered his house to be broken through" (Luke 12:39).

At the "catching away," or rapture, Christ is coming to take the Bride. The word *Harpzo* means to be "caught up" and it is from the phrase "caught up together" that we get the word "rapture." There are many in the Body of Christ who refute this very definition.

Why is Christ coming back for us compared with a thief in the night? First, remember when Christ comes for His Bride, it will be like lightning. It will be as fast as a flash of light. No one will notice right away—it will be that fast. Second, it is a mystery to the world, but believers left behind will know what took place. In the time of the tribulation, deception will find fertile ground.

When a thief enters a house, he takes only the best things. He does not take the old couch; he takes the jewels and the most precious things. All else he leaves behind.

When Christ comes for the Bride, whom will he leave behind? Those that held church in Jesus' name though worked in their own agendas will remain to be purified. When the Bride is raptured, the rest are going to fall over because God is going to tumble them. Then He is going to start to rebuild them to prepare them to be taken up. These people will not be part of the Bride because the door for that will be already closed.

God is saying, "BE READY, BE WATCHFUL!" God is coming for those who allowed Him to mature them now and we want to be part of that. We want every believer to be mature in Him. In **First Peter 4:17**, the Bible says, **"For the time is come that judgment must begin at the house of God: and if it first begin at us, what shall the end be of them that obey not the gospel of God?"** Cleansing judgment is not condemnation. God will bring a cleansing judgment down upon the earth. Jesus will appear on the clouds and take the general church up before the wrath of God comes down. During the last three and half years of the tribulation, at the end of the seven years, He comes back with the called, chosen, and faithful (Revelation 17:14). He will then destroy all His enemies and set up His one thousand year reign.

Speaking of the house of God, in Second Timothy, we find this:

¹⁹Nevertheless the foundation of God standeth sure, having this seal, The Lord knoweth them that are his. And, let every one that nameth the name of Christ

depart from iniquity. [20]But in a great house there are not only vessels of gold and of silver, but also of wood and of earth; and some to honour, and some to dishonour. [21]If a man therefore purge himself from these, he shall be a vessel unto honour, sanctified, and meet for the master's use, and prepared unto every good work" (2 Timothy 2:19-21).

The foundation of God stands firm and God knows whom His people are. There are times in our spiritual walk that we might doubt God is with us. This does not matter because He knows we are His children and we are saved. The covenant is not between the Lord and us but between the Father and His Son.

It also says everyone who confesses the name of the Lord must turn away from wickedness. He knows us and the truth is, not all of us are obedient children. Whether we walk the way the Lord wants us to, or we stumble and fall, we are all His children. Once you receive Christ, God's perfect will is to depart from wickedness and if we could do that perfectly, Jesus would not have needed to die for us on the Cross.

The reality is, every great house contains not only gold and silver, but wood and clay as well—some to honor, some to dishonor. There are not only vessels used for glory but also vessels used for common purposes. You would think that common purpose means you have toilet cleaning duties, but it is not. Common purpose means that some people in the house of God dishonor themselves by their own sinful actions.

Right now on this earth, in the house of God, there are noble vessels and ignoble vessels. We see both and we have all been both. God wants us to be sanctified by Him, to be a vessel of gold and silver so through us He can bring forth His plan. He is going to bring glory to His Name, and as much as we are willing to be a part of that, is as much of the glory we will receive. The amount of the glory received is determined by the amount we are willing to submit to God. Amen.

CHAPTER TEN

The Complete Meat Plate

God's Divine Order for His New Testament Church in Faith and Practice The Advanced Class

God's Mystery Church in Creation

Prophecies are fulfilling rapidly, proclaiming the near advent of Christ our Lord is near. He, who is the master Architect, and Builder, is building His glorious Church according to His plan and purpose. He ordered the life for all His creation and the Church within His spiritual kingdom. This newest creation began at our Lord's death, burial, and resurrection at Calvary. It was fully formed in His divine order at Pentecost. **"And they were all filled with the Holy Ghost, and began to speak with other tongues, as the Spirit gave them utterance" (Acts 2:4).**

It will be perfected at His coming, as promised in Ephesians, **"That he might present it to himself a glorious church, not having spot, or wrinkle, or any such thing; but that it should be holy and without blemish" (Ephesians 5:27).**

He promised and prophesied in Matthew, **"And I say also unto thee, That thou art Peter, and upon this rock I will build my church; and the gates of hell shall not prevail against it" (Matthew 16:18).**

We see God's divine purpose of man's creation, stated in the covenant in Genesis 1:

²⁶And God said, Let us make man in our image, after our likeness: and let them have dominion over the fish of the sea, and over the fowl of the air, and over the cattle, and over all the earth, and over every creeping thing that creepeth upon the earth. ²⁷So God created man in his own image, in the image of God created he him; male and female created he them. ²⁸And God blessed them, and God said unto them, Be fruitful, and multiply, and replenish the earth, and subdue it: and have dominion over the fish of the sea, and over the fowl of the air, and over every living thing that moveth upon the earth. (Genesis 1:26-28)

All of God's creation exists within the three dimensions of time, space and matter. We know the workman by his workmanship. His primal (basic) ministries are those of creation, redemption, and restoration. God did not make us to be defeated and driven by the storms of life, but that through faith in Him, we should be more than conquerors and have dominion over all things that now hold dominion over us. So let us lift our faith in Christ Jesus to the heavens, for practice never goes beyond our revelation.

As we look up into His vast universe, His workmanship proves Him omnipotent in foreknowledge, wisdom, and power. Man's largest telescope will not reveal the outer boundaries, within which whirl countless millions of celestial bodies, all created and set in perpetual motion by His Word. He, as the divine Architect, had to foreknow the size, weight, and magnetic attraction of every single star and planet. He had to figure accurately, its rotating speed in its prescribed orbit in age long cycles.

The giant Milky Way, the circle or equator of this entire universe, is a wheel of giant suns perfectly balanced. One giant sun out of its ordered place would have started a chain reaction and destroyed all of creation. God never fails or makes a mistake. He placed our moon at the proper distance from our earth so that its gravitational pull would lift the seas and forms the tides, yet not close enough to lift the crust of our earth and destroy it. One is amazed as we study God's balance in all nature.

In their proper order, He brought forth light, air, water, and food. Then properly mixed came the gases of oxygen, nitrogen, hydrogen, and carbon. Then came life into the earth, in its balanced order of vegetation, sea, and animal life and into this paradise came man, created out of the dust of the earth.

"The Lord has prepared His throne in the heavens: and His kingdom ruleth over all" (Psalm 103:19). God set up His throne room to reign from within His vast universe or kingdom in the heavens. In like manner, He set up His lesser spiritual kingdoms in the earth. One was the nation of Israel, and the other is the Kingdom of Heaven, known as the Church. This latter is His newest creation.

The new creation kingdom is a phase of God's heavenly kingdom our Lord set up in earth by his death, burial, and resurrection. Jesus our Lord tells us in **John 3**, the requirement for entrance is the new spiritual birth. **"Marvel not that I say unto thee, you must be born again" (John 3:7).** This is a kingdom of created spirits (1 John 3:9), and comes not by observation, but our Lord Jesus declared it to be within us. The Church is the material and visible aspect of this spiritual kingdom from which our Lord reigns in His Body of born again believers.

This new creation cannot lift itself up into a higher one, but the higher one can reach down and lift the lower life up. As an illustration, the vegetation creation reaches down with its roots, takes up the lower life of mineral creation, and assimilates it. The animal feeds upon the lower vegetable creation and lifts it up assimilated into a higher creation life. Man feeds upon the lower life of the animal and assimilates it. Christ had to reach down and enter our spirit to lift us up into His eternal standing as a child of God.

Jesus our Lord gave seven messages to the seven churches (Revelation 2-3). We are now in the last, the Laodicean, a time of spiritual declension before the Lord returns. The dry rot of modernism is bringing forth a clergy begotten of an apostate church where many have commercialized their calling and changed it into a profession.

The Bible speaks of them in **Matthew 15:9**, saying, **"But in vain they do worship me, teaching for doctrines the commandments of men."** Christ Jesus' body was broken on the cross before His resurrection and today His Church Body is broken and divided; and now it is time for full restoration of the prophet Joel's revival remnant. As we approach the last frontier, God is moving by His Spirit. In addition, a great host of small, independent assemblies is rising all over the earth. These are obeying our Lord's last command in **Acts 1:4, "And, being assembled together with them, commanded them that they should not depart from Jerusalem, but wait for the promise of the Father, which, saith he, ye have heard of me."** They were to "<u>wait for the promise of the Father</u>" the Holy Spirit. He would clothe Himself with the blood-washed believers, restore His dynamic miracle-working ministries, and restore God's order according to the pattern given on Calvary. True "body ministry" is rising up in the earth again and all the promised signs are following those who obey and believe.

Every believer in Christ has his or her own standard of righteousness, which usually mirrors the standard of righteousness of his particular church. Older Christians see the rapid declension (decline, deterioration) in denominational church standards. Older Christians saw many healed by the fervent prayers of righteous people. They were in services where numbers of deeply consecrated men and women were "slain" under the power of God.

In all of the churches of that day, there was a high standard of righteousness. The willful transgressor, if unwilling to repent was disciplined, and if that failed, the church would withdraw fellowship from him. In those days, the consecrated people lived separate lives, but today there is a lowering of the standards in the same church groups.

A spiritual standard has been replaced by a moral standard and a moral gospel prevails. Such churches have "sold" their birthright. God's high standard of Christian conduct, that gives the believer the right standing, is just the same today. When Israel's Ark of the Covenant was captured, God's glory was lifted. Truly today, under lower standards of discipline, God's Holy presence is in enemy hands. God's glory has departed and Ichabod is written over many church doors.

Out of this gloomy picture, the Lord has painted in Revelation:

And unto the angel of the church of the Laodiceans write; These things saith the Amen, the faithful and true witness, the beginning of the creation of God; [15]I know thy works, that thou art neither cold nor hot: I would thou wert cold or hot. [16]So then because thou art lukewarm, and neither cold nor hot, I will spue thee out of my mouth. [17]Because thou sayest, I am rich, and increased with goods, and have need of nothing; and knowest not that thou art wretched, and miserable, and poor, and blind, and naked: [18]I counsel thee to buy of me gold tried in the fire, that thou mayest be rich; and white raiment, that thou mayest be clothed, and that the shame of thy nakedness do not appear; and anoint thine eyes with eyesalve, that thou mayest see. [19]As many as I love, I rebuke and chasten: be zealous therefore, and

repent. [20]Behold, I stand at the door, and knock: if any man hear my voice, and open the door, I will come in to him, and will sup with him, and he with me. [21]To him that overcometh will I grant to sit with me in my throne, even as I also overcame, and am set down with my Father in his throne. (Revelation 3:14-21)

There is coming a day of restoration as we approach the pre-tribulation days. Today the visible Church stands in the same place as ancient Israel standing before the Red Sea, surrounded by their enemies. Today the Church, surrounded by her enemies, stands before the great tribulation and God is moving to prepare us for the crossing over.

We are now witnessing the third worldwide revival for Christ and His Church. The first worldwide revival came through the Apostle Paul and his revelation to the Church in the first century Apostolic Church. The second worldwide revival came out of the Dark Ages when Martin Luther rediscovered the truth, "The just (justified) shall live by faith" (Galatians 3:11). The Reformation spread rapidly over the earth.

At the turning of the twentieth century came the third worldwide revival and fulfillment of Joel 2:28-29 and Acts 2:16 as the mighty Holy Spirit was poured out as at Pentecost. Israel, set in due order at their first Pentecost, continued to celebrate the event each year, waiting for the day of Pentecost, which came to the disciples waiting in the upper room, bringing the three Jewish signs of: the voice of God heard at Sinai, the mighty wind of Sinai and the leaping fire seen at Sinai. Many millions of Christians have come under the power of this worldwide revival at Pentecost.

God's Order for a Christ-Centered Church

The Bible is full of records showing that God does judge His people who choose their own religious worship and church government. He began at Mount Sinai and had those naked dancers slain around the golden calf as a warning to the congregation of Israel. Aaron's two sons, the chief priests, died under judgment when they placed strange fire on the holy Altar. There are many other examples, but probably an outstanding one is the account of King David deciding to bring the Ark of the Covenant up to Jerusalem.

David disregarded God's due order of carrying it on the shoulders of consecrated priests. He had a beautiful cart made after the pattern of an idol cart and carried the Ark on it. When a priest fell dead, David stopped the procession and had it brought up later in God's due order, and wrote in First Chronicles, **"For because you did it not at the first, the Lord Our God made a breach upon us for that we sought Him not after the due order"** (1 Chronicles 15:13).

Numbers 16 we read of one of the leading priests named Korah who was rebelling against God's due order and endeavoring to lead rebellion against God's ordered plan. God opened up the earth and it swallowed him. Today if we would hold to God's Bible doctrines, they would reveal His order of worship and unite His Body, the Church. But ambitious church leaders, having passed these sacred words of Bible doctrine through carnal minds, have brought forth a Babylon of church traditions that have divided the Body of Christ.

"God is a Spirit: and they that worship him must worship him in spirit and in truth" (John 4:24) Restoring God's truth and consecration, or true worship, to every individual Christian is the place of beginning in God's restoration of the Church, as spoken of in the New Testament.

God will not accept a blemished offering. Living sacrifices were examined at the temple gates, and rejected if blemished. This is the main reason the average Christian is cursed with unanswered prayers. One could not think of the Lord praying unanswered prayers, or the apostle Paul either; so why should we have unanswered prayers return to mock us?

Great church systems of today are building on scaffoldings that are not in God's blueprint for the Church. They are building great houses of wood, hay, and stubble and likened to the house built on sand (Matthew 7:26). In Ezekiel 8-11, God reveals why their holy temple was destroyed and their nation carried off into captivity in Babylon. <u>It was because they profaned the four holy things of GOD on which divine order centers. Israel had profaned the holy House of God, as the Laodicean Church is today, then their priesthood became worldly, then God's Word was profaned, and lastly, the laity of worshippers was profaned. At each profaning, GOD lifted His glory.</u>

God still has the same divine order of Church government and discipline for the Church today as He had in the first century apostolic Church. Examine some of the patterns He has set in the Bible to guide us to the truth. The first national pattern is prefigured in Israel's tabernacle worship while they were in the wilderness.

Exodus 25:1 begins this planned pattern **"According to all that I shew thee, after the pattern of the tabernacle and the pattern of all the instruments thereof, even so shall ye make it."** Later, Israel's temple worship presented the same prefigured pattern for the New Testament Church to follow.

The perfect pattern is found in the life of our Lord Jesus who lived the very life He expected to live again in His Body, the Church. As one studies the four Gospels, it is evident that He divided His life into five ministries. They were lived separately and on different days. He ministered as the chief apostle, prophet, evangelist, pastor (or shepherd) and teacher. He did nothing outside of these five ministry offices and always exercised one or more of the nine spiritual gifts of First Corinthians 12:8-10.

Then another pattern is set in the Apostle Paul's revelations in Scripture and also in his practicing of them in his evangelistic journeys. At our Lord's ascension, He gave His five ministries to the New Covenant Church (Eph. 4:11), for the perfecting of the Body (Eph.4:12-13).

The local church was the center of all worship and activities for Christ's planned life in it. And the book of the Acts of the Apostles shows evangelistic ministry went out from it. Examine the contrasts between the early apostolic New Covenant Church of the Apostle Paul's day and the same Church as seen in its streamlined modern ministry of today. <u>In this simple comparison, one can see a great contrast between God's order and man's order</u>.

In the first century, the Church was born at Calvary and set in God's planned order at Pentecost where the Holy Spirit clothed Himself with Christ's church and began to manifest His spiritual gifts and ministries in it. In those days, all were Spirit-filled men and women who depended solely on God's Spirit leadership. In contrast, today our great church leaders rely more upon human wisdom and trained intellects.

In those days the evangelists went forth, empowered with God's tools for building new assemblies, while today we send forth men and women trained and schooled in denominational church discipline. In the first century they had no special educational training of great organizations to support and guide them. They had very little finance, communication or transportation systems to depend upon. Today our young people go forth with all these material things, but mostly without the spiritual gifts and ministries. In the first century, believers almost conquered the Roman Empire, while today we make little headway against the world's mockery of the Church.

Seeing then the need for us to return to God's due order, to see again a strong, militant Church going forth and burning down the gates of hell, examine further the Church of the first century.

In those days, each local church was sovereign, yet an integral part in the great one Body or organism of God. In those days, anointed witnesses went forth with an anointed Word and in an anointed ministry and the promised confirming signs, miracles and wonders followed. In the Apostle Paul's day, the local church was God's training school (Acts 13:1), where some are named teachers and prophets. These New Testament assemblies are today as they were then, schooled of practical experience.

In those local church training schools, those in training witnessed mighty miracles, and demons being cast out in the mighty name of Jesus Christ. In the divinely ordered assemblies one sees body ministry in operation. From time to time, the Holy Spirit sends in an apostle, with his anointing of faith and wisdom, to set foundational Bible truths established in the congregation. Then, at God's appointed time, the Spirit sends in a prophet with his stirring inspirational and prophetic ministry. Then, at another time, the teacher comes to minister and teach the truth and principles for practicing God's Holy Word. From these training centers there goes forth the anointed, Spirit-filled evangelist, to establish new assemblies. The pastor ministers in grace and divine wisdom as a balancing factor in the assembly worship and activities.

The great Roman Government with its military might had conquered the world in the first century. Our Lord came forth with a new power of nonviolent love that has conquered more people and set up a greater kingdom in the earth than any military power of violence. Our Lord became the Head and First Fruits of this great spiritual Kingdom in the earth. In His planned blueprint for this growing temple or Church, which is His Body, He gave an important place to His chosen eldership as a training school in these New Testament assemblies.

There are ranks of spiritual development in this great and important calling. In **Exodus,** we read of Moses appointing "elders" to rule over the great congregation of Israel. The seventy ruling elders were the legislative body who sought council together with God over His Law and Commandments. "**And Moses chose able men out of all Israel, and made them**

heads over the people, rulers of thousands, rulers of hundreds, rulers of fifties, and rulers of tens" (Exodus 18:25). These were ranks of elders where some who were qualified were set over a thousand; while those less qualified were set over the number they could minister to. Churches today are overlooking this great ministry of the elders to the Body of Christ who are watchmen over men's souls and the spiritual life of the local churches.

Is God's Plan Practical Today?

This is a challenging question and after all, revelation is only a theory until proven by experience. All Bible truth is set on exhibition in practice in the Old and New Testaments. Everything genuine has its counterfeit, but we can testify these spiritual gifts are genuine and real enablements for Christian service.

We are a home based fellowship used to minister and train people to go out into the fields, in His due order. Praise God! We are a teaching ministry more than a preaching church. God has a divine order for finances also and during our services, we never pass a collection plate. We have a miniature wooden church that sits on a small table at the church entrance, marked "Offering."

There is no limit to what one church can do when led and empowered by the Holy Spirit. Think of the one church of Antioch from which the apostle Paul went out. Think of the many New Testament churches that sprang up, and how much of Asia and known Europe were evangelized, largely from that one church. <u>The Lord can do the same through your church if you will burn the last bridge behind you and wholly follow your Lord.</u>

Apostolic Church Government

From the beginning, God set divinely ordained offices into the human race through which to govern His people. The offices of the priest, prophet, and elder are seen among the patriarchs. As the patriarch of old held his newborn son in his arms, the spirit of prophecy would come, and he prophesied the life of his own son, then named him according to how his life should be. One or more letters denoting the Lord were incorporated in the son's name.

In the New Testament Church, the Lord set His five ministry gifts as anointed offices (Ephesians 4:11). These were to minister to His Body. Then He ordained Spirit-filled men to anoint those He chose for the four lesser offices. The confirmation of their office would not be in their title, but in the anointing of the Holy Spirit on the offices. God's promised signs, miracles and wonders should confirm His presence working with them in His order. The proof of God's due order is peace and rest. We see this even in all nature, living and abiding in their ordered life and nature. For instance, the sparrow lives daily in the presence of death, but never fears nor worries but rests in the peace of God.

Church Government Order

Now examine the simple cross chart of all the offices of a balanced body ministry within the framework of Calvary's cross. Notice that the Head, Christ Jesus our Lord is atop the cross chart. In the cross arm of the chart, see the three places He meets His people in worship and government. The second place of importance in God's order is the local church. The third place of importance in the chart is that of the congregation. At times, for important local church decisions, a congregational call brings all the local churches together to consider issues, pray about them, and make decisions. The fourth place on the cross chart is that of the general assembly, as seen in Acts 15:1-30, where the apostles and elders came together to represent all the local churches and to clarify Church doctrine. They **did not** assemble to formulate new doctrine.

Now look at the three sets of nine ministries which are the supports by the Spirit for all church government. They are the nine spiritual offices, the nine ministry offices and the nine anointing graces of the Spirit's ministry in the Church.

	Christn the Head Eph.1:22 1 Peter 2:6-8 Col. 1:18	
Local Church (12 in Acts, 7 in Paul's Epistles and 7 in Revelation) 1 Cor. 14	Congregation (Special gatherings for the Body of Christ in conventions) Acts 15:30-33	General Assembly (Ministers Conference) Acts 15:1-29
	7 Anointed Offices Eph. 4:11 1 Cor. 12:5 1 Tim. 3 2 Basic Ministries	
	9 Anointing Gifts 1 Cor.12:8-11	
	9 Anointed Graces (Fruits) Matt. 7:16 Gal. 5:22-23	

Apostle

The first ministry office is that of the apostle to the Church. The twelve apostles of the Lord (the Lamb) were promised rulership over the twelve tribes of Israel (Matthew 19:28). But those mentioned in the Bible as New Testament Church apostles are the apostles Paul, Barnabas, Andronicus and Junia (Acts 15:22, Romans 16:7).

The Apostolic ministry is understood best when seen in full practice in the Apostle Paul's ministry: the laying of foundational truths, establishment of new assemblies, and a wide array of ministry in the power of the spiritual gifts. <u>They came not in the wisdom of men, but in the power of the Holy Spirit.</u>

Prophet

The second ministry office in the Church was the prophet's office. Spirit-inspired and anointed prophetic ministry stirred the hearts of the people with dynamic power and proved Christ by the fulfillments of their prophetic word. The miracles and wonders confirmed their ministry as the Holy Spirit exercised spiritual gifts in their lives. We find Silas and Agabus named among the New Testament prophets.

Evangelist

The third ministry office is that of the evangelist, as seen in Philip's ministry in Samaria where he went to start a new assembly. It is wise to note the Body Ministry pattern followed here (Acts 8:1-7).

Pastor (Shepherd)

The next ministry office in the chart is that of the pastor or shepherd. He is the undershepherd who cares for the local flock. The elders are his counselors and together they oversee the spiritual life of the local church. Many are called pastor who serve well, whether with or without a real teaching ministry.

Teacher

In the fifth office, that of the teacher, one sees many with a specially gifted teaching ministry who would not serve well as pastors.

Back in Israel's worship, God used only men who were born Levites, and then used only anointed priests in service at His holy altar. To serve properly in these holy ministries of God, we must be born again believers in God's spiritual family, the Church, and anointed by the Holy Spirit. Without the Spirit's anointing the promised confirming signs of the miraculous will not follow in your ministry.

Elder

The sixth ministry office is that of the elder. The elders or bishops of the aforementioned ministry offices served the Body as a whole, leaving the local flock to the home elders. At times, they go forth to minister to small assemblies. The eldership was the backbone of the early Church. **"When they had ordained them elders in every church" (Acts 14:23).** Those chosen out of Paul's new converts were those who fit the pattern of Titus 1:5-9, and 1 Timothy 3:1-10. Out of the maturing eldership, God chose the ones for higher offices.

Deacon

The institution of the office of the deacon is found in Acts 6:1-6. Spirit-led men chose other Spirit-filled people for this office, which was to minister primarily to the material needs of the local church. Philip served as a deacon and then later,

God mentions a woman named Phebe serving as a deaconess (Romans 16:1).

Helps and Governments

The next two ministry offices are helps and governments. First Corinthians states, **"And God hath set some in the church, first apostles, secondarily prophets, thirdly teachers, after that miracles, then gifts of healings, helps, governments, diversities of tongues"** (1 Corinthians 12:28). Faithful women of the church often accomplish these two ministry offices, helps and governments.

The helps consist of faithful and regular assisting service, such as bringing the aged to church, visitation, and a ministry of prayer. The governments deal with governing areas of church life, such as teaching Sunday school classes, serving as church secretaries, church treasurers, Sunday school superintendents and so on. Out of those in helps that prove faithful, Spirit-filled leaders choose those for the vacancies of the governments.

All nine ministry offices in which born-again believers in Christ minister, have a wider range of ministry than that to which many attain.

Every Christian must allow the Holy Spirit to assign him to one of these offices and then seek the Lord for a deeper consecration and better understanding of God's truth. Out of the lower offices come those later seen in the higher offices, each being a training school for expanding service for their Lord. Most ministers today began early life serving in helps, then governments, until the Lord could use them in some higher office and ministry.

One challenging question is, "What is the woman's place in the church?" Everyone agrees that without them man would have no Church. Their important position in the Church of the living God seems to have the same relationship to man as it has in the home life. All Christian men and women are witnesses for Christ. As such, they must win souls and encourage weak believers at every opportunity. More women go forth into foreign mission fields than men. Many women bring together groups in homes for prayer and study, and some have converts in all places.

The tabernacle and temple worship prefiguring the Church to follow did not have women ministers of the holy things of God. Our Lord chose men as apostles. As our Lord and Savior Jesus Christ is able to mature His nine spiritual fruits or graces in our life, all of these other things fall into God's ordained place.

God's Nine Spiritual Gifts

As we continue to study the cross chart let, look at the second nine, the nine anointed gifts in the lower supporting body of the cross chart. First Corinthians 12:8-10 records these nine spiritual gifts. The nine spiritual gifts are: the word of wisdom, the word of knowledge, the gifts of divine faith, healing, miracles, prophecy, discernment, tongues, and the interpretation of tongues. With these spiritual tools in the hands of the Holy Spirit, the Lord is building Himself a house to dwell in, the Church.

Wherever Spirit-filled men and women go, these spiritual gifts follow to confirm God's Holy word and presence. These gifts are exercised only to the extent of faith the believer has and should only be operated under the mighty anointing of the Holy Spirit.

"For the gifts and calling of God are without repentance" (Romans 11:29). Like the talents, the gifts and callings may be buried beneath worldly activities. God foreknew this but gave the one-talent believer his or her talent anyway. Sound teaching is needed on how best to try and prove these gifts when in operation. A balanced operation of gifts and beautiful order can be maintained, for the Lord has done this in our assembly.

satan strives always to pervert God's truth and blessing. In these spoken gifts, the gift bearer can operate at any time. However, if not operated with God's anointing, but with the fleshly mind instead, confusion will follow.

These nine spiritual gifts can also be divided into six for revelation and three for ministry. Some also divide these nine into three groups, with the three revelation gifts of God's omnipotent wisdom, knowledge and discernment exercised by God the Father as the Church's judicial Head. Then the three spoken revelation gifts of prophecy, tongues and interpretation exercised by God the Messianic Son as the Church's Legislative Head. The other three power gifts of faith, healings and miracles exercised by God the Holy Spirit as Administrator of the Church. Wherever the Spirit-filled believer goes, these spiritual gifts follow to prove and confirm by both God's Word and His presence.

Word of Wisdom

The first gift is a divine measure of God's unlimited wisdom, which is essential with the second gift of knowledge. For God's wisdom reveals how to exercise His knowledge to glorify His name.

Gift of Knowledge

The second gift is a measure of God's measureless knowledge. This is very important and has a wide range of expression in the Church. This "sixth sense" of knowing through the mind without seeing, was lost to Adam's race through sin in Eden, but retained to some extent in animals, such as in a cat or dog being able to find their way home from great distances when apparently lost.

This gift operates in the mind of the gift bearer, often as a flash, the revelation comes without thinking. Sometimes it is spoken forth under the anointing of the Spirit (1 Corinthians 14:26), and mistaken for prophecy. One should test revelation when it appears in one's mind. Ask these questions before sharing with the body: Is this scriptural? Is it a secret of the Lord to pray over before sharing? Will it edify the Church if spoken now, or is it for later?

The Anointing of God-Faith

The third spiritual gift is that of a super anointing of God-faith. Through the wide range of this gift, miracles, healings, and even financial turnarounds result. It is miracle-working faith. Any Christian can be an overcomer, have strong faith, speak the Word of God and see miracles as a result. As an illustration, Paul and Peter both spoke the Word in faith and the cripples who had never walked leaped to their feet and walked. At times, one sees all nine spiritual gifts manifested through deeply consecrated Christians.

Gift of Healing

The fourth mentioned are gifts of healing, the only one mentioned in the plural. Jesus our Lord is the Great Physician and desires a well Body so He has set various healing ministries in the Church. First is the gift of healing to the individual and then as a gift to His Body, the Church. **"And these signs shall follow them that believe; In my name shall they cast out devils; they shall speak with new tongues; They shall take up serpents; and if they drink any deadly thing, it shall not hurt them; they shall lay hands on the sick, and they shall recover" (Mark 16:17-18).** This gives authority through covenant rights to every believer who believes to exercise this ministry.

The elders have a covenant of healing for their ministry as seen in James. **"Is any sick among you? let him call for the elders of the church; and let them pray over him, anointing him with oil in the name of the Lord" (James 5:14).**

Luke unveils the authority of Christ's life within us. **"Behold, I give unto you power to tread on serpents and scorpions, and over all the power of the enemy: and nothing shall by any means hurt you" (Luke 10:19).**

Do not let the devil fool you any longer, you do not have to be sick or afflicted for **Matthew 8:17** says, **"That it might be fulfilled which was spoken by Esaias the prophet, saying, Himself took our infirmities, and bare our sicknesses."**

Working of Miracles

The fifth spiritual gift of the nine is that of the working of miracles. At times, through inspirational faith and a deep consecration, every Christian sees marvelous answers to prayer, problems solved, and miracles of grace in their life. This gift is a special anointing for this kind of ministry in the Church. All of these spiritual gifts are seen operating in our Lord's life through the apostles, prophets, evangelists, pastors and teachers in the early apostolic church. As the Lord exercised this ministry gift, the five thousand were fed, the lepers cleansed, water turned into wine, the storms stilled, and so much more.

Divine Prophecy

The sixth spiritual gift is that of divine prophecy, either forth-told or foretold. As foretold it is prewritten history that proves God's Word as divine and proves His deity. Our Lord used it to prove He is the Messiah in **John 13:19, "Now I tell you before it come, that, when it comes to pass ye may believe that I am he."** Prophecy forewarns and arms God's people for impending judgments. It is directive and edifying to the Body of Christ. It not only has the purpose of proving Christ and His Word but it also has creative power.

In 2001, two weeks prior to tropical storm Allison, the Lord gave me a prophetic vision of "rushing waters." He also instructed me to tell the pastor of the church my husband and I attended, that rushing waters were coming. Two weeks later the flood, the "rushing waters" that Allison dumped were extreme in some parts of the Houston metro area. The flooding was devastating, causing five billion dollars worth of damage in and around Houston.

Discerning of Evil Spirits

The seventh spiritual gift is that of discerning of evil spirits. The exercise of this gift has saved many people from demons which were cast after being discerned.

Tongues and Interpretation

The eighth and ninth gifts are tongues and interpretation. The heathen called this glossolalia and it was the marvel of heathendom, but despised and rejected today by all man-ruled systems. All of the spiritual gifts mentioned previously were exercised in the lives of Old and New Testament prophets. Yet among the Old Testament prophets, these last two, tongues or languages, and their interpretations were not necessary. Today the Church is composed of people who speak probably three thousand tongues and dialects so these gifts are needed today.

We have the pattern of it in Acts 2:4. This gift spoken in prayer, song or praise, edifies the Spirit-filled believer. But when spoken in a definite language, to be interpreted in the church, is directive or edifying to the congregation. An example of this, as a sign to the unbeliever, occurred at the Grace Gospel Church in Waco, Texas. An Indian brother visited the church years ago and doubted the exercising of spiritual gifts. The Lord gave a message in the Indian's native tongue through Robert Ewing, and then gave the correct interpretation in English through another of their brethren. The Indian understood both tongues and knew it was God speaking.

This brings us to the last of the three nines. The nine anointed graces found in Galatians 5:22-23 are the base to all these other anointings. The fruit of the Spirit comes from Christ's Spirit, which dwells in our heart, our human spirit. "Being filled with the fruits of righteousness, which are by Christ Jesus, unto the glory and praise of God" (Philippians 1:11). The basis for judging prophets is to examine the fruit of the prophet, not their accuracy in the prophecy. "You shall know them by their fruits" (Matthew 7:16).

God's Order of Dividing Our Spirit and Soul

The Apostle Paul reveals a difference in man's human spirit from the soul in Hebrew 4:12 and in First Thessalonians 5:23. This key unlocks many of the mysteries in the Bible. It has been lost in the lifeless creeds of man and in Babylonian sectarianism. Before Christ's earthly ministry, Oriental philosophers taught that man was a dual creature. In the end of the second century, this pagan philosophy found its way back into the Christian Church. The Bible teaches that man was created in the image of God. God is a Trinity, so man must be also.

As one examines the words for the spirit and soul in both languages of the Old and New Testaments, one finds each has a different meaning and a different ministry. In the New Testament, the word for spirit is *pneuma*, from which our English word *pneumatic* is derived (as in pneumatic tool). <u>Until one recognizes this difference, no line of demarcation can be clearly drawn between the body of scriptures concerning justification and sanctification. Though in a number of places, scriptures appear to contradict one another, when rightly placed, they substantiate each other.</u> ← Read the underlined one more time.

The entire Body of Christ has been divided into two great schools of thought, set against each other through the sin and error of not separating the spirit from the soul. Only truth can heal the Body and make us all one again. The "Baptists and Calvinists" see only the justification of the believer and are secure in the new birth until the day of redemption (Ephesians 4:30). While the "Methodist and Arminians" look at the need of daily sanctification of the believer's soul life. Each side battles the other with scriptures specific to each point. Here are scriptures that appear to contradict each other and a brief commentary on each.

Colossians 2:10 and Matthew 5:48

In Colossians 2:10 we read of justification, "And we are complete (or "perfect") in him (Jesus)..." While in Matthew 5:48, one reads of our imperfect sanctification, "Be ye therefore perfect (complete)..."

In the following scriptures we find another apparent contradiction of scriptures, one dealing with our justification and the other dealing with our sanctification.

1 John 3:9; 5:18 and 1 John 3:8

In First John 3:9 and 5:18 we read of our eternal standing in justification, "Whosoever is born of God (our spirit) doth not commit (practice) sin; for his seed remaineth in him; and he cannot sin because he is born of God." Yet we see the seeming opposite, dealing with our daily need of sanctification (made holy) in First John 3:8, "He that commiteth sin is of the devil." In these two scriptures adjoining each other and written to Christians, it reveals that the Christ-sealed, recreated spirit does not sin but the soul or mind of the believer does. The soul sins through the loaning of the mind to the devil.

The word *yeshua*, or *salvation*, means to make safe, and in the Bible applies to the believer's spirit, soul and body. The name of our Lord Jesus is from a word meaning "as one who makes safe." As the meaning of salvation is applied to man's spirit, soul and body, it deals with his justification, sanctification and glorification. It is a perfect work of Calvary for the believer. This gives to the believer a threefold salvation, with scriptures dealing with each.

Here is a simple illustration of threefold salvation. Place three books on a table before you. Book one represents our recreated spirit. Book two represents our soul or mind. Book three represents our physical body.

Book number one represents the believer's justification and scriptures are usually in the past tense, being unconditional. This delivers us or makes us safe from the guilt of sin through the shed blood and our eternal standing through the indwelling Christ.

Book number two represents our sanctification or daily work of God's grace in our heart through God's Word by the Holy Spirit. This is a daily need, making safe our imperfect state of spiritual growth as we obey or disobey God's Word. It saves us daily from the power of sinful habits. The "salvation" is usually conditional and used in the present tense. This is an act of Christ always striving to perfect (mature) our soul life.

The third book speaks of our physical body which is to be perfected in glorification at the coming of the Lord. The scriptures of salvation here used are in the future tense when He will make us safe from the presence of sin.

The greatest turnover in backsliding is among our dear brethren who do not see this difference between the spirit and the soul. <u>In other words they don't discern between their standing and their state</u>. An example from family life will help explain this. As a mother looks at her children and family, she loves one as much as the other, yet the only thing that sets them apart is their growth and that makes the difference in their state.

Similarly, as Christians we all have an eternal standing with one birth, but our spiritual growth from babyhood in Christ to maturity in Him varies, and upon this spiritual state we will receive our rewards.

The legalist taking the backslider to the altar never asks him to accept Christ into his life if he knows the backslider has ever been born again, but only asks him to repent. Repentance is the way to restore the joy of salvation and is essential, but repentance alone never saved anyone. It is Christ indwelling our spirit that makes us a new creation. Until the believer finds rest in his justification, he will never find rest in his sanctification.

Even the apostle Paul sought to perfect his soul sanctification daily, knowing he was eternally safe in his justification. He was striving to apprehend that for which he has already been apprehended (Philippians 3:12). There are thirty unconditional promises in the New Testament concerning eternal life for the believer in Christ. In John 10:28 we read, "And I give unto them eternal life; and they shall never perish." Even in John 3:16 one reads the same promise of unconditional safety.

Christians were redeemed from Satan's slave block by the redemption price of our Lord and Savior's own blood. The record stands today in the courts of heaven that we will never be enslaved again.

The Seven Covenants of Calvary

The seven covenants of Calvary wrought out in the sufferings of the man Christ Jesus in seven sorrows at Calvary, are prefigured in Israel's national worship. God, having led primitive Israel out of Egypt, brought them to rest before Him at Mount Sinai. They had lived many years under the idolatrous worship of the Egyptians who had ten primary deities and scores of lesser gods, one for each need.

At Sinai, God began to teach them that He, their one God, was sufficient for all their needs. They knew about Him through the God-ordained star constellations, which were figures of the truth. They knew that the seven head sins of satan, with their many lesser sins and hurts, were to be overcome in the sacrifice of God's Lamb. Abraham had prophesied in Genesis 22:8, " And Abraham said, My son, God will provide Himself a Lamb for a burnt offering: so they went both of them together" All Israel had waited through the long sojourn in Egypt for that One to come who would bind up all their hope of a perfect and sevenfold redemption. At Sinai, their almighty Jehovah began to make covenant promises that would deliver them from the hurts of sin.

God called Moses to the Mount and ordered their form of theocratic worship in which He was to be their Head, to govern their state affairs through the wilderness. In their order of worship, He set memorials of Calvary's sevenfold redemption to keep them constantly reminded of covenant promises.

These seven national memorials, to be annually before them, were each composed of seven individual acts of worship, thus forming forty-nine forms of worship. God covenanted with His people that on the forty-ninth or seven sevens of Sabbaths, He would usher in the fiftieth or "Pentecost" of blessings (Leviticus 25:8). This fifty year Pentecost was a time of rejoicing, for all they had lost would then be fully restored to them.

The first of the seven national memorials was in Jehovah's seven compound names, each denoting one of the coming seven covenants of Calvary. The second was in their seven annual feasts. The third was in their seven pieces of holy furniture of the Tabernacle. The fourth was in their seven sprinklings of sacrificial blood. The fifth was seen in the individual seven acts of sacrifice, and the sixth was the seven ministrations of the priesthood. The seventh of the seven national memorials of Israel's worship was the seven sufferings mentioned in Isaiah 53:4-7.

There were seven individual acts of worship incorporated into each of these seven national memorials, but we will only list here the seven individual memorials of the compound names of Jehovah. They are <u>Jehovah Jireh</u> (Supplies), <u>Jehovah Rapha</u> (Heals), <u>Jehovah Nissi</u> (Banner of Victory), <u>Jehovah Shalom</u> (Peace), <u>Jehovah Raah</u> (Shepherd), <u>Jehovah Tsidkenu</u> (Righteousness), and <u>Jehovah Shammah</u> (Helper).

God's ordained plan of sevenfold redemption, which was to be set in seven covenants with the believer, was first prefigured in Eden. There He slew the first sacrifice and the lamb slain at the beginning or foundation of the world or human race and its shed lifeblood became an atonement or covering for man's sin and the skins or covering from the hurts of sin.

The lifeblood of the animal substitution sacrifice could not redeem the sinner from his judgment but was only an atonement or covering. And his sin must be moved forward to Calvary where God's Lamb, even Jesus Christ our Lord, must die to provide redemption grace for all sins and believing sinners. For if animal blood could have redeemed the sinner, there would have been no need for God's Lamb to be offered. Sinners knew that the lifeblood of the innocent animal sacrifice was but a substitution for the lifeblood of the coming Messiah, whose lifeblood was a substitution for their own life, condemned by their sin. Thus, they looked forward by faith and received the seven benefits of the sevenfold covenants of Calvary, even as we now look back by faith and believe and receive these same benefits. The Psalmist David wrote to remind us in Psalm103:2, "Bless the Lord, O my soul and forget not all his benefits."

The individual sinner must show forth the earnest of his faith in God's coming sevenfold redemption through the Messianic sacrifice and identify himself with it by his acts of memorials at the brazen alter. There, as he entered the court of the tabernacle, leading his lamb sacrifice, he must walk through the blood of former sacrifices sprinkled on the ground. It was a blood walk to remind him of the penalty for sin.

At the altar, in the presence of the priests, he obeyed God's commandments and laid his hands upon the head of the sacrifice. This not only identified him with his sacrifice, but was to him a figure of laying or committing his sin upon the life of the innocent sacrifice. He confessed faith in the promises and faithfulness of almighty God.

Then he must slay his own sacrifice, and the priests, catching the warm lifeblood, sprinkled it over the four brass horns of the brazen altar. If one of the leaders of Israel sinned, they had to bring a larger sacrifice, a bullock, and go through the same acts of confession. As he slashed the throat of the sacrifice, the priests quickly lifted the animal, laid it back down into the burning flame of the altar, and tied the four legs to the four horns of the altar.

This last act was what the heavenly Father had to do, as Jesus Christ our sacrifice, with His bleeding, suffering back laid in the seven sufferings of the cross, has His hands and feet fastened to the four nails or horns of the brazen altar of the cross. The Psalmist saw this scene and wrote in Psalm 118:27, "bind the sacrifice with cords, even unto the horns of the altar." The priests of Israel laid the slain lamb in the burning flame of the altar each morning and evening as their daily sacrifice. It was a memorial for their faith to reach forward to Calvary and claim their deliverance from the hurts of sin. "The chastisement of our peace was upon Him" (Isaiah 53:5).

Today we look back to Calvary and see the chastisements of our peace upon Him, for they are upon Him or upon us, depending on where our faith reckons them to be. Can you, suffering one, see your daily chastisements being suffered by your Lord at Calvary? If you can, you go free; if not, you bear them for your sin of unbelief. Can you, sick or afflicted Christian, see your individual sickness suffered by Him back at Calvary? Can you believe, ".....Himself took your infirmities and bare your sickness"? (Matthew 8:17) It is impossible for two bodies, many miles apart, with centuries between them, to bear the same sickness or affliction. When you can see your individual suffering in Him at Calvary, your lying symptoms will pass away.

Now let us examine these seven covenants of Calvary that our Lord completed in His seven sufferings of the cross, where He fused life and death together to produce a new power: resurrection life. There are many scriptures for these seven covenants: Justification, Sanctification, Divine Healing for soul and body, Divine Health for soul and body, Divine Peace, Rest, Resurrection Life and the Glory of God. Until one finds rest in the first he never finds rest in the others. You must believe the work of redemption was finished at Calvary. Justification is for the believer's spirit, which was recreated in regeneration at our confession of faith in Christ's work at Calvary. His Spirit entered to seal us until the day of our redemption (Ephesians 4:30). It is eternal and secure, by His covenant Word and work, an eternal salvation and standing as God's child. The last six covenants are for the believer's soul life and our daily benefits.

God's Order of High Priesthood

Our Lord Jesus Christ, God's High Priest, is continuing as high priesthood in establishing His sevenfold redemption covenant in the Church. To establish His covenants in the Church He must first establish them in the individuals that compose His Body, the Church. To better understand how the Father established these Calvary covenants in Him, let us examine more closely our Lord's ministry of priesthood.

In Matthew 5:17, Jesus declared, "Think not that am come to destroy the law (Mosaic law) or the prophets (word of the prophets): I am come not to destroy but to **fulfill**." This challenging prophecy was to be the sign of our Lord's high priesthood. For no man could possibly fulfill these prophecies, commandments and ceremonial laws of the old covenant except Christ. To fulfill these, one must fulfill three sets of prophetic scriptures that deal with man's spirit, soul, and body and must fulfill all religious enactments of the same.

One of the principle annual enactments was that of the Day of Atonement (Leviticus 16). On that holy day each year, the ministry of the earthly high priest as he prefigured the ministry of the heavenly High Priest was to choose two goats for two sacrifices and two deaths. Thus our Lord, in fulfillment of this holy day, must fulfill the ministries of the high priest, and each of the two sacrifices also.

This would have been impossible for any one man to do except as the Lord did perform it in dividing His triune life into His Spirit, soul and body. This would fulfill the prophecies concerning man's justification, sanctification, and glorification. Jesus must (and did) fulfill His own prophecy involving both a time and place element. He had prophesied in **Matthew 12:40, "For as Jonas (Jonah) was three days and three nights in the whale's belly, so shall the Son of Man be three days and three nights in the heart of the earth."** Today most man-ruled churches refuse to believe their Lord's prophecy and celebrate the Lord's death as from Friday afternoon to the resurrection Sunday morning. This would leave His body in the tomb for only parts of two nights and one day. It could not be part of the night or days, but must be three days and three nights. Thus, our Lord prophesied that the time element would be of that length, and the place "in the heart of the earth."

We find the answer to these questions in the Scriptures by asking ourselves three questions. 1) Did our Lord's Spirit die on the cross? 2) Where was our Lord's soul during those three days and nights? 3) Where was our Lord's Spirit during those three days and nights? To fulfill His prophecies our Lord had to divide Himself into His three beings of body, soul and spirit.

1) Did our Lord's Spirit die on the cross? God's inspired Word begins to answer this question in Luke 23:46, "Father, into thy hands I commend my Spirit." His Spirit must have been holy and sinless, or the Father would not have received Him, for the Father had just looked away, not being able to look upon all of the sin of the human race placed upon our Lord's natural life, His soul, and body. Then again, God's Word proves that Jesus' Spirit did not die on the cross. In Luke 23:43, he declared to the dying thief on the cross, "Verily, I say unto thee, Today shalt thou be with me in paradise."

2) Where was our Lord's soul during those three days and nights? We read of Jesus' "soul-body" in Isaiah 52:14 where it declares His form was marred more than any man was. We know that millions of human bodies have been ground to pieces and marred more than His human body was, so this refers to His "soul-body" form. The Lord, in fulfillment of the Day of Atonement, had to be the High Priest and the two goats, and die the two deaths as they did. One of these goat sacrifices was chosen to die as the sin offering. Its blood was carried into the Holy of Holies on this day. The other goat was called the scapegoat and, after the death of the first goat, the High Priest would lay hands on it, committing in a figure all the sins atoned for in the death of the first goat sacrifice.

This second goat, the scapegoat, was then driven out into the wilderness between the Mount of Olives and the Dead Sea, wandering in the land of no return, bearing the atoned sins away, which speaks of purification and separation from our sins and sinful habits. As the scapegoat wandered in its loneliness, starving for food, water, and friendship, the circling vultures waited for it to stumble, and then descend to tear its flesh from its dying body. Our Lord's soul had to fulfill this ministry of the Scapegoat. This was prophesied by David in Psalm 103:12, when God promised to remove our sins away as far as the east is from the west.

In Psalm 16:10, the Bible says, **"For thou wilt not leave my soul in hell; neither wilt thou suffer thine Holy One to see corruption."** (This was also echoed in Acts 2:27 and 13:35.)

Corruption means "decay." This scripture shows clearly that our Lord's soul, fulfilling the scapegoat figure, became the scapegoat for us and that His soul did enter the heart of the earth in hell.

In Isaiah we read, "when thou shalt make his soul an offering for sin" (Isaiah 53:10)! He continues, "because He hath poured out His soul unto death" (Isaiah 53:12). Finally, Isaiah writes, "He shall see the travail of his soul, and be satisfied" (Isaiah 53:11). In Psalm 88, one sees the picture of our Lord's soul being tormented in death. Death does not mean a loss of consciousness. It does mean a complete separation from God. Every human soul will live forever, either completely separated from God, tormented in the lake of fire, or living forever in His Glorious Presence! The choice is ours to make. If His soul had not tasted death for every man, our souls would have to die.

In Psalm 88:6-7, 14 we read, **"Thou hast laid me in the lowest pit, in darkness, in the deeps. Thy wrath lieth hard upon me, and thou hast afflicted me with all thy waves.... LORD, why castest thou off my soul? why hidest thou thy face from me?"** Sin was conceived in highest heaven in the heart of Lucifer (Isaiah 14:12-14). God's holy Church was conceived in the suffering of Christ's soul in lowest hell. We read of it in **Psalm 139:15-16, "My substance was not hid from thee, when I was made in secret, and curiously wrought in the lowest parts of the earth. Thine eyes did see my substance, yet being unperfect; and in thy book all my members were written, which in continuance were fashioned, when as yet there was none of them**. We see, by the Scriptures, that the Lord's body and soul were both in the heart of the earth. Now let us follow the ministry of His sinless and righteous Spirit and see that He also ministered in the heart of the earth.

3) Where was our Lord's Spirit during those three days and nights? As our Lord's body died on the cross to furnish the Lamb of God's redemptive blood, His Spirit was committed into the hands and presence of the Father. In Hebrews, we read of Christ's Spirit fulfilling the ministry of the earthly high priest in carrying the freshly shed lifeblood of the sacrifice into the Holy of Holies:

> **Neither by the blood of goats and calves, but by his own blood he entered in once into the holy place,** (God's Throne Room) **having obtained eternal redemption for us. [13]For if the blood of bulls and of goats, and the ashes of an heifer sprinkling the unclean, sanctifieth to the purifying of the flesh: [14]How much more shall the blood of Christ, who through the eternal Spirit offered himself without spot to God, purge your conscience from dead works** (church traditions) **to serve the living God? (Hebrews 9:12-14)**

As heaven's High Priest, our Lord's Spirit must also fulfill the prophecy of the apostle Peter, **"quickened by the Spirit: by which also he went and preached unto the spirits in prison" (1 Peter 3:18-19).** To understand this scripture, it is important to realize that both paradise and Hades were in the heart of the earth before Calvary. Our Lord reveals this in Luke 16:19-31 when Lazarus and the rich man died and there was a great gulf between them. Samuel was seen coming up out of paradise in the earth in First Samuel 28:13-14. Paradise was as a city of refuge for the righteous whose sins were atoned for, but could not be redeemed until our Lord Jesus died as God's Lamb upon the cross.

Israel had six cities of refuge where the man, under judgment, found refuge from the avenger of blood until the High Priest died. Then all could go home and be free (Numbers 35:28). As Jesus Christ's Spirit entered paradise, the great city of refuge in the heart of the earth and proclaimed the death of heaven's High Priest, they could then go to heaven.

Then came the great Exodus and Passover as He, the Spirit High Priest, led all of those righteous ones up to heaven to the place God had prepared for them. In Ephesians 4:8-10, "....When he ascended up on high, he led captivity captive, and gave gifts unto men. (Now that he ascended, what is it but that He also descended first into the lower parts of the earth?" He that descended is the same also that ascended up far above all heavens, that he might fill all things.)

Then our Lord's Spirit as the high priest was sent by God to Hades and reentered His tormented soul still in death. At that instant the Father moved, to shake heaven and earth as He came down to impart His endless and resurrection life to the still soul of His only begotten Son (Psalm 18:1-20). As Christ's Spirit arose and entered His righteous soul, He placed His heel upon the neck of satan and took the keys of death and hell away from him. In Revelation 1:18, our Lord still holds those keys. Then quickly arising and entering His glorified body He stepped forth as the Head in a new creation of kings and priests.

God's Miracle Working Faith

God is moving by His Spirit to awaken a sleeping Church and restore His true faith through a restored Body Ministry model. Men have written many books on this subject but most of these have left the seekers trying instead of trusting. Much confusion prevails concerning this simple truth.

The word *confidence* is translated in the Old Testament as *trust,* and in the New Testament as *faith.* God's faith is really true worship, which is a balance between consecration and truth. We read in John 4:24, "God is a Spirit: and they that worship him must worship him in spirit (consecration) and in truth." A Christian living a daily, Spirit-filled life can alone maintain this balance, where God sees His promise in our heart and performs it with His Spirit.

God's eternal, immutable promises are our inheritances and are available to every believer. As a triune being, we live on three planes of life and there is a practice of faith for each plane. There is natural faith for natural life, mental faith for mental or soulish life, and spirit faith for our spirit's life. Do not substitute one for the other. Many exercise mental faith for pressing needs, but under adverse conditions it freezes over with fear. Only God can fully practice His spiritual faith.

Abraham is an example of one who maintained this balance between spiritual consecration and trust in God's Word, without doubting. This alone gives us right standing (the right to stand, or the righteous stand) before God. Paul calls this the "by faith" righteousness, or the righteousness of true faith which gives the believer the dominion over all things. Jesus gave us a creative word of faith in Mark 9:23 when He said, "all things are possible to him that believeth." In Matthew 9:29, our Lord said to the blind man, "According to your faith be it unto you." So we see that the word "faith" is both our revelation and practice of it. It is both an abstract noun and a practice of it.

There is only one gospel of true Bible doctrine, but every church under human headship has its own version of it. In most cases, some church tradition replaces some truth. This may be the main reason your prayers are not getting into the orbit of God's "faith-practice." It is important to know whose "faith" or doctrine to which you have subscribed.

In the teachings of man's church, we Christians have been taught a large amount of unbelief, for example that the days of miracles are over, and so on. God does not promise to watch over man's word and perform it when it is out of harmony with His, but He has promised to perform His own Word (Romans 4:21). Our responsibility is to know the truth so well that satan cannot make us doubt it; then it is God's responsibility to perform it. Leave the miracle to Him and rest in our confidence in His faithfulness.

In Ephesians, the apostle Paul reveals to us that our greatest need is not an active faith, but grace for God's faith to operate through. "For by grace are ye saved (delivered) through faith" (Ephesians 2:8). God's truth or His righteous Word in our heart gives us His grace. Instead of praying for faith, let us pray more for grace to believe God's promises so He can work them for us.

To do this one must have a purpose for faith in each test and trial. Our overall purpose is to live a Christ-centered life and our daily purpose should be toward that end. This adds to our consecration. When God gives us a vision of His righteousness and purpose for us, this vision becomes a picture of the purpose to encourage us on. This will help to establish the confession of our truth as our faith. In Matthew 12:37 we read, "For by thy words (confession of truth or tradition) thou shalt be justified and by thy words thou shalt be condemned."

Mark 9 records the Lord returning with Peter, James and John from the scene on the mount of transfiguration and finds His other nine disciples unable to cast an epileptic demon out of a child. They had cast out demons previously when the Lord sent them forth, but now the balance is broken, their consecration is lacking. The boy's father cried in Mark 9:24, "Lord, I believe; help thou mine unbelief."

He is here in the same position as most Christians who have acknowledged God's almighty power, yet fail to have God's grace to believe He will perform His promise. Sometimes, between the revelation and the practice, satan attacks the believer's confidence in the Lord's Word or ability. An illustration of this is when the apostle Peter walked on the water at the word of the Lord "come," then doubt came into his heart and he began to sink. God's Word challenges every trial of our faith to see if we believe the truth of His promise, as in Philippians, "But my God shall supply all your need (no condition) according to His riches in glory by Christ Jesus" (Philippians 4:19).

God's Word challenges us and when we act on His Word of promise, the responsibility is His. Our undisciplined, carnal mind breaks the balance and the sin of pride, or human reason defeats God's Word in us. Would we act, as Peter, and take an empty hook and cast it into the sea, expecting to catch a fish and get the tax money out of the fish's mouth?

Would we be like the old man who, when he was saved and baptized in the Holy Spirit, went into the country town bank, wrote out a check for $500, and signed Jesus Christ's name to it, payable to himself. He wanted the money to buy an old empty dance hall to begin a church in that town. The banker knew him to be honest but knew he had no funds in the bank. He looked at the check and said that Jesus Christ had no funds in that bank. A large landowner standing nearby, a Christian, overheard the conversation. He took the check, wrote his own name across the back, cashed it, and the building was bought and the church started.

These things do not test our faith as much as they test our grace to act on what we know. Some Christians live good, consecrated lives and really believe the promises of God but still fail to make contact. They need to stake their faith down on a certain day and meet God there in the promise. After all, our confession, even to ourselves, reveals the sin of doubt, fear and unbelief. In John 14:12-14 the Lord promises that we can do all that He did in miracle power and greater things, for He was to send back the Holy Spirit, which He did. "If ye shall ask any thing in my name, I will do it" (John 14:14).

Let us show reverence to our Lord's name. The word reverend is used only one time in the entire Bible and it denotes deity, yet men like to apply that title to themselves. Maybe this breaks the balance and keeps them from getting their prayers into God's faith orbit. I am sure our Lord Jesus never prayed an unanswered prayer, and I doubt if the apostles Paul and Peter did either, so why should we? Let us test our confidence, trust or faith in revelation and in God's grace to act on God's Word of many promises.

Where does our practice cease in our revelation? Ask yourself the question, "Can I feed five thousand men, besides women and children, with a few loaves of bread and fish? Can I walk on water?" The Lord said we can do all that He did. "Can I cleanse the lepers? Can I even raise the dead? Can I speak peace to the storm? Can I turn water into wine?" You have probably answered no to each of these challenging questions.

The apostle Paul confessed that he could do all things through Christ Jesus which strengthened him. The apostle John confessed in First John 4:17, "because as he is, so are we in this world." In First John 3:21-22, he writes, "Beloved, if our heart condemn us not, then have we confidence toward God. And whatsoever we ask, we receive of him, because we keep His commandments, and do those things that are pleasing in His sight."

The seven hundred commandments of the New Testament are summed up in the last one, in Jude 21, "Keep yourselves in the love of God." God desires you to have dominion over all things that now have dominion over you. It is not so much a matter of having faith, but of removing those negative confessions that you say to yourself, like "I cannot do that." Ask God for more grace to believe and meet Him in His own promises.

You have creative power in your own word, for God gives you the authority to create through your own word, when spoken in faith. "Whosoever shall say unto this mountain, Be thou removed, and be thou cast into the sea; and shall not doubt in his heart, but shall believe that those things which he hath said shall come to pass; he shall have whatsoever he saith" (Mark 11:23). You have a bank account in heaven. Start writing checks do business with God.

The Bible Doctrine of the Soul

All Bible doctrines are completed in the apostle Paul's epistles. Men have diluted and devitalized them by mingling in their church traditions. However, this one Bible doctrine of the mind or soul seems to have escaped. With their churches filled with mentally soul-sick people, pastors seek information in the psychology books of men. Many psychology books have been written by unregenerate men, using only human wisdom. Why not use God's study on this vital and important subject?

The Bible has four methods of revealing truth. The apostle Paul uses all four of these in his study of this subject, and they are set forth in <u>word, practice, comparison and contrast</u>. All life operates through given laws of God. There are natural laws, mental laws and spiritual laws. In the early chapters of the book of Romans, the apostle began his study concerning the law of sin, showing how it affects man's mind or soul life. He reveals man's two natures operating within these mental laws, and being the battleground between God and satan, as they struggle for possession of man's election and human will. In Romans 7, one sees a nominal, carnally minded Christian, in his spiritual ignorance, caught in an intense struggle, doing the things he does not want to do and failing to do the things he knows he should.

God is striving to make man "like Him", and Satan is striving to make a man or a machine like himself. Science has brought forth machines that think and make quick, accurate decisions in seconds of time. But this is nothing compared to the delicately balanced and operated mind or soul of man.

The word *mind* in the Greek is *psuche*, which also has the same meaning for soul, intellect, will and heart. Our mind or soul has three basic mental faculties of the <u>intellect, will and heart (the seat of the emotions).</u> These all operate in balanced precision through a set of mental laws, all recorded in the Word of God. Seven of these mental laws, are namely: the laws of attention, attraction, decision, action, possession, habitual nature and set direction. God ministers His life through these laws, while satan, for deception, must use these also.

God, foreknowing man's test and fall in Eden, created us with three rings of defense against sin. Man's outer ring is the natural senses or faculties of sight, hearing, smelling, tasting or feeling that examine and probe into all circumstances and environments of life. The second ring of our defense is our ring of mental and soulish functions or mental members, namely imagination, affection, conscience, memory and reason. The third ring of inner defense is that of the believer's spirit senses of faith, hope, love, fear or respect of God (true worship), and intuitive knowledge. Sin never enters the last ring, for Christ dwells there. Each of the above is based on numerous scriptures in the Bible.

Our "will-worship" of either God or satan determines our eternal destiny and rewards. Both those great forces strive to influence our life. We all know through experience and practice how these mental members operate. For instance, a person comes to your door and you go to meet him. Your intellect is alerted and you are conscious of his presence, and instantly your memory is alerted to determine if you know that person. Then your reason is alerted to know what action to take. With this information, in a split second, your human will decides and acts. Thus our human will is the directive part of our mind or soul system. What we consider important, our human will plants in our heart, the storehouse and seedbed of our life.

The heart makes all the final and important decisions of the will. Our mental senses, faculties or mental members give the information for all our will's decisions and acts. In Hebrews we read a command, "But strong meat (deep truths) belongs to them that are (matured) of full age, even those who by reason of use have their senses exercised (trained) to discern both good and evil" (Hebrews 5:14). We desire to examine these mental senses, that we are commanded to exercise or use under the discipline of God's Word and Spirit. Let us not confuse the mental sins of worry, fear, hate, greed, envy, jealousy, unbelief, and such, with these senses of the mind or soul.

The Bible is full of warnings of satan's "soul hazards" and show us how to put up roadblocks against them by using the name of our Lord in faith, and pleading His shed Blood in faith against them. We see satan using these soul senses in church services as someone suddenly looks vacantly at the floor. Their mind has wandered off into yesterday or tomorrow and maybe a thousand miles away. These are wandering souls that miss the message God had for them.

satan brings many under mental pressure, which weighs on their mind. If undisciplined, this condition often leaves the door open for demons to enter and make one allergic to certain things. Also, this is the prime cause of mental breakdowns. When you rest your mind and fail to use it in waking hours, satan will make his workshop out of it by injecting thoughts into it.

Learn to discipline your mind, for it is your soul. A deep daily consecration is your best protection. Study God's Word and strengthen your will to abide by its decisions. Through television, millions are filling their minds with carnal, worldly things. When your human will gets so weakened and bent out of God's divine order, watch for Him to put you in the fire to test and soften your will, so He can bend it back again. Let the mind of Christ dwell in you richly for we Christians know His will for us.

We must know the operation of our mental faculties, senses or members, and remember the picture of the frustrated, defeated Christian in Rom.7:23 suffering warfare in his members. Also in James we see this warfare in the mental members of faculties, "even of your lusts that war in your members" (James 4:1). When you loan one or more of these senses or faculties to satan and God holds the others, the warfare rages.

Let us look now at the mental senses or members of our imagination, affection, conscience, memory, and reason. There are numbers of scriptures concerning each of these showing us how to exercise them for Christ.

Take for instance our <u>imagination</u>. When we pray, we should immediately imagine that God heard that prayer and the answer is on the way. These senses are the nerve centers of our soul or mind system and should be the roots of our faith. If we do not control our own imagination when we pray, satan will use it to make us imagine that God didn't hear our prayer, and other deceptions. Through these senses, God plants His "faith-seeds" or satan plants his unbelief that robs you of the promises and blessings of God. The Bible commands us to cast down "imaginations, and every high thing that exalteth itself against the knowledge of God, and bringing into captivity every thought to the obedience of Christ" (2 Corinthians 10:5).

The next sense or faculty to examine is that of our <u>affection</u>. All of these mental senses have scriptures to show that they work in our hearts. The things that gain our attention (law) fascinate us and control our affections. Paul warns us in Colossians, "Set your affections on things above and not on things on the earth" (Colossians 3:2).

The third sense or mental member is that of <u>conscience</u>. In both Old and New Testament languages, this word means to "suffer." It is a mental member of our mind that has the sense of suffering when we do anything that we think is wrong. Paul warns the legalist who thinks it is wrong to not keep the law of Moses, "purge your conscience from dead works (error) to serve the living God" (Hebrews 9:14).

The next mental sense to train for Christ is our <u>memory</u> which has the ability of storing revelation for later use. An illustration of this is in our memorial of Calvary in the Lord's Supper.

The last of the mentioned mental faculties is <u>reason</u>. We have over-trained our reason to accept only that to which our natural senses testify. We should retrain our reason to think in terms of faith. It is, by faith, reasonable to expect answers to prayers and commands of faith, based in truth.

The Word and Spirit of God, are to be used consistently in the application of God's Word, which should discipline all of the senses mentioned above. Thus we receive covenant blessing through His promises. We are only touching on the primal teaching of the Bible on this subject, but through these, your present life has been formed and can be changed through the proper exercise of them. The attitude of your mind toward all circumstances creates an atmosphere in your heart of either faith or fear and God only ministers grace through a believing mind.

Your thoughts are weaving your destiny. You have the power of creation in your mind to create the rest of faith and a life of dominion power or to drive your life by fear and torments. Our relationship to God depends on our attitude to His Word. God is able to break stubborn wills and crucify pride in the purifying flames of sufferings. You as a Christian, have bound your souls with an oath to fully serve the Lord.

The Spirit of the Heart

In the Bible, the same word is used for man's spirit being and also for the "spirit" or characteristics of his or her mind. The heart of the fleshly body and the heart of the soul or mind are also of like meaning. <u>Man's natural life is known to others by his name (identification), by his personality, and by his influence</u>. Some people have a selfish "spirit," some a proud "spirit", and some a generous "spirit." We are all different, even as Christians, in this soulish nature, character or personality. Regardless of what your spirit, attitude, or your heart may be, it can change, which in turn changes your personality. For instance, a habitual drunkard, liar, or thief with his adamic (sinful) nature, has his passions ruling his life and despoiling his character. When that person is wonderfully saved and born again he suddenly becomes a sober, truthful, and honest person. Only God can change our character with its "spirit" or unrighteousness into a character and personality with God's nature and spirit of peace, joy and righteousness. So let us watch our spirit or the mental temper of our soul, and see which way it is being bent. The believer with two natures, that of Christ and that of sinful Adam, is God's only creature that can be double minded and change back and forth, even as two people living in one house.

Only a deeply spiritual soul life will anchor our heart and spirit to a Christ-centered life of joy, peace, and worship. Many man-ruled church systems of Babylon are used as satan's workshop to remold our thinking, revealed by our spirit, or acts of our will. The organized churches teach the hungry, born again child of God in their own church doctrines and traditions containing unbelief like "the days of God's miracles are over." Men attempt to steer the church into a "social justice" direction. This is not God's divine order of Church!

Often a man is saved out of the pitfalls of sin by the new birth and then has the church put him back into a religious sin of sectarianism and lifeless creeds and church practices. All of these things affect the new believer's heart or center of his or her soul life, which manifests later in their life "spirit" or attitude of mind. There are spirits of national customs that also influence the spirits of individuals. Just as at Christmas time, the spirit of Christmas affects and influences millions of people.

Today undisciplined guidance of the young shows the spirit of this age as cell phones and technical gadgets preoccupy nearly all, young and old. A mother should be creating a spirit in her small children each Sunday afternoon by reading Bible stories to them and telling them of His wonderful spirit of grace. Yet in the hearts of some, a spirit of liberalism is attempting to destroy the home and infect the hearts and minds of children through our schools.

The importance of this subject is reflected in literally hundreds of scriptures in both Testaments. Proverbs says, "Keep thy heart with all diligence; for out of it are the issues of life" (Proverbs 4:23). Proverbs 16:2 says, "but the Lord weigheth s the spirits." Proverbs 23:7 says, "For as a man thinketh in his heart so is he."

It is very important to watch the "spirit" or attitude of the five mental senses toward all circumstances and environments of life so that satan cannot be allowed to pressure your thinking and the acts of your will the wrong way. Do you have a "spirit" of love and forgiveness towards others at all times, regardless of how they may treat you? Remember, you can love the devilish spirit out of people but you cannot argue it out. Do not entertain vain arguments. The average person, when wronged, has a spirit or desire to get even by doing something to hurt them.

Watch your spirit and remember you are a Christian who is to maintain the true spirit of Christ in all deeds and actions. If you have a stubborn spirit, then make yourself do things you do not care to do and you can break it. If you have a spirit or habit Christ would not practice, then ask Him to take it away and cooperate with Him as He does. Man cannot change the leopard's spots, but he can change his own disposition as revealed in the spirit he shows in a test.

The Lord called us to yield our minds to a God-consciousness that will develop in us a righteous and Christlike "spirit" under all conditions. Guard against the spirit of worldliness, which would infiltrate our minds and bring us into the captivity of the world, flesh and the devil. God wants us to overcome. <u>Your spirit or attitude, unconsciously manifested at times, can destroy your Christian testimony.</u> Mental habits, if left unchecked, often change a person's personality. The spirit of criticism, if undisciplined, soon robs you of the gentleness and patience you once had.

The Bible tells of a place where Jesus healed all that were vexed with the devil. Today there are demon spirits that strive to vex weak-willed Christians, often pressuring their way into the person's mind. This is revealed in their spirit, which acts <u>as the thermometer of the feelings in their mind</u>.

Saints who are allergic to certain things actually can be tormented by them and need to be delivered from those oppressing little demons. The sure way to develop the "spirit" of Christ is to develop His nine spiritual gifts or graces of Galatians 5:22-23.

Every Christian shall stand at the Bema Judgment seat of Christ (Romans 14:10, 2 Corinthians 5:10). That is where our works will be judged and rewarded, if they stand the testing fire. In First Corinthians we read, **"Every man's work shall be made manifest: for the day shall declare it, because it shall be revealed by fire; and the fire shall try every man's work of what sort it is" (1 Corinthians 3:13).** This will take place at the beginning of the one thousand year reign of Christ.

Do not be like the wealthy businessman in this story: The businessman had been a nominal Christian for forty years, and he died. He stood trembling before the Judge and His Judgment Seat to have his life work judged for eternal rewards. The Lord asked, "What did you bring me out of your long Christian life?" The man stood paralyzed with shame, for he could not think of anything acceptable to give God as a present. Then pointing to nine large objects, the voice said: "<u>Those are the things you stole from God during your Christian life</u>."

The first object with his name on it was all the Lord's <u>tithes and offerings</u> he had used for himself. The second object was <u>God's time</u> which he had stolen. The third object was <u>broken vows</u>, the fourth was <u>buried talents</u>, the fifth was <u>lost opportunities</u>, the sixth was <u>dead testimonies</u>, the seventh was <u>all his idle words</u>, and the eighth was a <u>group of lost souls from hell</u>

who pointed their fingers at him and screamed that his life had "stumbled" them and sent them to hell. The ninth was the <u>glory of God he sold for the praises of men</u>. The spirit of your heart is the sounding board of your soul and denotes the way your life is going. The forty years as a leader in a fraternal society, the wealthy man thought to offer as a gift, was rejected and burned as wood, hay, and stubble.

God's Divine Revelation through Prophecy

"Watchman, what of the night?" says Isaiah (Isaiah 2:11). In the prophet's day, many were asking him, had the shadow of the king's moon dial revealed the prophetic time for them? Rapidly fulfilling Bible prophecies proclaim the nearing advent of our Lord Jesus. God in foreknowledge and mercy has actually revealed in prewritten history, called prophecy, all major events of the earth before they happened. Before He created man, He wrote the story of man's coming test, fall, and redemption. Man's first "bible" was the sixty constellations of the stars. In 12 of these prophetic and symbolic pictures or true imagery of truth, God wrote in the lunar, the completion of His plan. This universal language begins in our New Testament and ends with sign pictures set in parables and in picture stories.

God has other methods also of revealing His divine revelation of truth. He gave the spiritual people dreams, visions, and divine utterance, called prophecy. Our entire Bible is set in divine utterance, both as it forth-tells and foretells God's truths. Fulfilled prophecies prove God's Word to be divinely inspired and proved God to be infallible and all wise.

The Bible is full of prophetic predictions of events to come, even describing them in detail. No other book in the world does this. In Isaiah 41:21-26, God actually challenges all heathen religions to a prophecy contest. Our Lord Christ Jesus proved He was the Messiah also in this manner. John records Jesus saying, **"Now I tell you before it come, that, when it is come to pass, ye may believe that I am he"** (John 13:19).

The Old Testament prophets, at different places and times, delivered thirty prophecies that the Messiah must fulfill within three days and nights of His death, burial and resurrection. All of these were literally fulfilled at Calvary. Nearly all of the Old Testament prophets had prophetic visions that leaped over the silent centuries and gave spotlight pictures of this, our end-time days. All agreed it to be a time of unparalleled suffering as God purifies the earth with mighty judgments. But in Matthew 24, our Lord Himself gave to the Church a composite picture composed of twenty-one prophetic pictures of the last days period we are now in. These were to be the signs of His coming. Thus, the Old Testament and the New Testament prophets actually wrote the headlines for our newspapers of today and we see these things coming to pass.

The final book, closing of the canon of Holy Scripture, is the book of Revelation, composed of 12,000 words. The holy city described in it measures 12,000 furlongs cubed. (This is 1,500 miles). It pictures the last seven years of this world age and coincides with Daniel's prophecy of Daniel 9:24. In Daniel's prophecy of seven sevens of "day-years," the last week, or seven years are the last and lost week of Daniel's prophecy.

Let our vision leap forward with these end time Bible prophecies. We can now see the consummation of the ages in the conjunction of the prewritten outlines of the cycles of the Gentile nations, of Israel and of the Church. The Lord prophesied, **"But as the days of Noah were, so shall also the coming of the Son of Man be" (Matthew 24:37).** Noah's day was filled with violence, men's hearts were evil, and great building activity was in progress. Our Lord again forewarns us, **"For then shall be great tribulation, such as was not since the beginning of the world to this time, no, nor ever shall be" (Matthew 24:21).** As we locate ourselves in this pre-tribulation period, we realize that the Church is in the same position as Israel was at the Red Sea, surrounded by enemies and with no escape, except by God's miraculous power.

Today the Church stands before Great Tribulation, surrounded by her enemies, with no escape until the Lord comes to deliver us. Truly it is flood time in the earth again, but this time the earth will be purified by fiery judgments. Let us view with the prophetic vision of the apostle John, the unfulfilled Bible prophecies immediately ahead. He sets forth in symbolic and prophetic pictures the beast or federation of all world nations, rising out of the Gentile nations. The Bible speaks of a beast as a man or a group, who have no consciousness of God, even as an animal.

In Revelation 13, one sees two beasts rising for their last act in the earth, as satan strives to usher in a utopia without Christ. The first beast prefigures a federation of nations into a one world federated State. The second beast prefigures the forming of a likeness or image of it, by unifying all major religions into one state Church. The rising beast or federated state will have seven head nations and ten lesser or horn nations that control her military power.

We shall probably view a worldwide disarmament as seen by the prophet Isaiah "and they shall beat their swords into plowshares and their spears into pruning hooks" (Isaiah 2:4). In the picture of Revelation 13, the civil or state beast has no rider, but in the 17th chapter a "Scarlet Woman" the ecclesiastical formed state church, is riding and guiding the beast into view. This "Woman," rich in the wealth of this world, is covered with the blood of the saints, as also is the beast upon which she rides. The state church endeavors to unify all religions. It makes a patriotic appeal, and seeing many refusing to enter, uses her influence to have the federated state formulate laws to force all into this one ecclesiastical system.

In Revelation we read, "And it was given unto him to make war with the saints, and to overcome them" (Revelation 13:7). There will be saints in the earth then. As laws force all into this one state church, all other religious orders, denominations, and Christian churches that have not affiliated with them will be closed. This will be the end of all Protestantism.

Probably the last test of these pre-tribulation days before the Church is taken up (raptured) may be an effort to force all into this state church by making all people take the mark of the beast.

16And he causeth all, both small and great, rich and poor, free and bond, to receive a mark in their right hand, or in their foreheads. (Revelation 13:16) 9And the third angel followed them, saying with a loud voice, If any man worship the beast and his image, and receive his mark in his forehead, or in his hand, 10The same shall drink of the wine of the wrath of God, which is poured out without mixture into the cup of his indignation; and he shall be tormented with fire and brimstone in the presence of the holy angels, and in the presence of the Lamb. (Revelation 14:9-10)

As the vision moves forward, Armageddon comes into view and the curtain falls on man's embryo civilization. In removing sin from the earth by removing the sinner, God sends his seven last plagues of war, famine, pestilence and mighty earthquakes. Then the Revelation carries us forward to when our Lord returns with his Church and the armies of heaven to possess the earth for the millennium of peace. This scene shows all of the armies of the federated state present to withstand his coming. How can these things be? The vision opened with a scene of the general assembly of the federated nations of the earth in session. "**And I saw the beast, and the kings of the earth, and their armies, gathered together to make war against him that sat on the horse, and against his army**" (Revelation 19:19).

As they were discussing legal matters, suddenly a bright and mighty angel stood in their midst with a shining sword in his hand. He began to address the startled assembly, speaking in one language, yet understood by all in their own native tongue. He gave to them God's last call to repentance, then seeing them reject Christ, he stated that Christ would return in the future and stand upon the Mount of Olives and, with His armies of heaven, would possess the earth. As the angel vanished, consternation followed as they thought him to be a messenger from another planet. Orders immediately went forth for all armies to assemble and surround the Mount of Olives to meet the attack.

Then came the scene of Revelation 19:19, also pictured by the prophet Zechariah, in Zechariah 14:4. This scene is set for the consummation of the ages, for as our Lord Jesus Christ descends with His armies of heaven and His Church, all of the Gentile nations' armies are assembled at Armageddon to meet Him, and the last battle of this world age begins. As His feet touch the Mount of Olives, it divides and rolls back as the Red Sea, as in the time of the Passover. At that time the nation of Israel will march forth from their hiding places, the valley of Achor, accepting Him as their Messiah, and a nation is there born in a day. As they march singing through the divided Mount, and the heavenly hosts are singing a song of victory to the Lamb, all of the assembled Christ-rejecters are slain by the brightness of His coming. Then the curtain falls on man's civilization.

Millions now living will not be prepared to meet their God and they will have to meet Him unprepared. Why not confess your sins and call upon Him now? Tomorrow may be too late.

Watch ye therefore, and pray always, that ye may be accounted worthy to escape all these things that shall come to pass, and to stand before the Son of man. (Luke 21:36)

If by any means I might attain unto the resurrection of the dead. (Philippians 3:11)

Because thou hast kept the word of my patience, I also will keep thee from the hour of temptation, which shall come upon all the world, to try them that dwell upon the earth. (Revelation 3:10)

God's True Worship Restored

The full and true genealogy of all earth life is recorded in Genesis. The Almighty Creator **"The LORD hath prepared his throne in the heavens; and his kingdom ruleth over all."(Psalms 103:19).** The eternal God with no beginning nor ending, through His unlimited foreknowledge, has chosen His creations for each millennium. It was probably millions of billions of ages ago, that in the council of His own will, He the great Elohim, composed of the Father, Messianic Son, and the Holy Spirit, chose this seven thousand years we live in. He chose this tiny earth for His new creation, man.

The importance of this decision is seen when we realize that God would surely never set up the cross and offer up His only begotten Son as a Sacrifice again. He chose to have Spirit-filled children, **"Let us make man in our image, after our likeness" (Genesis 1:26).** In Ephesians 3:10, all of the hosts of heaven watched this, once for all eternity spectacle in the earth, with breathless interest, as God restored His rule to a rebellious earth.

Since the great God of love had no enemies, Lucifer, His covering cherub, was allowed to rebel against Him and to become satan, the tester (Ezekiel 28:1-19). satan, the devil, cast out of highest heaven, came to earth to overthrow the human race. Triune man, with his spirit, soul, and body, became the battleground of good and evil. Man was created with two relationships with his Creator, through his human spirit and his human soul or mind. The key to understanding these two relationships is in the dividing of our spirit and our soul (Hebrews 4:12; 1 Thessalonians 5:23). God is a Spirit (John 4:24). All life comes from God, and He chose to minister to man through man's spirit or life within.

In the paradise of Eden, before sin came, God ministered His divine wisdom and knowledge directly to Adam who named all fowl. God also ministered His knowledge to all life creations. The animals retain this sixth sense, and return to their homes after being seemingly lost. We call this "instinct," and even the blind earthworm lives by it, but man lost this in the fall from his sinless estate. satan reversed God's order by placing man's mental life above his spiritual life.

In Genesis 2:17 and 3:1-3, Adam and Eve stood before the tree of knowledge on which were the fruits of good and evil. (Never did the Bible say they ate an "apple.") This great family tree of the human race was to have the fruits of the Spirit (Galatians 5:22-23), and the fruits of the flesh or carnal mind (Galatians 5:19-21). Every human being must choose between the good fruits of the Spirit life and the evil fruits of the self-life of the mind.

God ordered the life habits of all creation, and His Word became the Law for their operation. In the human being, He set three sets of laws, one each for spirit, soul, and body. The laws of our inner man or spirit life are divine Faith, Hope, Love, Reverential Fear (True Worship), and Intuitive Knowledge. These are known as senses, faculties, or spiritual members. Our five mental or soulish laws are our senses, faculties or mental members of imagination, affection, conscience, memory and reason. Then our five natural or physical laws, are sight, hearing, smelling, tasting, and feeling. All human beings have these three sets of five laws and we live within their boundaries.

God as a Spirit has chosen our spirit and spirit "sense-laws" through which to minister to and through our mental or soulish senses or laws, and through these to our natural physical life. But Adam and Eve reversed God's order, and our life as an

214

overcoming Christian became governed by our election or will, using the mental laws or senses in decisions rather than by walking in the Spirit.

We see this sad, but now universal, cause and effect first in Genesis 11:1-6. There Nimrod and his organized church built the largest altar in the earth and after that, their order of worship was decided by their mental senses. From that broken order of worshipping sprang the oriental philosophies, and from them our Babel of "man-ruled" church systems and orders we see today. Each holds to their mental interpretation of their Christian philosophy and their lifeless programs, still building God's Son a House in His Kingdom, after their own plans and orders. It is this broken order of worship that brings the curse of God and satan's sin life of doubts, fears, envying, jealousies, greed, malice and unbelief.

God's coming Kingdom in the earth, with the growing human race, entered its second aspect at Mount Sinai, and its third aspect at the cross of Calvary. Little was known of the inner man or human spirit during this period before Calvary. Only a minority of the prophets and priests of God became full overcomers by restoring this order of God's true worship. These Old Testament prophets who restored God's order, and who lived and worshipped in His Spirit reigning through their spirit, lived an abandoned miracle life unto God. These were the overcomers who obtained a better resurrection (Matthew 27:52).

Then came Calvary, and God was able to restore true worship through their spirit above their soul reasoning and interpretations. But one sees Christian groups again, back in soul or sense knowledge worship, under human headships and programs of man. These mental Christian philosophies and orders hold their people under the bondage of mental fear of their church laws and under condemnation. But the Spirit frees us from condemnation. "He that believeth in Him (Christ) is not condemned" (John 3:18).

The first Man to completely fulfill the pattern of the Genesis 1:26 "man" was the Lord Jesus Christ. He alone was the first to fully obey God's first commandment with promises (Genesis 1:28), to subdue (self-life) and have dominion. He did it by fully restoring God's divine order of our spirit senses ruling our mental senses. His life in the Spirit found no limitations, and the miraculous became commonplace.

What He did, we are commanded to do (John 14:12-14). "If ye shall ask anything in my name, I will do it" (John 14:14). Here He gives us a creative power through the "power of attorney" to use His name. All of man's defeats and sorrows center on, or stem from, the soul or mental senses. There is no limitation or defeat ever in the regenerated spirit of any Christian. Christ is now the believer's High Priest, who daily ministers of His seven covenants of Calvary to our needs. These <u>seven covenants of Calvary are our justification, sanctification, healing, health, peace, abundant life, and God's glory</u>. The first is eternal for our recreated spirit at the new birth. The last six are daily benefits for our soul. All gifts and benefits of God must be claimed by faith to receive them.

Then suddenly came Calvary, and our Lord, at the height of His earthly ministry, was crucified. His forerunner, John the Baptist, at the height of his ministry, was beheaded. The early Church, at the end of seven years at the height of miracle power, was scattered abroad. "the kingdom of heaven suffereth violence" (Matthew 11:12). The impact of sin in Eden on the human race was nothing compared with the impact of Christ's righteousness in His seven sufferings of Calvary. In them, He fulfilled the seven compound names of Jehovah, the seven annual Feasts of Israel, the seven sprinklings of blood, and the seven sufferings unto death of Isaiah 53:4-8. The greatest of God's mysteries, hid in His mind, was the New Testament Church in God's divine order of government, truth, and discipline. This mystery church body was conceived in the lowest hell, in the soul sufferings of our Lord as the scapegoat (Leviticus 16:5-10, Psalms 139:15-16). It was born in the seven sufferings of the cross, and was set in God's divine order at Pentecost (Acts 2:4).

With the death, burial, and resurrection of our Lord Jesus, thousands of believing Jews were swept into the third phase of the heavenly kingdom set up in the earth. It was to be 15 or 20 years before the Lord gave the full revelation for the New Testament Church. In the early years, these Jewish converts thought the new move of God was the perfecting of Israel, according to their Jewish prophets. In this transition message, some endeavored to "Judaize" Christianity, by inserting some of Moses' gospel.

In Acts 21:20 we read that they were, "all zealous of the (Mosaic) law." Some were teaching, "Except ye be circumcised after the manner of Moses, ye cannot be saved" (Acts 15:1). Then when the apostle Paul came, with the full revelation of God's grace and salvation by grace through faith, he encountered great trouble from their legalistic, negative, conditional gospel. In Galatians 1:8-9, Paul warned of "other" gospels that held believers in the soulish interpretations and soul worship. Today, too many blood-washed Christians are worshipping under these negative, conditional, and "soul-sense" gospels of man's intellectual interpretations of spirit truth.

This life in the Spirit or with the Spirit-filled life reigning over the mental and physical life, is all about us today. The Bible pictures this great truth, of life beyond the veil of sense knowledge and above the realm of human reason, in the realm of faith. In Matthew 17:1-8, we see our Lord dividing His disciples, the overcomers from the overcome, at that time. He took Peter, James, and John up the mount of transfiguration, leaving the others behind, as their consecration at that time would not have stood the glory. There on the mount, the three New Testament apostles saw Moses and Elijah. Their Lord's Spirit so fully clothed His human body it almost blinded them. Today thousands of precious Christians are being baptized in the Holy

Spirit, speaking in tongues as the Spirit gives them utterance (Acts 2:4). Many millions have received this visitation since the turning of the twentieth century. Through this baptism, our inner man spirit is fully restored to preeminence over all soul or mental life, as the Holy Spirit clothes our mind, bringing it into captivity to our Christ-centered spirit of the new creation.

The Seven Covenants of Calvary form the gospel of Christ, and are set forth in two phases. We believers all have a provisional faith or revelation in our soul senses of the New Covenant truth and promises. We also can have an experimental faith by the spirit being in control. Many thousands of ministers have lived and died in the former, but never entered into the latter. We all have some revelation or message but too few ever enter into their full ministry, which is only by the Spirit. Many fail to understand the meaning of the word *spirit*. Scripture uses this word probably a thousand times, applying it to deity, angelic spirits, satanic spirits, and to human spirits. But in most scriptures, it refers to our mental attitude or spirit of our soul life. As an illustration, we have all said, "He has a wonderful spirit," or, "She has a humble, teachable, or gentle spirit." Today in church worship, one sees much of the "showmanship" spirit, or "religious entertainment" spirit. Many ministers even preach the truth, but destroy its power, with a jesting "spirit."

The apostle Paul, in his epistles, <u>teaches by precept, practice comparison, and contrast</u>. This makes all Scripture foolproof. In Romans 8, the ministry of the Holy Spirit is called "Spirit" by the apostle. The soul senses with their sense knowledge, are called the "flesh." He uses the word "flesh" thirteen times in thirteen verses in Romans 8:1-13, and in the same chapter, uses the word "spirit" nineteen times. This chapter, following the preceding ones in Romans, sets forth a strong contrast between righteousness of the Spirit-led life and the unrighteousness of our selfish self-centered mental life. "So then they that are in the flesh cannot please God" (Romans 8:8).

Every human being lives within the boundaries of the three sets of life faculties, senses, or laws mentioned previously. Our election decides in our human will, whether God or satan is allowed to exercise them. Often satan borrows our imagination or reason, while God controls the others, and there is warfare in the "members" (Romans 7:23). With our natural human wisdom and knowledge directing our life, and not God's Spirit within our Christian spirit in control, we are out of His order. Thus, we will remain weak and beggarly until we line back up and get into His order.

As in the life of Jesus our Lord, the will to do the Father's will, kept His Spirit, with its miracle power, completely in control of His mental senses. Mentally counterfeiting these five spirit senses is a common practice and sin. The spirit senses are divine faith, hope, love, reverential fear/worship, and intuitive knowledge. When we attempt these mentally, they become mental faith (intellectual assent), mental hope (unbelief), mental love (inordinate affection), mental fear/mental worship (torment), or mental knowledge.

With our spirit, soul, and body, we have need for a threefold salvation. This is seen in Scripture as justification by the blood and new birth, sanctification by the Spirit washing our minds daily with God's Word, and glorification of our body at the return of our Lord. The first is usually in Scripture in past tense and saves us from the guilt of sin. The second is present tense, saving us daily from the power of sin habits. The third is future tense, saving us from the presence of sin, at our Lord's return. "Who (Christ) delivered us from so great a death, and doth deliver: in whom we trust will yet deliver us" (2 Corinthians1:10).

God is the creator of order. His vast sidereal universe, set in perpetual motion in perfect gravitational balance, reveals His perfect workmanship. We also see this balance in nature. Through His law of propagation, all of the millions of species of earth life are living today. These creations all remain in God's created divine order, for there was no sin to break the harmony. Christ set His New Testament Church in His divine order for perfect spiritual propagation, but through man's election, satan has broken His order.

In Eden, by reversing His order of man's spirit, soul, and body, satan has man living and worshipping with the soul over the spirit and body. This gives our natural life rule over our spiritual life. In God's due order for the New Testament Church's government, the apostle Paul set forth nine spiritual anointed ministries, nine spiritual anointing gifts and nine anointing spiritual graces or fruits of the Spirit. Every born again believer is in Christ's Body and in one of these ministries of apostle, prophet, evangelist, pastor (shepherd), teacher, elder, deacon, helps, and lesser governments.

We should seek and receive the baptism of the Holy Spirit as in Acts 2:4, then receive one or more of the spiritual gifts of divine wisdom, knowledge, faith, healing, miracles, prophecy, discernment, tongues, and interpretation (1 Corinthians 12:8-10). The nine graces or fruits of the Spirit life are listed in Galatians 5:22-23. Christ is the Head of His Body, an organism and not a human organization. All activity was centered in the local churches and elders were ordained in every church (Acts 14:23).

Today, highly organized church groups, under centralized human headships have swallowed up the local churches and rejected the Holy Spirit gifts and ministry, replacing God's order with their own "program-ized," powerless, "elder-less" orders. Spiritual ignorance is the curse and mildew of death in the "man-ruled" streamlined church striving in greater annual budgets to build towers of Babel. Liberalism or modernism has infiltrated their foundations, and all major organized churches are breaking up from within. But God is raising up true New Testament Churches all over the earth by restoring the spiritual over the mental; God will restore the true Church.

The scarlet thread that runs through the Bible is the story of redemption. Redemption is two-fold. It is by the shed blood of our Lord Jesus on the cross, and it is also by the Spirit, as He redeems according to God's covenant Word. We see this pre-figured in the nation of Israel's Passover. There they sprinkled the Passover lamb's blood on their doorposts, to redeem them from the death angel when the Lord's Passover came. But they were led and delivered out of Egypt by the Spirit of God, in the overshadowing cloud, which was Israel's Passover.

They were three days passing out of Egypt, and then for forty years, the Spirit redeemed their lives daily by raining bread from heaven in the manna. He also sheltered them, as under the wings of the Almighty, from their desert enemies. Today, all Christian groups believe the blood redemption, but few teach concerning the Spirit daily redeeming God's Word of promise, for divine healing, and so on. The shed blood speaks of our eternal justification while Spirit redemption is daily sanctification.

Adam knew the origin of life. King Solomon sought for the profit of natural life. But the apostle Paul discovered the prize of life.

In Philippians, Paul declared, "I press toward the mark for the prize of the high calling of God in Christ Jesus" (Philippians 3:14). He also says, "If by any means I might attain unto the resurrection of the dead" (Philippians 3:11). The word used here for *resurrection* means *out-resurrection*, or "out from among the sleeping ones." This is the "better resurrection" (Hebrews 11:35, Matthew 27:52). This was the prize for the overcomers, and they are depicted in Ezekiel, the first and tenth chapters, as living creatures in the form of the Cherubim. This words *cherub* and *cherubim* are used ninety times in Scripture. They were figures in the Holy of Holies of the tabernacle.

The apostle John, in Revelation 4:6 sees these same four living creatures as forms of Cherubim, composing probably countless millions of Christian overcoming saints out of all the

Church Age. They are upon the throne reigning as our Lord promised (Revelation 3:21). They are the raptured "inner-body" of the Church. The outer Body of the Church, the over-comers of the Church age, appear in the general resurrection of Revelation 7:14, and are before the throne or outer court. The qualifications for the prize are in Ephesians 5:27, "a glorious Church, not having spot, or wrinkle, or any such thing, but that it should be holy and without blemish." Which group are you in?

Our Christian failures in life can easily be traced to the fact that we make decisions based on our mental reasoning, rather than allowing the indwelling Spirit to lead us. Our natural wisdom, based on sense knowledge taught in the books of men, lacks God's grace to believe God's miracle Word. We give mental assent to the promises of God, our inheritance, but with our mental faculties, are unable to get our prayers into orbit. Our self life rushes ahead to meet the issues of life that test our testimony, and fails to fully reckon, recognize, or even realize the reality of the new creation life within. It is surprising to find so many Christians who will not believe the plain wording of the Bible, believing some church law or tradition instead.

In the plain wording of the Bible, Jesus says, in John 10:28, "And I give unto them eternal life and they shall *never* perish." In John 3:16, Jesus says, "That whosoever believeth in him should not perish, but have everlasting life." Matthew 8:17 says, "Himself took our infirmities and bare our sicknesses." In spite of this, man's unwritten church tradition, believed by millions, teaches that the days of miracles are over.

Jesus came preaching the laws or principles of the Kingdom. Paul came preaching the laws or principles of righteousness for the Church. After our Lord had fully set forth the revelation, He entered into the ministry of it. We must be like Him, filled with the Holy Spirit for power to enter into the second phase of the gospel. In Mark 4:33-35 our Lord begins the ministry of His miracle Word, which was to confirm and prove it. "Let us pass over unto the other side" (Mark 4:35). We have to cross over also from revelation to experience. Other small ships followed His gospel ship. A sudden storm frightened the other ships back, but His kept on through the storm. His frightened disciples called on Him and He rebuked the destroying wind, and it instantly ceased. "Why are you so fearful? How is it you have no faith?" he asked. This enacted parable depicts for us the picture of the storms of life we must face in crossing over to the other side.

As they approached the other side, a demon-crazed wild man met them. Jesus met him with a rest of faith in His Spirit and cast the demons out. Every Christian has this power of authority. "Behold I give you power (authority)... over all the power of the enemy; and nothing shall by any means hurt you" (Luke 10:19). With the baptism of the Holy Spirit, as in Acts 2:4, you will be crossing over to the other side, from the lower moral self life to higher spiritual warfare. God has restored His divine order of worship in you. Do not allow the devil to drive you back to the lower soul sense worship again.

Let us not spend our entire lives with only a revelation about our Lord and His miracle ministry, but let us be filled with the Spirit and enter into the miracle ministry that awaits every Christian. In Mark 9:24, a man challenged by the afflictions of his son, cried, "Lord, I believe; help thou mine unbelief." He believed in his mind, but his inner spirit could not break through the crystallized unbelief in his heart, to allow God's Word to work. Another enacted prophetic prophecy illustrating this challenge of the "other side" is found in the last chapter of the gospel of John. There the disciples, becoming discouraged with their gospel not expressed in miracle power of the Spirit, had returned to their old order of fishing. They had labored hard in self-effort all night, and as the new day broke, they were returning with empty nets. What a picture of much of modern ministry.

The Lord, in His resurrection Body, stood on the shore waiting for their return. He challenged them to step over into the Spirit and cast their nets down on the right (righteous) side, to find a catch. They obeyed His Word and came in with their nets filled with fish. God's miracle Word of covenant promise must be believed. We must reckon with God by fully recognizing that "God watches over His Word and performs it." On the shore, in a new day, they feasted with the Lord, for by His miracle Spirit-empowered Word, the affinity of the atoms were changed from sand to fire, fish, frying pan and bread. Let us go over to the other side.

As a blood-washed Christian, you have the full authority of God to speak with miracle power, and when you are living in the spirit over the soulish reasoning senses, you also can speak the Word in faith. The apostle Paul, living in the spirit over the weak natural soul senses, spoke the Word with authority, and the cripple leaped for joy.

We are truly living in Bible days again and we are seeing God's Word working in miracle power. "These signs shall follow them that believe; In my name shall they cast out devils; they shall speak with new tongues; They shall take up serpents; and if they drink any deadly thing, it shall not hurt them; they shall lay hands on the sick, and they shall recover.... And they went forth, and preached every where, the Lord working with them, and confirming the word with signs following. Amen" (Mark 16:17-20).

"....Whatsoever things you desire, when you pray, believe that you receive them, and you shall have them." (Mark 11:24). Amen.

CHAPTER ELEVEN
Doctrine of Baptisms

There are three phases of baptism: A teaching session.

Here is a list of fundamental doctrines every babe in Christ should learn, "doctrine of baptisms, and of laying on of hands, and of resurrection of the dead, and of eternal judgment" (Hebrews 6:2).

FIRST:
Ownership of the soul **must be** the very first baptism.

    A. When one is <u>baptized into the Body of Christ,</u> it transfers the soul from enemy hands to Christ's hands. "For by one Spirit are we all baptized into one body, whether we be Jews or Gentiles, whether we be bond or free; and have been all made to drink into one Spirit. (1 Corinthians 12:13). In plain terms, we are baptized into the Body of Christ. This is JUSTIFICATION taking place in our human spirit.

    The next two baptisms can come in either order or at the same time, according to Scripture.

    B. Baptized by water
    C. Baptized by the Holy Spirit.

A BREAKDOWN OF ALL THREE
(A) Baptized into the Body of Christ:

Who is baptized? The lost, repentant sinner; whosever will call upon the name of the Lord. "And it shall come to pass, that whosoever shall call on the name of the Lord shall be saved." (Acts 2:21)

What is received? JUSTIFICATION "Therefore we conclude that a man is justified by faith without the deeds of the law" (Romans 3:28). The law is not in effect anymore. We receive forgiveness of sins. "If we confess our sins, he is faithful and just to forgive us our sins, and to cleanse us from all unrighteousness" (1 John 1: **9**).

Why? To escape hell and to have eternal life. "For God so loved the world, that he gave his only begotten Son, that whosoever believeth in him should not perish, but have everlasting life" (John 3: 16).

Who baptizes? It is God who baptizes the sinner into the Body of Christ by sending the Spirit of Jesus into the human spirit of the lost repentant sinner. **"And because ye are sons, God hath sent forth the Spirit of his Son into your hearts, crying, Abba, Father" (Galatians 4: 6).**

(B) Baptized in water:
Who is baptized? The saved person only. As the old saying goes, "If you go down a dry sinner, you come up a wet hypocrite." "And as they went on their way, they came unto a certain water: and the eunuch said, See, here is water; what doth hinder me to be baptized? And Philip said, If thou believest with all thine heart, thou mayest. And he answered and said, I believe that Jesus Christ is the Son of God. And he commanded the chariot to stand still: and they went down both into the water, both Philip and the eunuch; and he baptized him" (Acts 8:36-38).

<u>Why should you be baptized in water?</u> To be obedient to God. **"Therefore we are buried with him by baptism into death: that like as Christ was raised up from the dead by the glory of the Father, even so we also should walk in newness of life" (Romans 6:4).**

Obedience is the key element here and we can see that as well when Jesus was baptized.

"Then cometh Jesus from Galilee to Jordan unto John, to be baptized of him. But John forbad him, saying, I have need to be baptized of thee, and comest thou to me? And Jesus answering said unto him, Suffer it to be so now: for thus it becometh us to fulfill all righteousness. Then he suffered him. And Jesus, when he was baptized, went up straightway out of the water: and, lo, the heavens were opened unto him, and he saw the Spirit of God descending like a dove, and lighting upon him: <u>And lo a voice from heaven, saying, This is my beloved Son, in whom I am well pleased</u>" (Matthew 3:13-17). Verse 17 is where the foundation (Jesus) was judged.

To take that further, the foundation upon which our works shall be judged is found in First Corinthians:

¹And I, brethren, could not speak unto you as unto spiritual, but as unto carnal, even as unto babes in Christ. ²I have fed you with milk, and not with meat: for hitherto ye were not able to bear it, neither yet now are ye able. ³For ye are yet carnal: for whereas there is among you envying, and strife, and divisions, are ye not carnal, and walk as men? ⁴For while one saith, I am of Paul; and another, I am of Apollos; are ye not carnal? ⁵Who then is Paul, and who is Apollos, but ministers by whom ye believed, even as the Lord

gave to every man? [6]I have planted, Apollos watered; but God gave the increase. [7]So then neither is he that planteth any thing, neither he that watereth; but God that giveth the increase. [8]Now he that planteth and he that watereth are one: and every man shall receive his own reward according to his own labour. [9]For we are labourers together with God: ye are God's husbandry, ye are God's building. [10]According to the grace of God which is given unto me, as a wise masterbuilder, I have laid the foundation, and another buildeth thereon. But let every man take heed how he buildeth thereupon. [11]For other foundation can no man lay than that is laid, which is Jesus Christ. [12]Now if any man build upon this foundation gold, silver, precious stones, wood, hay, stubble; [13]Every man's work shall be made manifest: for the day shall declare it, because it shall be revealed by fire; and the fire shall try every man's work of what sort it is. [14]If any man's work abide which he hath built thereupon, he shall receive a reward. [15]If any man's work shall be burned, he shall suffer loss: but he himself shall be saved; yet so as by fire. [16]Know ye not that ye are the temple of God, and that the Spirit of God dwelleth in you? [17]If any man defile the temple of God, him shall God destroy; for the temple of God is holy, which temple ye are. [18]Let no man deceive himself. If any man among you seemeth to be wise in this world, let him become a fool, that he may be wise. [19]For the wisdom of this world is foolishness with God. For it is written, He taketh the wise in their own craftiness. [20]And again, The Lord knoweth the thoughts of the wise, that they are vain. [21]Therefore let no man glory in men. For all things are your's; [22]Whether Paul, or Apollos, or Cephas, or the world, or life, or death, or things present, or things to come;

all are your's; ²³And ye are Christ's; and Christ is God's" (1 Corinthians 3:1-23). Fulfillment.

Who baptizes? The God ordained minister. **"I thank God that I baptized none of you, but Crispus and Gaius; Lest any should say that I had baptized in mine own name" (1 Corinthians 1:14-15).** Attention was being given to the baptizer and that needed correcting. Not just anyone should be baptizing, only God ordained ministers. God is a God of order, and His order should be followed and not what man feels is correct.

(C) Baptized in the Holy Spirit:

Who is baptized? The born again, spiritually hungry Christian. **"For John truly baptized with water; but ye shall be baptized with the Holy Ghost not many days hence" (Acts 1: 5).** To get here, you have to be one who is seeking God, and hungry for God. It is our "will" that comes into play here. How? Our will is directed by our soul and we know that is where our emotions come into play. Our will determines how far we will allow ourselves to grow into maturity. **"He said unto them, Have ye received the Holy Ghost since ye believed? And they said unto him, We have not so much as heard whether there be any Holy Ghost. And he said unto them, Unto what then were ye baptized? And they said, Unto John's baptism. Then said Paul, John verily baptized with the baptism of repentance, saying unto the people, that they should believe on him which should come after him, that is, on Christ Jesus. When they heard this, they were baptized in the name of the Lord Jesus. And when Paul had laid his hands upon them, the Holy Ghost came on them; and they spake with tongues, and prophesied" (Acts 19:2-6).**
An example of the order is found in Acts 10:42-48. **"To him give all the prophets witness, that through his name whoso-**

ever believeth in him shall receive remission of sins" (Acts 10:43). Peter explains what a lost, repentant sinner receives. While he was speaking, the Holy Ghost skipped the pattern of **(B)** and **(C)**. They spoke in tongues and then they were baptized in water. So **(B)** and/or **(C)** can happen in either order.

<u>What is received?</u> The power of the Holy Spirit, with evidence of Gifts. **"And when Paul had laid his hands upon them, the Holy Ghost came on them; and they spake with tongues, and prophesied" (Acts 19:6).**

<u>Why should you be baptized?</u> To live an overcoming life. In John, chapters 14, 15, and 16, in the Upper Room, Jesus gives seven major points about the Holy Spirit. They all begin with "C."

<u>Who baptizes?</u> Jesus baptizes in the Holy Spirit. **"I indeed baptize you with water unto repentance. but he that cometh after me is mightier than I, whose shoes I am not worthy to bear: <u>he shall baptize you with the Holy Ghost, and with fire:</u> Whose fan is in his hand, and he will throughly purge his floor, and gather his wheat into the garner; but he will burn up the chaff with unquenchable fire" (Matthew 3:11-12).**

To summarize who is to baptize, you must first understand that there is more than one baptism. At each stage, there is a different baptizer. God is first as He leads a person to Him, that person listens to Him calling, then makes the decision to be saved, undergoing transference of the soul. He is baptized by God into the Body of Christ and is now saved, and his soul no longer belongs to the enemy.

The second baptism is the baptism in water. (This can actually be the second or third baptism.) Neither this baptism, nor the next will save the person, only the first one does. This baptism in water is an act of obedience and fulfills a part of God's will in your life. It it was not important it would not be there. Too many people toss it out and say it is not necessary, which comes through their own lack of understanding. Baptism in the Greek is *baptizo* which means total immersion, not sprinkling.

The third baptism is where growth explodes in the spiritually hungry. Gaining spiritual understanding of God's Word is beginning to be attained and the operation of gifts are evident. Some people believe that if there is no evidence of the gifts in operation, the person is not saved. This is simply not true. What is true is that the evidence must follow those who are at this stage in their relationship with Christ. The reason evidence must follow is that it shows truth in the believer. What is truth? Christ. Christ is living through that person more so, as that person allows less of themselves to come through, and more of Christ to shine through. It is a process, the race we should be running daily, without fainting. **"Jesus saith unto him, I AM THE WAY, THE TRUTH, AND THE LIFE: no man cometh unto the Father, but by me" (John 14:6).**

Part Four

Self Searching and Teachings

Searching your heart truthfully is the important part of dying to self. It is the building block of truth, coupled with love, which allows you to stand in "right relationship" (righteousness) before God and others.

The final chapters in this book are some of the key "sicknesses" that have infected the body of Christ. There is too much division and infighting in churches today.

Are you ready to truly search within yourself to see what may lie hidden in your heart that prevents you from moving forward in Christ?

Are you wondering why you are still weak and beggarly?

Are you a person who has caused division in the Body of Christ? If so, why?

Church leader, are you brave enough to admit that you may have caused hurt because of a lack of understanding? Are you brave enough to ratify old hurts and heal wounds? Repentance and forgiveness break the root of bitterness.

Can you honestly search within yourself and ask, "Am I agenda driven or am I God driven?

Sitting in church or being in a leadership position does nothing but harm the body of Christ if you are there with the wrong motivation.

CHAPTER TWELVE
The Discipline of Your Conscience
A Weak Conscience

Learning some things about your own conscience can expose some of the enemy's strongholds set up in your mind that you may not currently recognize. Let's do a little housecleaning so your spirit can be in God's divine order. Make room for the richness of God's revelation to pour in and bring healing to your soul! AMEN!

T he blood of Jesus Christ gives us a clean conscience. The word *conscience* in the Greek (Strong's #4893) means *co-perception* or *to know together*. The conscience is that voice within us that tells us whether we are going in the right or wrong direction. Conscience is that still, small voice that is within us.

We have physical senses we use to distinguish the world around us. We have "soul senses" we use so we can know what is going on within our own hearts. We have a "spirit sense" so we can have contact with God. Within these senses, our spirit and soul line up when our hearing perceives the word of God. Hearing is a physical sense and our conscience is our soul sense so we can hear what is going on within our own hearts. Faith is what we hear from God.

Hearing: Conscience: Faith

Conviction is the work of the conscience stirred up by God. Conviction motivates us toward good and motivates us to change. Condemnation and shame are the work of the flesh, stirred up by the enemy. Condemnation and shame paralyzes us and causes us to retreat and hide from those things we need to change.

Conviction will point out sin but it also gives us the motivation and hope to change. It will not bring shame to us when we take appropriate action. If we do not deal with conviction, it will fester and become condemnation.

In order to fix our own conscience, we must learn how to diagnose it so it can function properly. It is akin to seeking help from a doctor. A doctor will begin to ask questions to get to the root of your illness. You must do this to your own conscience to be able to determine what is wrong.

Six Types of Consciences

1. A Weak Conscience
2. An Over-Sensitive Conscience
3. A Defiled Conscience
4. A Seared Conscience
5. A False Conscience
6. A Good Conscience

What is a weak conscience and how do you deal with one? First, you must look at how HEARING and FAITH operate.

Romans: 10:8-17 gives us valuable insight on how hearing and faith operate.

"But what saith it? The word is nigh thee, even in thy mouth, and in thy heart: that is, the word of faith, which we preach" (Romans 10:8). The Word tells us, "As we preach the Word, there is faith rising up, speaking words that bring forth faith."

"That if thou shalt confess with thy mouth the Lord Jesus, and shalt believe in thine heart that God hath raised him from the dead, thou shalt be saved. For with the heart man believeth unto righteousness; and with the mouth confession is made unto salvation" (Romans 10:9-10). When you hear the Word of faith do you know what it does? It gives you something to say. When you hear preaching, you know how to respond because you begin to realize that there is salvation, that there is a purpose, and there is a plan. God has set forth a plan to set us free and redeem us, and that is what we are to act upon!

"For the scripture saith, Whosoever believeth on him shall not be ashamed" (Romans 10:11). Hearing produces faith—faith then gives us the ability to feel no shame. That works within our conscience as well because the Word takes us to a place of not being ashamed.

When one hears the truth, it usually sounds negative initially. When one hears it again and again, the tone and sound begin to change. The hearing begins to line up and the word begins to sound positive. For instance, when you first hear the gospel, you discover that you are a sinner. "WELL! What do you mean I am a sinner?" When the mind begins to hear things about itself, it may not be ready to accept them, so it shuts down the rest of the message. It will just stay focused on, "What do you mean I am a sinner?"

When the mind and the heart begin to open again to hear the entire story, that God has a plan to redeem us, it all starts to come into proper perspective. Then the gospel is accepted in its proper truth and the shame is no longer attached. Our pride and ego weaken and our flesh moves out of the way, as more and more of Christ lives through us.

Where faith exists, there is freedom for our conscience. When we place our faith in Christ, we are in a place that has no shame. Many believers are afraid to be honest with God because we feel shame. Shame prohibits us from admitting our true sin to God and sometimes, even to ourselves. Why is this?

We are afraid that if we admit our sins, God may notice. Romans 10:11 is key because we need to have confidence that God is not going to shame us. Faith gives us the conviction to have the courage to step into the arena of TRUTHFUL confession.

"For there is no difference between the Jew and the Greek; for the same Lord over all is rich unto all that call upon him. For whosoever shall call upon the name of the Lord shall be saved" (Romans 10:12-13). There is no difference—your past failures and heritage do not matter. ALL that matters is, whosoever calls upon the Lord Jesus Christ will be saved! There is no shame in the Lord Jesus! Amen! The word says He is, "rich unto all that call upon Him!"

You know what hearing does? Not only does faith come by hearing, but as our faith increases, it gives us a voice! Without faith, God cannot hear us, because it is all unbelief and then our words become meaningless! But when we have faith we have a voice and that voice can call upon the Lord God and HE will answer us, AMEN!

"How then shall they call on him in whom they have not believed? and how shall they believe in him of whom they have not heard? and how shall they hear without a preacher?" (Romans 10:14). This clearly shows the relationship between HEARING and FAITH. We must understand this to grasp what faith is in the context of the conscience and in the context of salvation.

"Knowing that a man is not justified by the works of the law, but by the faith of Jesus Christ, even we have believed in Jesus Christ, that we might be justified by the faith of Christ, and not by the works of the law: for the works of the law shall no flesh by justified" (Galatians 2:16).

There are two important aspects of faith covered here. First, whose faith is it? It says the faith of Jesus Christ. In other words it is not our faith, it is Christ's. It is not only faith in Jesus Christ but it is actually Christ's faith. We cannot make faith up. We cannot produce faith. Faith is a spiritual thing and God is spirit. We can stir ourselves up, but if we are just stirring ourselves up in the flesh, nothing will result from it. We can even go as far as claiming we are stirring up our faith but that is not what the Word tells us.

If you are trying to lead someone to Christ by trying to convince them of the truth, you misunderstand what faith is. We are not supposed to argue to convince someone of the truth because that just creates a meaningless debate. What we do is speak forth the Word and live a spiritually mature life. The Holy Spirit touches them with faith. Understand that it is Christ's faith, not our faith, it is the faith of Jesus Christ.

Some mistranslate that into believing it is faith in Jesus Christ but the word states otherwise, *"by the faith of Jesus Christ."(Italics added)*

Second, we see in the last verse WHO believes in Jesus Christ, *"even we have believed in Jesus Christ."(Italics added)* In other words, that is OUR part. God's part is that He gives us faith. Our part is the responsibility of carrying out the act of believing. We must respond with the action of our believing.

When we are preaching or teaching, we are not trying to convince people to believe. We are speaking the truth and the Holy Spirit gives the people faith. The people have to choose the act of believing just as you have chosen to believe.

When sharing the gospel with someone, you have prob-ably witnessed their heart being moved as faith is imparted by the Holy Spirit. Some choose not to act upon that faith. At that point, faith withdraws, leaving them in unbelief. The resis-tance in their heart to the truth still remains. They may desire to believe but they do not act on it. At the very moment they decide to act upon that faith, it becomes part of their spirit.

When we share the truth with others, we encourage them to begin seeking understanding. We encourage them to respond to the faith that they are **already** experiencing. When you are born again you have faith imparted into you by Jesus Christ **but we must learn how to respond to that faith being imparted.**

Difficult situations can sometimes keep us from praying, because we feel overwhelmed. When we are born again, faith is within our spirit and we make a choice within our soul to turn to God. As we choose to worship God and turn to Him, the faith within our spirit is activated in our soul. Whenever we choose to activate our faith, <u>NOT our feelings</u>, we begin to worship God and meditate on the Word. Our faith rises up within our soul and we are strengthened in the Lord.

> **"And how shall they preach, except they be sent? as it is written, How beautiful are the feet of them that preach the gospel of peace, and bring glad tidings of good things! But they have not all obeyed the gospel. For Esaias saith, Lord, who hath believed our report? So then faith *cometh* by hearing, and hearing by the word of God" (Romans 10:15-17).**

He concludes by saying faith comes by hearing and hearing by the word of God. That concludes this aspect of faith. If faith is something spiritual and faith is something God imparts into our spirit, then what is the connection between PREACHING, HEARING and BELIEVING?

If we say it's God's faith and God imparts that faith, then how does hearing affect that faith? How does it correlate? Yes, faith is something that originates in the spirit, however, the act of believing occurs in the soul. So when the Word is spoken or taught, what happens? It is not that our spirit understands, for our spirit is perfect in Christ and is not what acts upon faith. Our soul has to act upon faith. Our soul has to make the decision to believe. Our soul needs to know how to believe. When we are hearing the Word spoken or taught, it imparts to our intellect and affects our will and emotions.

In other words if we have faith, our soul needs to know how to act upon that faith. How do we respond to that faith and how do we move forward in that faith? That's when we begin to teach the Word, we begin to move our soul into that intellect and say, "OH! This is what God demands! This is what God expects! This is how God operates! This is how God is!"

Once we recognize our soul understands, we walk in that faith that is already in us. We have a conviction of what is true in our hearts and we begin to understand how to walk it out. "Intellect" as used here is not intellectual understanding, it is revelation revealed to our intellect.

"And he said unto them, Take heed what ye hear; with what you measure ye mete, it shall be measured to you: and unto you that hear shall more be given" (Mark 4:24).

Take heed what you hear. Why? Hearing wrong things will confuse you. It will confuse your soul. The Word warns us to be careful about what we hear. If we hear everything, read everything, and go everywhere, it will confuse your soul and you will not know how to walk out your faith.

"Take heed therefore how ye hear: for whosoever hath, to him shall be given; and whosoever hath not, from him shall be taken even that which he seemeth to have" (Luke 8:18). Take heed in HOW you hear and in what WAY you hear. When we listen to something, we can hear the truth, but hear it in the wrong way. Having a bias or being tainted gives us preconceived ideas that result in us filtering out things, distorting the whole conversation. The Word warns us not only to be careful what we hear but how we hear it as well.

God makes us active participants in developing our faith. He gives us His Word and the responsibility to read it, study it, and to receive instructions from others through it. We are to live it through the gifts in the Body of Christ. We are to discuss it, share it, teach it, preach it and not debate it.

"Therefore shall ye lay up these my words in your heart and in your soul, and bind them for a sign upon your hand, that they may be as frontlets between your eyes. And ye shall teach them your children, speaking of them when thou sittest in thine house, and when thou walkest by the way, when thou liest down, and when thou risest up. And thou shalt write them upon the door posts of thine house, and upon thy gates" (Deuteronomy 11:18-20). This tells us the Word of God is to be before you at all times. If not, there is a great chance you will become confused. If the Word is not your primary source of truth, you will go off course. Faith is always keeping the Word before you. When you sit down, when you talk, when you write it on the doorposts, when you lie down, and when you go about your day. God wants the Word in front of us always. So wherever you go, the word goes with you.

"And be not conformed to this world: but be ye transformed by the renewing of your mind, that ye may prove what is that good, and acceptable, and perfect, will of God" (Romans 12:2). Correct believing! The Word renews your mind and transforms you in truth, which results in correct believing. If you have wrong beliefs, the Word will affect us in the wrong way. Correct believing and correct hearing are the two warnings we should take heed of.

Romans 10 gives us the correlation between hearing and faith. Romans 14 give us the correlation between conscience and faith, specifically a weak conscience. **"Him that is weak in the faith receive ye, but not to doubtful disputations" (Romans 14:1).**

The first thing we are told is NOT to argue with a person who has weak faith and a weak conscience. Do not try to convince them that they should do things in a particular way. Weak faith does not translate to a person being weak in their belief in Christ Jesus. It translates to that person being weak in their soul in understanding.

"For one believeth that he may eat all things; another, who is weak, eateth herbs" (Romans 14:2). This gives us an example of what a weak conscience does. Read verse two again. Here we have a person who goes to Burger King and only eats french fries because he feels eating meat is wrong. A weak conscience does NOT cause a person to sin. A weak conscience does two things. First, it restricts one from doing things that are not sinful. It restricts a person from doing things one does not need to be restricted from. Second, a weak conscience compels one to do things that hold NO spiritual value, such as keeping the Sabbath or holding rituals.

A weak conscience:

1. Restricts one from doing things that are not sinful.
2. Causes one to do things that hold no spiritual value.

"Let not him that eateth despise him that eateth not; and let not him which eateth not judge him that eateth: for God hath received him" (Romans 14:3). The principle here is, do not despise one another. It applies to both ways here. The person with a weak conscience may respond to the person eating and claim that what he is eating is wrong. But the person who is free may respond by claiming that the other is legalistic.

"Who art thou that judgest another man's servant? To his own master he standeth or falleth. Yea, he shall be holden up: for God is able to make him stand" (Romans 14:4). God can make a man with a weak conscience stand. We are not to be his judge! This is NOT speaking about Christians who are involved in immorality. It is speaking about people who have a weak conscience. Why will God make a person with a weak conscience stand? His faith may be weak BUT if his heart is sincere and his motivation is to please God, He will make that person stand.

If a Christian is walking in hypocrisy, he will NOT stand and God will cause him to fall. God will honor the one with the right heart and motivation, regardless of how much faith one has. One must remember to remain in right standing before the Lord. Always remember, God looks at the heart of each person.

"One man esteemeth one day above another: another esteemeth every day alike. Let every man be fully persuaded in his own mind" (Romans 14:5). This is another example of a person with a weak conscience. One person claims we cannot work on Sundays because it is a holy day. This is not to condemn others, it just shows a weak conscience. Paul says, "Let every man be persuaded in his own mind." He is saying it is OUR responsibility to receive instruction. THEN we go into the Word and study it out until we have a greater understanding of the truth. THEN we can live by that and walk that out in faith.

"He that regardeth the day, regardeth it unto the Lord; and he that regardeth not the day, to the Lord he doth not regard it. He that eateth, eateth to the Lord, for he giveth God thanks; and he that eateth not, to the Lord he eateth not, and giveth God thanks. 7 For none of us liveth to himself, and no man dieth to himself. 8 For whether we live, we live unto the Lord; and whether we die, we die unto the Lord: whether we live live therefore, or die, we are the Lord's" (Romans 14:6-8). The key point here is motivation. When you are walking in your relationship with God, do it with a sincere heart. You may do everything right but if your heart is not in the right place, or you are motivated by hypocrisy, it's not pleasing to God.

"For to this end Christ both died, and rose, and revived, that he might be Lord both of the dead and living" (Romans 14:9). We make Christ the Lord of our lives.

"But why dost thou judge thy brother? or why dost thou set at nought thy brother? for we shall all stand before the judgment seat of Christ. For it is written, As I live, saith the Lord, every knee shall bow to me, and every tongue confess to God. So then every one of us shall give account of himself to God. Let us not therefore judge one another any more; but judge this rather, that no man put a stumblingblock or an occasion to fall in his brother's way" (Romans 14:10-13). There is one purpose when you are dealing with a person with a weak conscience. DO NOT cause him to stumble. You are not there to cause him to stumble, to argue, or to debate. You are there to encourage him.

"I know, and am persuaded by the Lord Jesus, that there is nothing unclean of itself: but to him that esteemeth any thing to be unclean, to him it is unclean" (Romans 14:14). If a person has chosen to believe that something is unclean and chose to participate in that unclean thing anyway, that person's conscience may feel they have displeased God. He has made a resolution that it is wrong in his heart but it is only made unclean by his own belief. If he feels something is wrong in his heart even though it is not, that is called condemnation.

"But if thy brother be grieved with *thy* meat, now walkest thou not charitably. Destroy not him with thy meat, for whom Christ died. Let not then your good be evil spoken of" (Romans 14:15-16). There is nothing wrong with eating pork, but if your brother is offended by it, the good you are doing now becomes evil. Why? You are offending your brother by your action and harming his faith as well. If you are doing something that is causing your brother to stumble, stop it.

"For the Kingdom of God is not meat and drink; but righteousness, and peace, and joy in the Holy Ghost. For he that is in these things serveth Christ is acceptable to God, and approved of men. Let us therefore follow after the things which make for peace, and things wherewith one may edify another. For meat destroy not the work of God. All things indeed are pure; but it is evil for that man who eateth with offence" (Romans 14:17-20). What are we to pursue? We are to pursue peace, happiness and joy—those things that build one another up! How are we to decide what to do in everyday situations? Ask yourself if what you are about to do is going to build up or tear down. Will this action bring peace or discord?

Our words can tear a person down quickly. When representing Christ you are not there to convince people. You are there to spread the gospel and to love one another. In verse 20 it states, "all things are indeed pure," but if we handle it wrongly, it becomes evil. The point is, do what brings about peace and joy.

"It is good neither to eat flesh, nor to drink wine, nor any thing whereby thy brother stumbleth, or is offended, or is made weak" (Romans 14:21).

We are instructed in three areas here for when we are dealing with our brethren:

1. Do not cause others to stumble
2. Do not offend
3. Do not make another weak.

Stumble means to trip up. Many Christians today get tripped up by legalism. Offense means to entice into sin. To make one weak means to throw one into turmoil that zaps their resolve in the Lord. When we abstain from something, do it graciously. It doesn't have to be announced to the world.

"Hast thou faith? have it to thyself before God. Happy is he that condemneth not himself in that thing which he alloweth. And he that doubteth is damned if he eat, because he eateth not of faith: for whatsoever is not of faith is sin" (Romans 14:22-23). If you do not have faith to do something and you do it, its sin. If someone believes its sin to eat a BLT and they eat it, it's sin to them. Well, how could that be sin? Because they have a weak conscience and they have believed wrong, their conscience tells them that eating the BLT is wrong and they eat it in an act of rebellion against their own belief. It is not that God condemns them, they are condemning themselves. In fact, if they do something they believe is wrong, even though it is not wrong, it will make them feel ashamed and condemned that may even cause them to backslide.

What does it matter then? Paul in Galatians 4:9 is trying to grasp why the people want to go back to weak and beggarly things. He is saying, "WHAT'S GOING ON?" In the same chapter, verses 19-20, it says, <u>My little children, of whom, I travail in birth again until Christ be formed in you, 20 I desire to be present with you now, and to change my voice; for I stand in doubt of you.</u> The word *doubt* there means *to be perplexed*. Paul is beside himself, asking essentially, "What am I going to do with you guys?"

Paul wrote both Romans and Galatians. In Romans, he instructs us how we deal with one another. Paul even said in Romans, "but you need to be fully convinced, so don't be lazy!" (paraphrasing.) He asks them, "Why do you want to go back to weak and beggarly things that put you in bondage?" This is where our doctrine comes in, because it affects our image of God. In return, it dictates how we relate to God and how we serve God. Our walk is much bigger than doctrine because it is about relationship.

What is doctrine? It is not about having the right set of rules. Doctrine is not some intellectual exercise. Doctrine is having the right image of God and how we relate to Him. It is about knowing the truth, according to His word. It is about obtaining REVEALED knowledge via the Holy Spirit (not man's opinion of what he feels the Word is telling him). YOU must seek the truth. The largest spiritual stumbling block for most people is, they do not take the time to seek out the truth for themselves.

Too many people rely solely on what is preached from the pulpit and never take the time to study it out.

When we have misconceptions, even out of sincerity, our view of God is distorted, our relationship is incomplete, and our ability to relate to God becomes confusing. When we have this distorted or incomplete view of God, we find our self always grasping to be accepted by God. We do not need to grasp for God's acceptance, because Jesus paid that price for us already. If we accept Him as our Savior, then it is a done deal. Instead of enjoying all that God has for us, walking in ALL the authority that Christ has given to us, we remain restricted because of wrong doctrine and wrong understanding.

As believers, we need to understand God's Word. As we hear the word of God, as we study the Word of God, understanding fills our soul. Our faith begins to increase within our spirit and then that faith begins to manifest properly into our soul life. Otherwise, we will live our faith incorrectly, prohibited from enjoying God and hindered from serving and sharing Him with others. That is why doctrine is so important; it is our image of who God is. Who is God? IT IS IN THE WORD!!!!!

As we read the Word, experience the Holy Spirit, and begin to attain understanding of God's Word, the reality of God grows within us. If we continue to have a distorted reality of who God is and how we relate to Him, it will hinder our ability to grow in the relationship.

A weak conscience hinders us from enjoying an unhindered relationship and fellowship with God. Christ's redemptive blood is sufficient to give us a good conscience. It is sufficient so our relationship with God can be complete. We do not need to add anything to it.

[1]Now as touching things offered unto idols, we know that we all have knowledge. Knowledge puffeth up, but charity edifieth. [2]And if any man think that he knoweth any thing, he knoweth nothing yet as he

ought to know. ³But if any man love God, the same is known of him. ⁴As concerning therefore the eating of those things that are offered in sacrifice unto idols, we know that an idol is nothing in the world, and that there is none other God but one. ⁵For though there be that are called gods, whether in heaven or in earth, (as there be gods many, and lords many,) ⁶But to us there is but one God, the Father, of whom are all things, and we in him; and one Lord Jesus Christ, by whom are all things, and we by him. ⁷Howbeit there is not in every man that knowledge: for some with conscience of the idol unto this hour eat it as a thing offered unto an idol; and their conscience being weak is defiled. ⁸But meat commendeth us not to God: for neither, if we eat, are we the better; neither, if we eat not, are we the worse. ⁹But take heed lest by any means this liberty of yours become a stumblingblock to them that are weak. ¹⁰For if any man see thee which hast knowledge sit at meat in the idol's temple, shall not the conscience of him which is weak be emboldened to eat those things which are offered to idols; ¹¹And through thy knowledge shall the weak brother perish, for whom Christ died? ¹²But when ye sin so against the brethren, and wound their weak conscience, ye sin against Christ. ¹³Wherefore, if meat make my brother to offend, I will eat no flesh while the world standeth, lest I make my brother to offend. (1 Corinthians 8:1-13)

Knowledge is not the thing. Love is the thing. We can have so much knowledge that we can use it to hurt others. Even if knowledge is correct, it can be used to hurt others. Paul is saying that idols are nothing and they have no power or authority over us.

In verse 7, look at what he says about the conscience. The word *defiled* here means, *to make blackened, to ink*. In other words, if a person comes out of idolatry or believes an idol has power or reality over them, then goes back and "eats" from that idolatry again, his conscience is blackened or stained—even if he has become a Christian. Because in his own mind and conscience, he still believes there is some kind of significance to the idol. While it will not affect anyone but him, it shows that his conscience is still weak. He does not yet have the understanding or full reality of what Christ did on the cross, nor does he have the full understanding that those idolatrous things are nothing any longer in his life. When it blackens his conscience, he will feel he is doing something wrong.

If you go into an idolatrous temple and eat there and a new Christian passes by and sees you eating, your action of eating in an idol's temple may embolden him to think, "Well, maybe I should be doing that too." He may not realize that you are just there to have a meal. At that moment, all he may see is you eating food offered to idols. Then he goes and eats food offered to idols. Why? Because his conscience is still weak and his reality will continue to affect him until he attains a better understanding. Do not allow your knowledge to affect your weaker brother. That will cause him to stumble or backslide. Remember it can wound their weak conscience because their faith is weak.

[19]What say I then? That the idol is any thing, or that which is offered in sacrifice to idols in any thing? 20 But I say, that the things which the Gentiles sacrifice, they sacrifice to devils, and not to God and I would not that ye should have fellowship with devils. 21 Ye cannot drink the cup of the Lord, and the cup of devils; ye cannot be partakers of the Lord's table, and of the table of devils. 22 Do we provoke the Lord

to jealousy? Are we stronger than he? (1 Corinthians 10:19-22)

Paul says something interesting and gives a warning here. If you are a believer in Christ Jesus and you go and partake in idol worship, you are provoking God to jealousy. He also states that they are serving demons and not idols. He tells us this not because demons are going to get us, but because these actions are provocative and elicit jealousy from God. He is not saying not to go because it is spooky, but because God is holy.

All things are lawful for me, but all things are not expedient; all things are lawful for me, but all things edify not. In other words—do those things that build up people! 24 Let no man seek his own, but every man another's wealth. 25 Whatsoever is sold in the shambles, that eat, asking no question for conscience sake: 26 For the earth is the Lord's and the fullness there of. 27 If any of them believe not bid you to a feast, and ye be disposed to go; whatsoever is set before you, eat, asking no question for conscience sake. (1 Corinthians 10:23-27)

If you go to a home of a known idolater who offers food up to idols and he offers you some of that food, eat it. Do not allow your first thought to be, "Ah! Nope! Can't eat that food, it was offered to idols and now it's cursed!" Do not worry about it because the Word just instructed you not to worry about it. It has no power and authority over you. Paul said he has no problem eating food that was sacrificed to idols. Paul would give thanks and praise God for that food, even though the idolater sacrificed it to idols.

"That ye abstain from meats offered to idols, and from blood, and from things strangled, and from fornication: from which if ye keep yourselves, ye shall do well. Fare ye well"

(Acts 15:29). This is written in context for those in Antioch, many of whom had come out of paganism and still had a weak conscience. If we eat the food offered to idols as if it has some meaning, it is sin. If we just eat the food, knowing it has no meaning, it is okay. As a believer, eat that food and offer it up to God. It is the belief you have in how that food is received that matters.

> **"But if any man says unto you, "this is offered in sacrifice unto idols, eat not for his sake that shewed it, and for conscience sake; for the earth is the Lord's and the fullness thereof. Conscience I say, not thine own, but of the other; for why is my liberty judged of another man's conscience" (1 Cor. 10:28-29).**

Paul instructs us if that the person says to you that the food they are serving you has been sacrificed to idols, do not eat it. This is not for your conscience sake, but for the person's sake. Because if you continue to eat the food sacrificed to idols, he will begin to think you are eating food unto idols. That would reinforce that you agree to eat food sacrificed to idols. Though you are not, he will think you are. Because of that, you cannot continue to eat food offered up to idols. You decline because you do not partake in food sacrifice to idols. You do this not for your sake, but for his conscience sake. Why? Because his conscience still believes there is power and a reality in that sacrifice.

Our purpose on this earth is not to please ourselves. It is to be a witness of Christ Jesus and in being that witness to be pleasing to God.

"Ye are of your father the devil, and the lusts of your father ye will do. He was a murderer from the beginning, and abode not in the truth, because there is no truth in him. When he speaketh a lie, he speaketh of his own: for he is a liar, and the father of it" (John 8:44). We see here the devil is the father of all lies and he can have power over Christians when we begin to believe his lies. The enemy's power over us is when we believe his lies. He will attain power over us through lies. That is why, when we begin to see who Christ is, we no longer try to fight the devil. We then move over into the category of serving God. Did you get that? If you spend all day long rebuking the devil, where is your focus? Your time and attention is on the devil. Do not spend your time talking to the devil; God has him under control. Use your time getting to know God and developing a relationship with him.

I am not saying that there is never a time to take authority over the devil, what I am saying is that our focus should remain on Jesus Christ and the works of God. If you allow him too, the devil can take you on countless, twisted, dead end journeys. God will take you, mature you, and set you on a path that He created and designed just for you. Amen.

CHAPTER THIRTEEN
An Over Sensitive and False Conscience

If we have an overly sensitive conscience, it makes it difficult to feel forgiven. Even if we ask for forgiveness, we do not feel forgiven right away. We feel we need to suffer a little bit first. An overly sensitive conscience tells us that it's not so easy to be forgiven. It makes us feel like we need to be sad or feel pain first before we are forgiven. The simple act of asking forgiveness is never good enough for those who have an overly sensitive conscience. In feeling this way, we are actually putting our conscience above Christ. We say to ourselves that we will serve our conscience until we feel good enough and have suffered enough, and *then* we will accept that we are forgiven.

When we stop serving our conscience and accept the act of forgiveness, we need to start disciplining our conscience by grabbing hold of those vain thoughts and tossing them out. We do this until our conscience comes into right faith.

Romans 14:1-23 gives us the relationship between conscience and faith, and Romans 10: 1-17 gives us the correlation concerning faith and hearing.

When someone with a weak conscience does something he feels is against God, it makes him feel guilty and is an indicator of weak faith. The things I am referring to that people "feel" are against God, but are not, are things such as believing one cannot eat pork and you end up eating pork, and so on.

We want to recognize the relationship between right believing and having a conscience that works correctly versus having a wrong belief and our conscience not lining up correctly.

Whenever you do something you feel is wrong, it will actually feel wrong within your heart. Why? Whatever is without faith is sin. For example, the person who believes eating pork is a sin, eats a sandwich with bacon on it. How do you believe he is going to feel? He is going to feel guilty because he now believes he must have sinned against God because he ate bacon. Eating pork is not a sin against God but this person believes he has just sinned. What has taken place? Not a sin against God, but condemnation has just taken place and is trying to settle into his conscience. Why? He has placed himself under condemnation through feeling guilty, believing he has just sinned against God.

When a person does something she believes is wrong, even if it is not, that condemnation has a good chance of making her backslide. In the previous chapter we looked at how a weak conscience won't make one do immoral things. It restricts one from doing things that are not sinful or impels them to do things that hold NO SPIRITUAL value.

An example of something that holds no spiritual value is food sacrificed to idols (1 Corinthians 8:10). A weak conscience leads some into superstitious acts. As you read First Corinthians 8, you see Paul would eat food offered to idols because it held no spiritual value, authority or power and he knew it. Paul also tells us to take great caution when it came to eating food offered to idols because if one with a weak conscience sees you eating it, it could cause them to stumble. To eat the offered meat is not sin because it holds no spiritual value, but be careful in your deeds concerning it, because it could cause someone to believe that you are agreeing with the ways of the man offering food to idols. It can also embolden the man to continue to offer food to idols.

If a weak conscience makes us do things that hold no spiritual value, what does an overly sensitive conscience do to us? A key for contrasting an overly sensitive conscience with a proper conscience is understanding how CONVICTION and CONDEMNATION work.

Conviction is our awareness of the Holy Spirit at work in our heart. It will speak to our conscience. If we are doing something wrong, the Holy Spirit will prompt our conscience and lead us into the understanding that we just did something wrong. Conviction motivates us and we move closer to God. It will move you into a place of confessing your sins and the result will land you into a place of rest and forgiveness.

Condemnation is the response of our conscience through the works of the flesh and through the works of the devil. Condemnation pulls us under and can become destructive. It motivates us to flee from God and causes us to run right into our sin. Why? Because God is holy and when we allow ourselves to be put under condemnation, we flee to where God is not and we hide in our sin.

Failure to respond properly to our conscience when it convicts us of our sins, results in us having a conscience infected with condemnation.

[1]There is therefore now no condemnation to them which are in Christ Jesus, who walk not after the flesh, but after the Spirit. [2]For the law of the Spirit of life in Christ Jesus hath made me free from the law of sin and death. [3]For what the law could not do, in that it was weak through the flesh, God sending his own Son in the likeness of sinful flesh, and for sin, condemned sin in the flesh: [4]That the righteousness of the law might be fulfilled in us, who walk not after the flesh, but after the Spirit. (Romans 8:1-4)

There is not condemnation for those whose are in Christ Jesus. Who is it that condemns the believer? It is our own conscience listening to the voice of the enemy. Condemnation is not of God.

Symptoms of an overly sensitive conscience are: a general sense of shame; a general sense of guilt; unworthiness; condemnation.

After we confess our sin we still allow ourselves to feel those things. You can spot a person who has an overly sensitive conscience because they are always going up to the altar for every altar call. An overly sensitive conscience speaks to you by saying, "I am not good enough," or "I don't pray enough" and the like. An overly sensitive conscience gives us that overwhelming cloud of guilt, feelings of shame and worthlessness, all of which make up the ingredients of condemnation.

First John speaks about how to deal with an over sensitive conscience:

18My little children, let us not love in word, neither in tongue; but in deed and in truth. 19And hereby we know that we are of the truth, and shall assure our hearts before him. 20For if our heart condemn us, God is greater than our heart, and knoweth all things. 21Beloved, if our heart condemn us not, then have we confidence toward God. 22And whatsoever we ask, we receive of him, because we keep his commandments, and do those things that are pleasing in his sight. 23And this is his commandment, That we should believe on the name of his Son Jesus Christ, and love one another, as he gave us commandment. 24And he that keepeth his commandments dwelleth in him, and he in him. And hereby we know that he abideth in us, by the Spirit which he hath given us. (1 John 3:18-24)

Some people say things they are going to do, but never do them. When you speak about what you are going to do, really do those things. When we are doing the things God has called us into, we will be persuaded, encouraged and assured. Our hearts will assure us before the Lord God! God looks at the heart because in our heart is found the truth about us. The benefit of a good conscience that is working properly is that it assures us before God. When we have confidence in God and go before Him in prayer or communication, our conscience is prepared and clear and tells us, "YES! I can stand before God without shame! AMEN!"

First John 3:20 is an interesting verse: **"For if our heart condemn us, God is greater than our heart, and knoweth all things."**

When you are assured and walking before the Lord, you have boldness and can really enjoy His presence. Your worship and service to Him are pure. When people come to church and feel their life is not right, their attitude can be one of, "Oh, I hate to be here!" Why? Because that overly sensitive conscience is making them feel unworthy. Here is one thing we need to grasp: our conscience does not know everything, only God does.

The word *CONDEMN* is not the typical word used in the New Testament. When used, it is in the context of judgment: to blame or find fault. But if your heart is always finding fault, casting judgment or blaming, there is good news—the Word tells us that God is greater than our heart. Your conscience may be wrong, but God is never wrong. There are times when your conscience makes you feel wrong, but hold tight to the truth in First John 3:20. If your believing and understanding is not right, your conscience will work improperly and you won't be able to rely on it until it becomes healthy. An over sensitive conscience will make us believe we are supposed to be miserable.

I remember sitting in a church many years ago. All around me, people were praying very loudly. I wondered if this was what praying to God was all about. My conscience kept telling me no, but after a while I worked up the nerve to join in. I fell to the ground and began to cry. I rocked back and forth and began to feel so unworthy. I thought to myself, "I'm doing a great job." I must really be impressing Jesus, right? I worked up some misery, got some prayers so I could feel better and thought to myself, job well done! That is what an overly sensitive conscience makes one do! It makes you work up unworthiness and makes you feel shame and guilt.

You do not have to work up those kinds of actions and feelings before asking for forgiveness. Those kinds of works are not of God but of the flesh! Did you see how many "I's" were in what I shared about myself in the previous paragraph? There was no part of God in what I chose to start doing those years ago. I praise God that He freed me from myself.

There is no such thing as groveling before God. If you are one who thinks you must grovel and feel shame before you ask for forgiveness, STOP IT! It is not of God but of your flesh and is not pleasing to God. God wants you to have freedom and liberty so you can serve Him with a servant's heart. Groveling in your shame turns your focus AWAY from God and onto YOUR failures and past sins. One can easily remain focused on their past failures and sins for the rest of their life. God does not want us to do that. He wants us to confess failures and sins with a sincere heart and then move forward in Him. Look at God's goodness and do not focus on failures. When the Holy Spirit speaks, it is amazing how CLEAR and BRIEF He is. If you are focused on your poor miserable self, you will miss what He is saying to you.

A weak conscience adds rules and laws on how to please God. An overly sensitive conscience fails to see that Christ's redemption brings us complete and total forgiveness. An overly sensitive conscience hinders our faith from believing that when we confess our sins, we are forgiven, totally and freely. The overly sensitive conscience puts our conscience before Jesus' work on the cross. In effect we stop serving God and begin serving our own conscience. We no longer try to please Christ, but become enslaved in seeking ways to make our conscience feel better.

An overly sensitive conscience will constantly tell us the fleshly works we are creating to make ourselves feel better are never enough. The overly sensitive conscience constantly seeks itself out and stops seeking Christ. It will stop caring about what Christ has to say because it is consumed with what it thinks and will continue to be consumed until it feels it has done enough fleshly works (that only appear holy), to finally say, "Okay, now I am forgiven."

I do not know where or when it began to seep into the Church that one must grovel, feel shame or carry guilt before feeling forgiven. Think about how much time one could free up to serve God in spirit and truth if everyone would grasp the act of asking for forgiveness, walking in that forgiveness and then moving forward. Jesus must be looking down upon us and thinking, "HEY! I died on the cross so you can be forgiven. I made sure your salvation, so STOP your groveling! My work was enough for you!"

[21]Beloved, if our heart condemn us not, then have we confidence toward God. [22]And whatsoever we ask, we receive of him, because we keep his commandments, and do those things that are pleasing in his sight. [23]And this is his commandment, That we should believe on the name of his Son Jesus Christ, and love one another, as he gave us commandment. [24]And he that keepeth his commandments dwelleth in him, and he in him. And hereby we know that he

abideth in us, by the Spirit which he hath given us. (1 John 3:21-24)

Every time we open our heart to God in prayer, we can have confidence that He is hearing us and that He will answer. A properly working conscience has confidence before the Lord God. No matter how bad things look, rest assured He is hearing our prayers and petitions. We do not have to wait to see a manifestation of God to answer our prayer because we are confident that He is hearing us. AMEN!

So, how do you discipline an overly sensitive conscience? Build up your faith according to God's Word. You must make God greater than your conscience.

When we study the Word, we take in what the Word of God says about what Christ did. Walking with Christ is not about a need to do some kind of penance. Working out penance is a false reality and a false work. Jesus' suffering was sufficient. Now that's reality!

We cannot add any type of suffering of our own to improve on what Christ did on the cross. We need to grasp that reality! Why does man believe we need to add things? Man's concept of God is that He is not a generous God and that His mercy is not sufficient. In pagan worship, they always have to do things to please their god or to win favor in the eyes of their god.

Stop trying to do things you feel will finally make God happy with you. Stop believing that after you sin you need to make yourself suffer awhile before asking for forgiveness. We need to begin to remove this theology of "self works" that has seeped into the Church and caused our conscience to be infected with wrong belief.

Train yourself to receive forgiveness by faith. How? Understand that forgiveness is NOT a FEELING! Sometimes we will not *feel* forgiven when we confess our sins. We must push through those feelings and take on the forgiveness of God!

1. As soon as you recognize you have sinned, confess it. Do not ignore it, do not ponder it, confess it!

2. After you have confessed it, immediately give thanks to God for his complete forgiveness. By faith, receive that forgiveness. Your thought process should line up something like this: "Lord I have sinned. Forgive me of that thought/ action/ deed. (Then begin to give thanks.) Thank you Lord, for forgiving me! Receive that forgiveness by faith and begin to walk in the forgiveness the Lord has given you. Make the choice to walk in that forgiveness and exercise that faith immediately. DO NOT wait to feel forgiveness! Speaking out words of thanksgiving after confession is a key to not falling into condemnation and works of the flesh.

3. Rejoice that God is so faithful to forgive. For an overflow of faith, begin to rejoice in Him. Begin to add praise to your thankfulness!

Confess your sins by faith.
Thank Him for forgiving you.
Rejoice that He forgave you.

DO NOT WAIT ON FEELINGS TO LINE UP! RECEIVE WHAT HE HAS ALREADY GIVEN YOU!

The type of walk described above goes contrary to any type of religious doctrine. Appearing holy and desiring to be religious is not pleasing to God, period! God did not call us to be religious, He called us to be followers of Jesus Christ. We do not need to be miserable, we need to be forgiven!

When a person first comes to Christ, we rejoice. We need to continue to maintain that rejoicing but for some reason, it gets lost. It is terribly hard to rejoice if one continues to wear their robes of past failure and sin. Exercise your faith by walking out of the robes of condemnation and putting on the robes of righteousness!

1. Do not allow your mind to dwell on past sins and failures. Have you ever caught your mind wondering off into your past sins and failures, even as you pray? It is easy to veer off the course of prayer and drive down the road of "self-works"!

"But with me it is a very small thing that I should be judged of you, or of man's judgment: yea, I judge not mine own self. For I know nothing by myself; yet am I not hereby justified: but he that judgeth me is the Lord" (1 Corinthians 4:3-4).

This is an important concept. It gets inside the one's of us with an overly sensitive conscience who try to be circumspect or look inside ourselves, wondering what is wrong with us. We can sometimes dig stuff up that we have confessed long ago—stuff that was long ago cast into the sea of forgetfulness. We can even dig stuff up in our mind that was not really sin, all the while distracting us from prayer.

In First Corinthians 4, Paul states he does not worry when people are judging him, nor even judging himself because it is God who judges him. When we come to the Lord and ask Him to show us things that are wrong in our lives (or He sends someone to show us a wrong thing in our life) we are not to become circumspect, turning over every rock to find more wrong things. We are to simply ask God to show us those things that are sinful and hindering us from walking forward with Him. That is it! Simple, easy, breezy! Do not waste time searching for what is wrong. We need to simply look to Jesus with faith and trust that He will show us.

2. Seek a mentor to help discern if you have an overly sensitive conscience or are truly being convicted by the Holy

Spirit. This mentor must be someone you can trust because this steps into the area of discipleship. Everyone needs a person she can trust to speak into her life and correct her as needed. A mentor can pray with you, and work with you.

In most things, a person with an overly sensitive conscience has no issues. The person recognizes the enemy is trying to make a mountain out of a molehill, to burden him down before making a full attack. When we resist the enemy and begin to struggle with an overly sensitive conscience, he will most likely get us to walk in condemnation. That's what he counts on because he wants you to stop resisting and give in to the sin. If he can get you to feel guilty about the lack of resistance you are giving toward temptation, he knows he can get you to drop your resistance. For some people, guilt is enough to make them stop resisting. The guilt of the thought of sin is enough to get them to go ahead and commit that sin. They will reason in their mind that they have already been tempted so they are already condemned. That is a wrong belief system that needs to be let go and replaced by the truth.

Even if you are struggling in temptation, it is okay. The key is, do not give in to the sin. The goal is to get your conscience working properly so you can be a powerful witness for Jesus Christ. When you have confidence in God, that He has forgiven you, that Christ has given you right standing, then you can stand before anyone, no matter what you've done in your past, and be a bold testimony for Jesus Christ.

A False Conscience

A false conscience listens to the voice of the enemy. A false conscience agrees with the devil when he accuses you, making you feel like you will never be forgiven. It will take what it feels were your biggest and worst sins and make you feel like you will have to live with them for the rest of your life. A false conscience produces hopelessness.

¹Beloved, believe not every spirit, but try the spirits whether they are of God: because many false prophets are gone out into the world. ²Hereby know ye the Spirit of God: Every spirit that confesseth that Jesus Christ is come in the flesh is of God: ³And every spirit that confesseth not that Jesus Christ is come in the flesh is not of God: and this is that spirit of antichrist, whereof ye have heard that it should come; and even now already is it in the world. ⁴Ye are of God, little children, and have overcome them: because greater is he that is in you, than he that is in the world. (1 John 4:1-4)

If we do not deal with an overly sensitive conscience, it can easily grow into a false conscience. A false conscience is one that has fallen under control of the VOICE of the enemy. Read First John 4:1 again. There are many voices speaking to our hearts and in our minds. If we have an overly sensitive conscience, those voices can be our own thoughts, the voice of the Lord or the voice of the enemy. The Word tells us to DISCERN because not every voice we hear is from God. We need to discern them so we know what is from God and what is not.

How do we know what is not from God? If someone says to you that Jesus Christ did not come in the flesh, that person is confessing they have no Savior. When a voice says to us that Christ's suffering was not enough for us and that we will be stuck with our sins and their consequences for the rest of our life, that is the voice of the enemy.

When my youngest son was six or seven years old, I dreamed he was sitting in my car parked in our driveway. I was standing behind the car when he suddenly put the car in reverse and crashed into me, which jarred me awake. This little dream settled into the back of my mind. A few years later, I had a dream that we were driving down a road near our home and an oncoming car ran us off the road. We careened into a bayou and flipped upside down. I was floating above the car and could see both of us lying there. Both of us had cracked through the windshield. We were run off the road while I was driving, but now my youngest son was on the driver's side. I saw my body lying still, but saw no wounds. I saw my son's body lying dead, the blood seeping out of his body so fast, I was instantly overcome with great sorrow.

At a very early stage, the enemy began to disturb my peace about my son behind the wheel of a car. It did not help when my oldest son was 16 and was involved in a terrible accident. My sons are eight years apart in age. The enemy had planted thoughts in my mind that did not testify to God. It created a fear in me that would cause me to have thoughts that did not line up to God's Word. From that fear, I would see pictures in my mind about my youngest son crashing or getting lost on our maze of highways. The enemy threw so many terrible thoughts at my mind, hoping to embed them there.

My son drives today and I pray each day for God's protection over him as he drives. It is still a struggle for me at times, but as time passes, God has strengthened me in this area. I have to continue to do my part in the thought arena. When those terrible thoughts come to my mind, I hand them over to God instantly. (See Psalm 55 for more about how the enemy tries to oppress or create anguish in us.)

How do we know it is from God? **"Hereby know ye the Spirit of God: Every spirit that confesseth that Jesus Christ is come in the flesh is of God" (1 John 4:2).**

Everything that testifies to goodness and truth according to God's Word is of God. It's up to you to seek out that truth so you will know what it is and how to apply it to your everyday life. If you have an overly sensitive conscience, it can be deceived and become a false conscience causing you to believe the lies of the enemy. Giving in to those lies will build up walls around you, causing you to feel there is no way out of the glass house you have built for yourself.

A false conscience will say it does not matter what Jesus Christ did on the Cross. A false conscience will always dwell on past sins and bad deeds, giving voice to an antichrist spirit. The word *Christ* means, *the Anointed One.* The word *antichrist* means, *against the Anointed One.* The antichrist is against the anointing. The antichrist spirit is trying to speak into people that God has no power to redeem them, that there is no anointing, that God has no power to save them or forgive them, that God has no power to lift them up out of their failures and that no matter what; they cannot be changed by God. The antichrist spirit wants them to live the rest of their life in and beneath the WEIGHT and CONDEMNATION of their past sins and failures.

"Ye are of God, little children, and have overcome them: because greater is he that is in you, than he that is in the world" (1 John 4:4).

What is this verse? It is the TRUTH! That is the anointing! He is in you and is greater than he who is in the world. Because you have received Christ, the anointing that is in you is greater than he who is in the world. He has given you the power by His grace and mercy to give you freedom from whatever you have done or will do. He has given you freedom from your failures, and freedom from the sins you have committed!

The opposite of freedom is slavery! The enemy wants to keep you locked down in a depressive life of slavery to your sins. The enemy wants you to walk down a road to destruction. A false conscience leads to a loss of hope where the overly sensitive conscience allows room for little hope.

We must pull one another up, sharpen one another, correct one another and love one another as Christ loves the Church. Instead, church is more about who can build the biggest church, drive the fanciest car, or be in the most popular clique. Sad to say, "church" has turned into a big gossip mill for the devil's works. Over the years, I have found "church" people can be the meanest people toward those they deem lower than themselves.

"Fearfulness and trembling are come upon me, and horror hath overwhelmed me" (Psalm 55:5). When we have a false conscience we are overwhelmed with horror and that is what the enemy was trying to do to me concerning my son driving. Give those voices NO MORE POWER! If the enemy is trying to overwhelm you with voices, give them over to God! When our conscience speaks, test it to see if it is God speaking, because sometimes it is not Him. We have a false conscience when our conscience has been deceived. It feels it is justified in what it is doing. It feels totally justified in condemning itself and leaves it feeling that there is no hope. A false conscience says, "You're condemned. Your life will be destroyed, no matter what you have done. You will never have rest. You will never be good enough." It will keep you immersed in that internal turmoil. When we have a false conscience, life is black and we cannot see the light.

Ah! But we have rest! **"Cast thy burden upon the LORD, and he shall sustain thee: he shall never suffer the righteous to be moved" (Psalm 55:22).** Trust in God and do not be moved! I am forgiven and I am not going to allow what the enemy means for evil. God has redeemed me and no matter what I face, He will bring me forth as a greater warrior. I will cast my burden upon the Lord no matter how I feel. I know that I am not condemned. The Lord shall sustain me and He will not suffer or permit me to be moved!

What is to be our response to the voice of the enemy? **"And we know that all things work together for good to them that love God, to them who are the called according to his purpose" (Romans 8:28).**

Our response to the enemy is, "God's redemptive promise for our lives is that all things work together for good." It does not mean that all things are good. We may have done horrible things in our lives, but God's redemptive promise is that if we will serve Him, He will weave those horrible things together and work them out together for good. God is able to transform us, if we allow Him to.

"For whom he did foreknow, he also did predestinate to be conformed to the image of his Son, that he might be the firstborn among many brethren" (Romans 8:29). It is God's redemptive purpose for our lives that we will be conformed to His image, no matter what we have done. We will be transformed into God's image. That righteousness in our spirit will be manifest into our soul through the sanctification process, daily.

"Moreover whom he did predestinate, them he also called: and whom he called, them he also justified: and whom he justified, them he also glorified" (Romans 8:30). It is God's redemptive foreknowledge of our lives. No matter how many mistakes we have made, no matter how many sins we have committed, God is prepared. Do not believe that something will happen in your life that will surprise God.

"What shall we then say to these things? If God be for us, who can be against us?" (Romans 8:31). It is God's redemptive power for our lives! If we put our faith in the Lord and received Him, He is for us, not against us. God weaves all the circumstances of our life in a redemptive way, if we will trust Him. No matter how we may feel, or what shame the enemy tries to bring down on us, if we are willing to walk through the process, He will bring about His glory in our life.

Conscience and faith are linked together. We need to trust the Lord that He is able and willing to do what He promises and we need to discipline our conscience, making it subject to Jesus Christ. Amen.

CHAPTER FOURTEEN
A Defiled and Seared Conscience

¹²**One of themselves, even a prophet of their own, said, the Cretians are alway liars, evil beasts, slow bellies. ¹³This witness is true. Wherefore rebuke them sharply, that they may be sound in the faith; ¹⁴Not giving heed to Jewish fables, and commandments of men, that turn from the truth. ¹⁵Unto the pure all things are pure: but unto them that are defiled and unbelieving is nothing pure; but even their mind and conscience is defiled. ¹⁶They profess that they know God; but in works they deny him, being abominable, and disobedient, and unto every good work reprobate. (Titus 1:12-16)**

Paul is speaking to Titus who pastors a church among the Cretians. Read Titus 1:12 again and you will realize Paul says this is true of those people. Imagine if a pastor stated that all Americans are liars, evil beasts and lazy gluttons! How fast do you think that pastor would be excused from that church? People do not want to hear the truth, sitting in their cozy pew in today's ideal world of church.

How and why can Paul say such a thing that sounds so bad? It is a true witness. What they said about themselves was true. It is not because they are genetically liars, evil beasts or lazy gluttons. It was the society. In a society, when everyone starts doing the same thing generation after generation, they can lose sight of the fact that some of their actions are wrong. This is the way society affects individual people.

Walk into a society where immorality is accepted and everyone is involved, and they won't realize that it is wrong. We have so many different types of societies in our world. Consider a sinner walking into a Christian society for the very first time, having never heard the gospel before. He receives Christ and is saved. You begin to discuss with him the aspects of Christian living and find out he is living with his girlfriend. You explain to him that it is wrong to live together outside of marriage. His previous society accepted it, so he is puzzled. In his society, his mother accepted the concept of fornication, as did her mother, and so on. You do what you know and you give what you know to give until you learn another way that way is THE WAY, Jesus Christ.

Similarly, in Cretian culture, their sinful attributes were ingrained to such an extent that it was transparent to them. Paul's exhortation on how to deal with that was, **"Wherefore rebuke them sharply."** That does not mean we are to condemn people, nor does it mean that we should say, "Well I don't think it's good to fornicate so often" or "Why don't you lie a little bit less?" NO! What they were doing is wrong, it was sin, and it was destructive. Paul says to rebuke them sharply because their sin will destroy them. People who live in sin, even though they believe it is okay, will ultimately be destroyed by it. When you meet someone with a defiled conscience, tell them clearly that what they are doing is sin and destructive. Do not condemn them to turn them off to the message, but love them enough to rebuke them sharply so they will not be destroyed.

"That they may be sound in the faith." The word *sound* in the Greek means *healthy*. Rebuke them so that they may have a healthy faith. He is not saying the Cretians were an inferior race or group. He is instructing us to deal with those who are living in a society that is sinful and destructive, who do not know it. We are to tell them so they may have a healthy faith and repent to gain a pure conscience.

Then he says, **"Not giving heed to Jewish fables, and commandments of men, that turn from the truth."** Keep in mind He is speaking to Titus, the pastor of a Gentile church. There are two things that cause us to have unhealthy doctrine or unhealthy faith: <u>1.A bad lifestyle, and; **2.** Fables and/or commandments of men</u>. Examples of fables or commandments of men are religious superstition and legalism. Paul was stating this because there were some Jews who thought they had to keep the law. Not only were they teaching to keep the law but they were also teaching that Gentiles were inferior. Paul was assuring them they didn't have to keep these fables and commandments of men, and that Gentile Christians are not inferior to the Jewish Christians. We are one new man in Christ so put those things away and do not let them think you are inferior.

If you feel you are inferior, you will believe you are inferior and so shall you act as if you are inferior. Though what Paul said of the Cretians was true, he did not say, "That's the way you're always going to be!" He said, "Your lifestyle is sinful, but you are God's people and God has a plan for you to have a godly faith, a faith in which Christ will live through you." That was his purpose. God did not want them to give heed to Jewish fables! God wanted them to have a healthy faith so they could have a boldness to serve Jesus! AMEN!

"Unto the pure all things are pure: but unto them that are defiled and unbelieving is nothing pure" (Titus 1:15). This verse gives us insight into how the conscience works. The Greek word for *defiled* here means, *to dye with another color*. If we dip a white napkin into dye, its color will change. That is what defile means, to color something a different color.

Let us picture a good conscience as being white. A way to know when something is wrong is by comparing it to other things. When you compare something brown with something white, you realize something is wrong. There are times when you can see something that looks right but discern something is off about it. It is only when you peel back the layers of the situation do you discover that something was off. When we have a good, pure conscience we may see things that appear to be true, but discover they are not true only after we compare it to the truth. The Word will expose the impurities in the "color" and the truth will shine forth.

If we are exposed to sin around us and we begin to give into that sin, after awhile our conscience becomes stained. What once was a very clearly right or wrong becomes murky. Sin makes it difficult for us to determine right from wrong, and our conscience begins to grow confused—it is stained. That is why, when a person grows used to sinning, it will bother them no longer. The conviction that lets you know when you are doing wrong is no longer working. Your worn down conscience no longer bothers you.

A person can feel convicted in certain areas of their life, such as lying. They know it is wrong to lie and feel conviction when they do. Say this person thinks sexual immorality is okay, so they participate in that sin and feel no conviction. A defiled conscience will not feel shame or guilt because it no longer feels the action is wrong.

"But unto them that are defiled and unbelieving is nothing pure; but even their mind and conscience is defiled" (1 Titus 1:15). Unbelief affects how a defiled conscience operates. A person with a defiled conscience, when rebuked for a wrong, will respond with something like, "How do you know it's really wrong?" That is unbelief. In John, Pilate serves as an example of this:

> **[37]Pilate therefore said unto him, Art thou a king then? Jesus answered, Thou sayest that I am a king. To this end was I born, and for this cause came I into the world, that I should bear witness unto the truth. Every one that is of the truth heareth my voice.**

³⁸Pilate saith unto him, What is truth? And when he had said this, he went out again unto the Jews, and saith unto them, I find in him no fault at all. (John 18:37-38)

When Jesus was before Pilate, He talked about the truth because Pilate's conscience had been defiled in the area of truth, due to his cultural and politics beliefs. Pilate would do anything necessary for him to stay in his position as ruler or to advance his position. It would be expedient for him to put an innocent man to death and grant leniency to a man who was truly guilty. In others words, it was in Pilate's best self-interest to do it.

Pilate's conscience was defiled or stained. He did not know what truth was. His political environment had become so self-serving that he could no longer determine truth. His "truth" was whatever was best for him and his promotion. His conscience could not work on any level of faith at this point so that he became skeptical.

A man with a defiled conscience becomes skeptical about everything that goes on around him. You will hear him say, "Oh, come on, what's wrong with that?" or "What's the big deal?" That is a defiled conscience speaking unbelief.

Christ stood before Pilate and He was the Truth. Pilate could not recognize the Truth even then. He was staring at The One, The Way, The Truth, and The Life, The Light of the world and he failed to recognize it. He questioned what the truth was. His skepticism was so open that he goes before the people and says in effect, "I find no fault with this man, but scourge him and then crucify him anyway." His conscience was so defiled in the area of truth that his actions made no sense. Unknowingly, with this action, he fulfilled a prophecy. While he was proclaiming Jesus to be faultless, at the same time, the earthly high priest was saying the same thing about the Passover lamb!

"They profess that they know God; but in works they deny him, being abominable, and disobedient, and unto every good work reprobate" (Titus 1:16). Those with a defiled conscience have no sense of guilt because they believe they are doing nothing wrong. They can even be religious. Their conscience can be so defiled that they have backslidden, come back to the Lord, out there witnessing, but still living in a sinful lifestyle. They do not even feel there is anything wrong with it either.

They profess to know God but their lifestyle is not Christian. A defiled conscience can be singing on the front row of the church choir. A defiled conscience can be teaching your children in Sunday school. They minister in spite of the fact that their sinful lifestyle disqualifies them for every good work!

A defiled conscience will make excuses for their lifestyle and might even claim it is no big deal to lead a sinful lifestyle. This type of person has a false sense of righteousness because they will not recognize their sin. They will claim that they are a good person.

How do you deal with a defiled conscience? We need to be submitted to someone who can speak to our life and correct us when they see that our conscience is not operating properly. How does one find such a person? They will be someone who seeks God's will, and who is bold enough in faith to rebuke you by clearly stating what you are doing is wrong.

Then we must be humble enough to submit ourselves to receive understanding of what they are saying. At first we may not understand or even see what they are saying is true. We then need to confess and repent in those areas that we have allowed our conscience to become defiled. The blood of Jesus cleanses us from that sin. **"If we confess our sins, he is faithful and just to forgive us our sins, and to cleanse us from all unrighteousness" (1 John 1:9).** There is a cleansing of our conscience upon confession! Amen.

Lastly, we need to renew our mind in the Word of God so we can receive His standard of righteousness for our lives. We need to study the Word so we can see things from God's point of view.

One of the problems we ALL have is that we weigh things from a temporal point of view versus an eternal point of view. We look at things as if we are going to be here forever. We measure what it means to be faithful or unfaithful according to a temporal standard versus an eternal standard.

Look at Stephens's life, the first martyr in the Bible. He was a faithful man, full of God's grace and power and yet he was killed. In our temporal eyes we see this and say, "Wow, what a waste, he could have done much for God if God, had let him live." In God's eternal eyes it was precious that Stephen, when he stood before those who mocked him and he had only a blessing on his lips, looked up and saw Jesus standing there. God was blessed to see faithful Stephen! What we may have considered a wasted life was precious in the sight of God. I believe as well that Stephen's death had such a great impact on Saul that he would later become the apostle Paul.

We need to evaluate things from God's perspective. Sometimes we become discouraged when our expectations fail us because we have deemed success to be of material things. We need to know what God's vision of success is.

We see that a defiled conscience is nearly opposite to the weak conscience. A weak conscience makes us feel guilty even when things are not wrong, while a defiled conscience makes us feel free when we are wrong.

A Seared Conscience

[1]Now the Spirit speaketh expressly, that in the latter times some shall depart from the faith, giving heed to seducing spirits, and doctrines of devils; [2]Speaking lies in hypocrisy; having their conscience seared with

a hot iron; ³Forbidding to marry, and commanding to abstain from meats, which God hath created to be received with thanksgiving of them which believe and know the truth. ⁴For every creature of God is good, and nothing to be refused, if it be received with thanksgiving. (1 Timothy 4:1-4)

Some will depart from the faith, those who have a seared conscience, which is a rejection of faith. In a defiled conscience there is skepticism, but a seared conscience is a rejection. Not only a rejection because the Word says, "giving heed to seducing spirits, and doctrine of devils."

To *give heed* means to *bring near something* and in the Greek means, *to hold the mind* (Strong's #4337). They are receiving those seducing spirits and embracing them by inviting them into their lives. When we have a seared conscience it appears that there is a demonic aspect to it.

Read verse 2 again. The difference between a seared conscience and a defiled conscience is that a person with a seared conscience knows what he is doing is wrong and it does not bother him at all. A person with a defiled conscience does not recognize what they are doing is wrong, because if he did he would feel guilty about it. A person with a seared conscience can do what is totally evil and feel no remorse, guilt, shame or conviction. In the medical field this type of person is considered a psychopath or sociopath, as they have no conscience.

In verse 3 those with seared conscience forbid marriage, and command people to abstain from food God created to be received with thanksgiving by those who believe and know the truth. A person with a seared conscience wants to torment other people. They are people who want to place such heavy burdens on others that it destroys them. An example of this is satanic cults. They take away anything that is natural and guide people to becoming animalistic. They remove anything for which one could be thankful.

When God gives us something, we respond with our hearts by being thankful. Those who are demented develop a cold heart. They try to make sure there is no contentment, no thanksgiving, no enjoyment in life and they turn them into lustful beasts. They do all this knowing it leads to destruction and is evil, but yet they delight in doing it. They feel no shame, filled with hate, and committed to torture. This is the philosophy of liberalism in government.

A seared conscience wants to rob others of any consciousness of God and faith. This is why prayer and Bible reading were taken out of public schools. This is why crosses and monuments to the Ten Commandments are removed from public property. If these types of people are allowed to continue to *rule* (they are not governing) God's severe judgment will fall.

How to deal with a seared conscience?

1. Surrender to Christ
2. Engage in a supernatural intervention of God to bring reverence and restoration to the seared conscience. It needs to happen that way because there are demonic elements to it.

God is able to deliver one from his seared conscience and restore him to Christ. Amen!

CHAPTER FIFTEEN
The "Ants"

*Do you have an antagonist spirit? Can you recognize
an antagonistic spirit operating in your life or in your
fellowship group?*

W e need to know how to recognize church antagonists, because they are either for you or against you and you do not know which until they are on you. Whether it's one antagonist, or a group of antagonists, their bite is not realized until they either expose their purpose, or are exposed by others. Most of the time, the antagonist's plan is not realized until they begin to *bite*.

Ants work nonstop when building their beds or searching for food. If you observe ants, you will see them form a line to building their bed. Each ant carries in its pincers, one piece of dirt. After much effort, evidence of their ant bed building begins to show on the surface of your lawn. The result is a nice little home where they live, hidden away, and are only brought to the surface when their cozy little ant bed is disturbed.

An antagonist is just like that ant, constantly in motion to build a bed of destruction. They go from person to person seeking tidbits of news they can use to build a bed of destruction. Their motive remains hidden until they have collected enough pieces to begin to "bite" and bring hurt and pain to those they have targeted. Those targeted often do not know what is happening until they suffer the bite!

An antagonistic spirit is one of the many characteristics of the Jezebel spirit. They move around with a motive known only to them. Their goal is to control those in leadership positions. The Jezebel is the "queen" in the ant bed who sends out her "worker ants" to bring about destruction, or to gain control.

Through the rest of this chapter I will be referring to an antagonist as an "ant."

"Now I beseech you, brethren, mark them which cause divisions and offences contrary to the doctrine which ye have learned; and avoid them. For they that are such serve not our Lord Jesus Christ, but their own belly; and by good words and fair speeches deceive the hearts of the simple" (Roman 16:17-18).

"Ants" are individuals who work on "poor" evidence of any situation. They go out of their way to make impossible demands, usually attacking the person or performance of others. In the body of Christ, they even attack the ministry to which a person has been called.

Their attacks are aggressive in nature and selfish. They tear down rather than build up, typically directed against those in leadership. They have a tremendous potential to destroy a church and its vision, leaving behind discouraged, broken and apathetic people. They go out of their way to initiate trouble and are highly sensitive. Their hypersensitivity can cause them to take anything as a personal attack. The aim of their attacks are to gain control, regardless of the cost to others.

The ant does not reflect or represent anyone. They are a law unto themselves. Their purpose is to tear down, rip up and destroy. Ants never draw people together; they divide and conquer. They can be one person or work in a group of people.

Three Major Categories of Church "Ants"

1. Hardcore ants (industrial strength ants)
2. Major ants
3. Moderate ants

Hardcore and Major ants will go out of their way to cause problems.

Hardcore ants: They are seriously disturbed people, out of touch with reality. They have a root of bitterness described in Hebrews, **"Looking diligently lest any man fail of the grace of God; lest any root of bitterness springing up trouble you, and thereby many be defiled" (Hebrews 12:15).** They drive the "simple" out of the church and have incredible venom and poison. They are blind to right and wrong and they have an incredible persistence. Their whole objective is to destroy you, the ministry Christ established you in, your marriage, family, and children.

> **"Take heed therefore unto yourselves, and to all the flock, over the which the Holy Ghost hath made you overseers, to feed the church of God, which he hath purchased with his own blood. ²⁹For I know this, that after my departing shall grievous wolves enter in among you, not sparing the flock. ³⁰Also of your own selves shall men arise, speaking perverse things, to draw away disciples after them" (Acts 20:28-30).**

Major ants: These ants can be reasoned with, but they do not desire reason or understanding. They carry a big load of hostility and have serious demonic issues coupled with a great drive for power. They carry very little guilt and have no desire to change. Their hunger for power overrides everything.

<u>Moderate ants:</u> Theses ants lack self-starting power. They follow the hardcore and major ants. They will not go out of their way to cause problems.

Ants are different from activists in that ants are oriented to destroy people while REAL activists are about change. Activists are genuinely concerned about the issues of all people. It is vital to know which you are dealing with, ant or activist. Problems come when we misjudge between the two. When dealing with ants and activists, you need tremendous discernment.

Ant activities happen in a church because:

1. The nature of an ant is that, wherever they go, they cause problems. It does not matter whether it is a social gathering, social or professional organization, church, workplace, or political position.
2. They need the support of other people in order to operate effectively. If they cannot gain the support of those around them, they will lose steam.

Why people follow ants.

A. They mistake ants for activists.
B. For them, the truth is less exciting than half truths and lies.
C. They are gullible.
D. They are intimidated by the ants.
E. To express their own feelings.
F. Due to misguided loyalties.
G. The ants validate their *feelings* causing them to feel important. The ant may have even promised them a position of authority and ministry.

The structure of some churches tends to placate ants. Churches tolerate behavior that other organizations would not.

Whereas other organizations (offices, businesses) would order an ant out of the situation or place.

The congregational form of church government or one-man rule is susceptible to attacks, as are home groups, new members classes, care groups, prayer meetings, and so on.

Activists are "loud" people with compassion toward a cause. They strive to build up a group or community for the better of all those affected. Their motives are pure and rooted in truth and stability. A true activist will never tear down another group or cause to gain footing for their cause. They will never take advantage of individuals, groups, governments, and churches to further their cause.

Red Flags of Church Ants

1. Church Track Record: They tend to repeat their behavior at successive churches. They are "Mr. Vocal" about everything. Do not be quick to believe you can reform them.
2. Parallel Track Record: They are antagonistic in the other areas of their life (work, social, etc.)
3. The Nameless Others: When someone offers you a word of criticism and adds, "There are 'X' number of people that feel the same way." You need to give them the litmus test by asking them, "Who are they and what are their names?" If they give names, they may not be an "ant." But if they say, "Well! They came to me in strictest of confidence and I cannot betray their confidence." RED FLAG!
4. The Predecessor Downer: Beware of when they criticize their previous pastor and praise you at the same time.
5. An Instant Buddy: New people who are overly friendly. Familiarity breeds contempt: They overpower you to get on your good side, pump you for information, want to know every detail about every thing. They will not need you after contempt sets in.

6. Gushing Praise: Gushing praise soon breeds criticism. Those who are overly generous with their praise will often be overly generous with their criticism later on. Unrealistic expectations cause the shift from praise to criticism. If your reaction does not line up to their expectation, the shift will occur.

7. A Church Hopper: People who move from church to church because they have not liked any Pastor. You will not be an exception unless you let them run roughshod over you. The ant will not settle in a church until she finds a pastor she can control.

8. A Different Drummer: They resist established policy and insist on their own way. You will hear them make such statements as, "Don't give me oversight! I am my own man! I hear God for myself! Rules are for other people so don't apply the rule to me!" A "man on his own island."

9. The Situational Loser: Dissention creates sides and some ants do not lose well. Ants avoid making decisions.

Learn to Get a Feel for Ants

After some flags drop, you will notice the following four early warning signs of an ant.

1. A chill in relationship: A distant coolness will occur where there once was warmth. They avoid being alone with you and will challenge and confront you in a group.

2. The New Concerns: They go outside of their measure of rule by meddling in other people's affairs instead of their own concerns. They will address you with a "letter of concern" or visit, which translates to, "I'm mad!" Their other actions will follow based on your reaction. To defuse, go straight to the elders and department heads.

3. Meddling: Interested in areas outside their measure of rule. Will sniff out a problem or potential weakness and exploit it by sending you a "letter of concern."

4. Resistance and Independence: They withdraw from activities and ministry. They will resist approving anything in committees or board meetings.

A letter of concern is a list of implied notions the ant will use against you. These notions are the tidbits they will use to build their bed of destruction. If you react to the letter of concern by being upset, the ant knows he has hit a sore spot and will cause more trouble by getting others to rally around him.

Six Later Warning Signs

1. Sloganeering: Using emotional slogans to spread troublesome dissention.
2. Accusing: They can approach this in one or more of these ways: sex, money, or power.

A. They may accuse you of some sex sin which is not true. A pastor or any male staff member should never counsel a troubled woman alone. One scream from her could cause a ministry untold misery, if not ruin it. His wife or a mature female should be present.
B. They may accuse you of misusing church funds for yourself.
C. They may accuse you of "taking over" when you are merely following the Lord's leading.
3. Distorting: Distorts incidents, leaving grains of truth to maintain credibility.
4. Judas Kissing: A common greeting in the bible was a slight kiss on the neck as an act of endearment. Judas distorted this in an act of betrayal toward Jesus. An ant will use this act and make such statements such as, "I'm your friend, but I have to do this." They will proclaim they love you, yet will step on you. They will distort, accuse, and sloganeer and will do it all in the name of the Lord.

5. Pretense: Often portrays self as a friend of the underdog. He sides with the hurting minority. People will either cheer for the underdog or for the cause.
6. Lobbying: Out to get power, followers, and credibility. They lobby interests with home groups, prayer groups and vulnerable new members.

SOLUTION

If the church has properly addressed the ants behavior, yet they persist, they must be asked to leave the church. Their unrepentant nature is the evidence that follows them, that they are intent on causing dissention.

CHAPTER SIXTEEN
Bitterness in the Body of Christ

*"Looking diligently lest any man fail of the grace of
God; lest any root of bitterness springing up trouble
you, and thereby many be defiled" (Hebrews 12:15)
The only way to be free of bitterness is to let go of past
offenses and refuse to collect them.*

The dictionary defines *bitter* as *sharp, sour tasting,
unpleasant, angry, resentful; sarcastic.* [a] It stems from
deep-seated anger and a lack of forgiveness that embeds itself
into one's soul. Bitterness is watered, and fertilized by playing
and replaying in one's mind the video of the offense(s). If one
pays close attention, a second plot begins that leads to a possible third plot and so on. These are the "shoots" of the roots
that spread off into different directions and produce rotten
"fruit."

Recall a time in your life where you were wronged and
an angry confrontation resulted. After that confrontation, were
you still stewing and thinking about one more thing you could
have done or said to get in just one more "shot"? This is what is
called "plotting destruction" which goes against planting life-
bearing seeds! That behavior cuddles the bitterness spirit.

Paul warns us that having a "root of bitterness" can grow
up and "defile many" (Hebrews 12:15). James tell us that bitterness is from the devil (James 3:14-15). Peter cautions that

bitterness can keep us from being effective in ministry (Acts 8:22-24). Bitterness in our hearts will produce bitterness in our actions. This opposes the will of God for the believer to whom He has given powerful, abundant, victorious life.

Jesus said in John, "The thief cometh not, but for to steal, and to kill, and to destroy: <u>I am come that they might have life, and that they might have it more abundantly</u>" (John 10:10). Do not confuse the words "abundant life" with worldly riches. By abundant life, Jesus is speaking about the abundance God's Word brings to us when it operates in our lives. In the simplicity of this verse, Jesus presents to us our choices in life. Either we can walk down the road that leads to destruction or we can walk down the road that develops abundant life within us. Your choice determines your rewards on your day of judgment. If you are an unbeliever, though, this verse does not speak to that, your road dead ends in the lake of fire.

Many believers live below their privileges and do not experience the abundant life. This is largely due to the defeats we experience, often from hurtful experiences and because of sins we commit. In Galatians 4:9 we read, **"But now, after that ye have known God, or rather are known of God, how turn ye again to the weak and beggarly elements, whereunto ye desire again to be in bondage?"**

Most of us understand that we experience defeat when these things come into our lives. However, many of us do not understand their long-term effect on us if we do not resolved them due to reluctance, rebellion, or ignorance. Our subconscious memory is a vast storehouse. Everything we have experienced in life is stored there, including memories of sin and hurt. The experience of hurt and memory of it is one of the most powerfully destructive forces there is in the human heart. It can destroy lives, relationships, families and nations.

The dictionary defines *HURT* as, 1) **a:** to, <u>INJURE</u> **b:** to do substantial or material harm to: <u>DAMAGE</u>. **2 a :** to cause emotional pain or anguish to : <u>WOUND</u> **b :** to be detrimental to <u>DIS-</u>

<u>TRESS</u> **1 a :** to suffer pain or grief **b :** to be in need **2) :** to cause damage or distress. [b]

The enemy wants to cause injuries and wounds that will damage us and bring us pain. He wants to cause us distress to hamper our walk. Hurt is a big stick used by the enemy's camp and the root of most hurt turns into some form of bitterness. That is why it is vital to address a hurt as soon as it takes place so there is no time for it to stew.

Hurt is **an** offense taken as a perceived injustice by the attitude or actions of one whom we hold in high regard. There is a difference between being involved in a hurtful situation and actually receiving the hurt from it. There are two basic options when confronted with a hurtful situation: (Remember John 10:10 and those two roads previously mentioned when reading these two options.)

1. We can obtain the grace of God for **healing** through immediate forgiveness. (Hebrews 4:15-16; 12:15)
2. We can accept the hurt as our "right" in view of the injustice we have suffered and as a result, refuse to forgive.

There are three reasons why we do not forgive:

1. We do not feel that the offender deserves to be forgiven, though the Word tells us in Ephesians, **"And be ye kind one to another, tenderhearted, forgiving one another, even as God for Christ's sake hath forgiven you" (Ephesians 4:32)**
2. We do not feel that the other person has been punished enough, though the Word tells us in Hebrews, **"For we know him that hath said, Vengeance belongeth unto me, I will recompense, saith the Lord. And again, The Lord shall judge his people" (Hebrews 10:30).**
3. We do not want to make ourselves vulnerable again, though the Word tells us in Matthew:

³⁸Ye have heard that it hath been said, An eye for an eye, and a tooth for a tooth: ³⁹But I say unto you, That ye resist not evil: but whosoever shall smite thee on thy right cheek, turn to him the other also. ⁴⁰And if any man will sue thee at the law, and take away thy coat, let him have thy cloak also. ⁴¹And whosoever shall compel thee to go a mile, go with him twain. ⁴²Give to him that asketh thee, and from him that would borrow of thee turn not thou away. (Matthew 5:38-42)

We most often find that we are following the fleshly reaction instead of living the way the Word of God instructs us. We do this and then question why we are in the state that we are in!

We are affected the most when the source of the hurt comes from someone we love, trust, or for whom we have had high expectations. **"For it was not an enemy that reproached me; then I could have borne it: neither was it he that hated me that did magnify himself against me; then I would have hid myself from him: ¹³But it was thou, a man mine equal, my guide, and mine acquaintance" (Psalms 55:12-13).**

That sense of injustice, which is the seed-bed of hurt, comes from the feeling of being abused, rejected or betrayed. **"And one shall say unto him, What are these wounds in thine hands? Then he shall answer, Those with which I was wounded in the house of my friends" (Zechariah 13:6).**

As a result of hurt, our trust changes to cynicism, high expectations to disillusionment, and love turns to hatred. Our personality and attitude are strongly affected, based on our continued perception of the offense. If we "water" this perception, the formulation stage begins and this is when the attitude of bitterness begins to form. As the sense of injustice grows stronger, powerful and formidable reactions spring forth in response to our hurt. The final stage is when our whole personality is formatted with the imprint of bitterness.

When the grace of God, which enables us to forgive, is not expressed by us at the time of the offenses, we will internalize them as hurt. All offenses are the result of feeling a sense of injustice, a reaction to being deprived of something good that we deserved. It could also be injustice over having something bad put on us that we did not deserve. Such personalized offenses result in a sense of hurt that is compounded in the heart (mind, will and emotions).

Unforgiveness is **an** act or choice of the will. How we respond to such situations is very telling. We choose to charge or not charge wrongful intent to the offender. We choose to accept and to internalize the hurt or release it to the grace of God. The afflicted chooses whether to forgive. Choose correctly.

Forgiveness is always a choice. It requires addressing the hurtful incidents which we tend to avoid because of the discomfort involved. There are costs involved, in terms of restoring the offenders, which they may not want to bear. Most times, the offenders want to avoid confrontation because of the gossip and lies involved in the situation and they do not want to get caught in them. (Recall in the Ants chapter, one of the reasons the offenders may avoid addressing the situation is because they thrive on half-truths and lies. They love to stir the pot and cook "bitterness stew.")

The Root the Shoot the Fruit

The **"root"** grows from the heart: **"For as he thinketh in his heart, so is he: Eat and drink, saith he to thee; but his heart is not with thee" (Proverbs 23:7).**

The total personality of man is affected by the experience of hurt. It expresses itself emotionally, mentally and volitionally.

Then the **"shoot"** that results in **"fruit"** springs forth and produces "works." The bitter person produces various types of trouble in her life. Bitterness manifests itself in attitudinal changes. It produces a profane attitude toward God (i.e. taking the things of God lightly. See Hebrews 12:13) It produces compulsive desires, like lust and greed.

A bitter person walks around wounded. They have internalized hurts but do not address them for various reasons. They think they can handle them, are choosing to try to ignore them or simply believe they will pass or "blow over." They do not accept responsibility for internalizing the hurt and will feel that their offender owes them reconciliation or some evidence of repentance. Since they do not address their hurts, they will ultimately go through a hardening process. When confronted about their attitude of bitterness, clear indications that the hardening process has developed in their heart is seen if they respond in the following ways:

1. Denial of bitterness
2. Projection of hurt and bitterness
3. Justification of a negative attitude toward those who caused the hurt.

There is a spiral of bitterness. When a person is bitter over the hurt in his life, a chain reaction occurs which is not of God. The bitter person progresses through deep behavioral changes. They become more introverted, causing alienation from others. Ultimately, they can become capable of bringing harm or destruction to him and others. This is why it is vital to pull up roots of bitterness quickly and decisively.

When bitterness is unresolved, it causes a succession of stages of bondage. Luke records the basic levels of bondage resulting in bitterness. **"The Spirit of the Lord is upon me, because he hath anointed me to preach the gospel to the poor; he hath sent me to heal the <u>brokenhearted</u>, to preach deliverance to <u>the captives</u>, and recovering of sight to <u>the blind</u>, to set at liberty <u>them that are bruised</u>" (Luke 4:18).**

The Bruised: A person who is bruised sees the tribulation in their life as bondage. He has either refused to choose grace or is ignorant of that privilege. He burns his "wick" only, and carries no "oil" in his lamp. He will view his life as always having to "bite the bullet."

The bruised will view his bitterness on three levels:

He will deny its existence.

He will admit its existence but will project the responsibility for it onto someone else.

He will justify its existence.

The bruised person, at any point, can choose to receive the grace of God for healing and freedom. Failure to make this choice will place him in line for God to allow tribulations to come to him, unto restoration. When he suppresses his hurt and pain, as opposed to confronting it with the grace of God, he will be plagued with emotional and mental ills. The result is, he will be bowed down with the weight of bitterness, and be vulnerable to the enemy's desire to drive him into a depression or worse.

The Blind: This person justifies their bitterness. They follow the basic path written in Romans 1:21-23. The blind gives no glory to God in their hurt. They are devoid of the spirit of thanksgiving. They are arrogant in their own wisdom. They create a god of their own design, having rejected the sovereign design of God in their life. They are spiritually blinded to the degree that they have totally suppressed all desire for and confidence in God. The desire for material things drives the blind. If they have anything to do with God, it will be from a selfish motive (Acts 8:18-24). The result is that their foolish heart is darkened (Romans 1:21-23). They cannot "see" what they are walking into.

The Captives i.e., The Bound: This person has chosen to walk in the ways of darkness instead of in the glory of God. In their bitterness a stronghold will be erected which will pull them under and into a demonic oppression. In this state, their choices become limited. Whereas once they could not see, now the bound is unable to resist. They are now compulsive in bitterness, anger and unforgiveness. They will blame their problems on others even though they created them themselves. They will be obsessed with their anger toward their offender. They will not be able to hear God and it will require help from the Body of Christ to pull them out.

The Brokenhearted: God's commitment is so great that He will not leave His children in the condition described above. He is committed to the restoration of His children. He will bring to bear **an** array of circumstances upon them to break their stubbornness. He comes with grace and mercy for **healing** when that brokenness has occurred. The broken is one who God has shattered through difficult circumstances to bring them to a place of forgiveness and healing. God's grace will set the captive free, give sight to the blind, and set at liberty those that are bruised. **"The Spirit of the Lord is upon me, because he hath anointed me to preach the gospel to the poor; he hath sent me to heal the brokenhearted, to preach deliverance to the captives, and recovering of sight to the blind, to set at liberty them that are bruised" (Luke 4:18).** AMEN!

Bitterness will draw upon its environment to supply its needs. **"Looking diligently lest any man fail of the grace of God; lest any root of bitterness springing up trouble you, and thereby many be defiled" (Hebrews 12:15).**

There seems to be a sequence, from experience and witnessing, to the development of bitterness. Unresolved hurt produces unforgiveness. Unforgiveness produces a sense of rejection. Rejection causes a person to judge those whom they deem to have hurt them. A judgmental attitude will produce a form of rebellion, causing one to allow a rebellious spirit to operate through them. A rebellious person's spirit will find ways to retaliate toward the perceived offender believing it to be a need to "self-protect." A form of self-protection could be isolate oneself from others, which in turn causes loneliness.

Adding up all those factors, depression sets in. Depression can cause destructive behavior.

How do you fight this sequence? **"For if ye forgive men their trespasses, your heavenly Father will also forgive you"** (Matthew 6:14). How many times do you forgive? **"Jesus saith unto him, I say not unto thee, Until seven times: but, Until seventy times seven" (Matthew 18:22).** If one chooses to follow this road, instead of blindness, bondage, and captivity one can develop love, peace, and joy.

You must forgive the offender unconditionally. That means dropping ALL charges brought against the offender before God, man and the counsel of YOUR OWN heart. Releasing the offender from the responsibility of ALL hurt which they caused. The last one is, restore the offender, **"Wherefore receive ye one another, as Christ also received us to the glory of God"** (Romans 15:7).

Restoring Love Toward an Offender

I felt I needed to share this chapter because of all the roadblocks of bitterness, anger and unforgiveness the enemy has tried to put up in my life. In order for one to walk toward Jesus; to be able to put on the robe of righteousness, believers in Christ Jesus must learn how to crucify our flesh and line up our minds to His ways and thoughts. When we do this, He will lead us out of the wilderness.

How do we restore love?

Renounce any right to feel negative. **"But I say unto you which hear, Love your enemies, do good to them which hate you" (Luke 6:27).**

Receive the person as they are. **"Ye have heard that it hath been said, Thou shalt love thy neighbour, and hate thine enemy. But I say unto you, Love your enemies, bless them that curse you, do good to them that hate you, and** pray for them which despitefully use you, and persecute you" (Matthew 5:43-44).

Restore him to your personal favor. "Brethren, if a man be overtaken in a fault, ye which are spiritual, restore such an one in the spirit of meekness; considering thyself, lest thou also be tempted" (Galatians 6:1).

Rejoice about him in and out of your presence. "Rejoice in the Lord always: and again I say, Rejoice" (Philippians 4:4).

Respond to him in love. "This is my commandment, That ye love one another, as I have loved you" (John 15:12).

Resist the enemy. "Be sober, be vigilant; because your adversary the devil, as a roaring lion, walketh about, seeking whom he may devour: Whom resist steadfast in the faith, knowing that the same afflictions are accomplished in your brethren that are in the world" (1 Peter 5:8-9).

Rest in the Lord. "Come unto me, all ye that labour and are heavy laden, and I will give you rest. Take my yoke upon you, and learn of me; for I am meek and lowly in heart: and ye shall find rest unto your souls. For my yoke is easy, and my burden is light" (Matthew 11:28-30).

Resist your feelings and go with what God said in His Word. I know it is a struggle, but that is why it is called warfare. Go through the motions by faith to put on the armor of Ephesians 6:14-18 every day. Remember, the things of this world are temporary. Our permanent home awaits us in Heaven and no problem while here on earth is too big to conquer as long as God is in the lead, both in your mind and in your heart. AMEN!

CHAPTER SEVENTEEN
Discipleship and Prayer Life

M y oldest son tells me from time to time, that he is thankful to have a mother who he can talk to concerning about matters like those in this book. Growing up, my parents could only share with me as much knowledge as they had concerning Christ. Because I made a decision to go further in my walk, the Lord revealed more aspects of Him that have allowed me to explain more of God to him. We can never go further than the revelations God has given unto us.

For example, when I was growing up, I had no clue what gift the Lord had given me. In my testimony, I shared that I knew I had gift, but I didn't know what to call it, and I certainly didn't know what to do with it. I never asked my parents in-depth questions concerning it because I never thought to do so, and I was always asking God about it. It was something in me that just seemed automatic to do it that way. Maybe that was God's plan to begin with as I no longer question it and I have rest and peace concerning it.

Because of the relationship I desire in Christ, my children, when they choose to do so, can come to me and ask me in-depth questions, deeper questions that I did not know to ask my own parents. I too can only share the depth of the knowledge that the Lord has given me. I can only pray that in my children's walk that they go further than I do and that their walk is even more blessed with the richness of God's revelations than mine, and that they will also share with their children. As a matter of fact, I proclaim that right now in Jesus name, amen!

I know the struggles and the experiences I have had and have on my walk toward Jesus. I have talked with many people and it seems like most of us have the same questions. I have also come across some of the rudest and cruel people in the church, who with one breath claim they love me yet with the next breath behind my back gossip and lie about me. Some of those people are even family. That kind of circumstance is created when people establish their own righteousness instead of allowing God to set the "stones" in place.

By sharing what I have shared above, I am not expressing unforgiveness, believe me. I hold no unforgiveness toward any of those people. They are just parts of the wilderness I have had to walk through to get to what God has promised to me and to put me on that path He wants me to walk down. I thank God that He sent me through the many wilderness walks because, through them, God has molded me into the person He has called me to be. We are always a work in progress and the finished project awaits us in heaven.

It is through those uncomfortable wilderness walks that God desires to do the most work in us centrally directed on our character. Yes, they are uncomfortable and the flesh gets wounded, but I realize that is when Christ in us should soar the most. This is where we miss it the most sometimes, our flesh desires to be satisfied with a "war of words" yet God's still small voice is telling us, "I will handle it." We miss His voice because our own has drowned His out.

Though I still miss the mark sometimes, through each pass of the mountain, a little more of me is gone and a little more of Christ is birthed in me, because I recognize that it is not me, but Christ in me.

In early 2005, my husband and I were attending a church, and had been for some time. Prior to service one morning we were informed that some people were talking negatively about us. While sitting in that service, my mind was focused on what I was just told and I just kept asking God "Why did that happen? What did I do? Is this what church is all about?" I was wounded by the words I heard.

God revealed to me that Christians, in general, did not understand who HE wanted us to be in HIM. While sitting in that service I recognized that the characteristics of Christ must replace our characteristics (Romans 8:29; 2 Corinthians 3:18).

Because I chose not to confront those people and went to God about it instead, He showed me through His Word that what they were doing would eventually lead to their destruction. The destruction would not be by anything that I said or did. God's Word did come to pass by sending those involved into various levels of wilderness walks.

It is sad when people go into a church, equipped with the ministries God has called them to do, but then get accused by that body of wanting to "take over" what they have built. They totally missed the mark and caused many to stumble. The enemy had me tied up in self-doubt about who I was in Christ Jesus, so I was sent through a "why me and what did I do" wilderness walk.

When someone who is truly seeking a relationship with Jesus walks into a church that people have built, those people will **TRY** to push them out, tear them apart, or attempt to leave them devastated. It is in them to protect "their" work and what "they" have built and it is that attitude that will cause the tumbling of stones. Our part, being mature, is to recognize all this and grow from the experience. If they reject Christ in you, dust off and move on.

It was not until I understood the truth of God's Word concerning these matters that I then found rest and peace in it and I ate from the "meat plate" of the Word, and it was filling! Amen! I gained the understanding of what God was showing me and the false accusations no longer consumed me. God's

Word consumed me! That is why today I can say that they are forgiven and I can pray for them unhindered.

How do we avoid becoming like those who build their own things yet call them holy? We become a true disciple of Jesus Christ. A disciple will develop seven attributes which become the evidence in their lives that they are truly walking on the path lined with God's Word, that God has placed them on.

1. He will be like his Master. (Luke 6:40)
2. He will lay down his "psuche/flesh" life to obtain "Zoe" life. (Luke 14:26)
3. He will bear his own cross. (Luke 14:27)
4. He will forsake all he has and deny himself to serve Jesus. (Matthew 16:24; Luke 14:33)
5. He will bear the fruit of the Holy Spirit. (John 15:8)
6. A disciple will have love for other disciples. (John 13:34-34; 1 John 4:7)
7. He will continue to grow in God's Word. (John 8:32)

The proper motivation for all this to grow in the life of the believer is LOVE. **"The disciple is not above his master: but every one that is perfect shall be as his master" (Luke 6:40).** Being perfect, or "spiritually mature," you will be like Jesus.

"²And it shall come to pass in the last days, that the mountain of the LORD's house shall be established in the top of the mountains, and shall be exalted above the hills; and all nations shall flow unto it. ³And many people shall go and say, Come ye, and let us go up to the mountain of the LORD, to the house of the God of Jacob; and he will teach us of his ways, and we will walk in his paths: for out of Zion shall go forth the law, and the word of the LORD from Jerusalem" (Isaiah 2:2-3). We can see that the goal of Christianity, is not just to get people converted but to lead people into the development of becoming disciples. That development is the <u>sanctification process</u>. We lead them to the knowledge of it, as this book does, and that is where we step out. It is for the individual to seek God on what he is presented.

It is my prayer that this book makes what seem to be "mysteries," understandable to all who seek Him, are spoken to, ministered to, and called by God. I pray that you will understand that the pastor is not exclusive in the Church, and that God has called us to be a Body of Christ that works together to bring about the works of God, for His glory. We should be working together, interlocking the joints in fivefold ministry.

> **"And he gave some, apostles; and some, prophets; and some, evangelists; and some, pastors and teachers.... Till we all come in the unity of the faith, and of the knowledge of the Son of God, unto a perfect man, unto the measure of the stature of the fulness of Christ" (Ephesians 4:11,13).**

A Disciplined Prayer Life

To begin, we should have a disciplined prayer life. **"That the trial of your faith, being much more precious than of gold that perisheth, though it be tried with fire, might be found unto praise and honour and glory at the appearing of Jesus Christ: Whom having not seen, ye love; in whom, though now ye see him not, yet believing, ye rejoice with joy unspeakable and full of glory" (1 Peter 1:7-8).**

One "acid test" of a victorious Christian is their ability to have a God conscious faith that can express joy unspeakable, one that can praise, honor, and glorify God when tried by fire. This decisive test is part of that race that we have to keep running, without growing weary. I do not pass it yet, but I am getting better because I stay aware and learn through each trial. **"Be sober, be vigilant; because your adversary the devil, as a roaring lion, walketh about, seeking whom he may devour" (1 Peter 5:8).**

Most new Christians struggle in their walk to begin a consistent prayer life and lack an understanding of what they are walking toward. This is mainly because of a lack of confidence in God. At the altar, in the beginning, there is great joy, but once the first trial by fire comes, most new believers "flatline." Their heart stops because it was not properly motivated to grow in the Lord yet. At that crossroad point there is either a "feeling" to give up on God and go back into the world, or stick with God but allow the experience to hinder our progression in Christ. It leaves them unable to enter into the purpose He has for their lives.

Sometimes we can get frustrated because "a change" does not seem to be happening for us. (Remember that man who went to that large convention in an earlier chapter?) If we allow that frustration to drive us, then we will eat our way right into a dry bag of crackers. We will feel nothing and simply feel frustrated.

What comes before prayer in your priorities? What keeps you from prayer? Are those things zapping you so much that you don't have time left to pray? Are you one of those who go through the entire day milling about in your business until finally, at bedtime, you pull out the Bible, and read two or three minutes before falling asleep?

If you answer yes to these questions and yet you ask God, "Why aren't you moving me in my life? Why is it such a struggle to serve you Lord?" Do you find yourself making fresh commitments to the Lord, yet nothing truly changes? You know in your heart you haven't made a change, so you need to stop questioning and get walking toward Jesus for real! You have a flatlined relationship with Christ if you just go through the "motions" of Christianity.

Do you want some heart pumping reality? Read the book of Malachi, all four chapters and things will begin to become clearer to you. There are a few key verses that will really bring it into a clearer context.

⁶A son honoureth his father, and a servant his master: if then I be a father, where is mine honour? and if I be a master, where is my fear? saith the LORD of hosts unto you, O priests, that despise my name. And ye say, Wherein have we despised thy name? ⁷Ye offer polluted bread upon mine altar; and ye say, Wherein have we polluted thee? In that ye say, The table of the LORD is contemptible. ⁸And if ye offer the blind for sacrifice, is it not evil? and if ye offer the lame and sick, is it not evil? offer it now unto thy governor; will he be pleased with thee, or accept thy person? saith the LORD of hosts. (Malachi 1:6-8)

Are you treating God with contempt? Are you giving Him the least amount of your time at the lamest part of your day? Are you giving the last five minutes of your day, yet failing to do even that as you fall asleep? You may feel the desire to change, yet still you do not.

We are all guilty of these things and we need to pray and ask the Lord to forgive us. We must seek a deeper relationship with Christ. Take your Bible each morning, first thing, even if you do not feel like it, and begin to read it. As you do, you will begin to develop a consistent prayer life. Without a consistent prayer life, you will remain in a spiritual "rut." If you do not develop one, then you do NOT have a right to question WHY things are not happening in your walk with Christ.

"Let us therefore fear, lest, a promise being left us of entering into his rest, any of you should seem to come short of it. For unto us was the gospel preached, as well as unto them: but the word preached did not profit them, not being mixed with faith in them that heard it" (Hebrews 4:1-2). In other words, the promises of God are valid to us but we need to respond to it. God's promises are an open invitation to each of His children and it is our responsibility to respond, to act upon them and to receive them. Our response is one of faith and obedience.

God touched me many times, urging me forward, but I just did not seem to respond. It is not that I did not want to respond but I did not take that faith and obedience step. It is up to each one of us to respond when will feel God touching our lives. When you have a move of Christ in your life and the next week, you are still in the same place you were before God touched you, that is evidence you did not respond.

A few months ago when I picked this book back up to finish writing it, I could have *not* responded and you would not be reading it right now. Sometimes I need confirmation to make sure I am hearing from God, which is okay; we should test every spirit. This time, He made sure I heard it three times, back to back, and I responded in faith and obedience to His calling.

I could have pushed aside the calling and that nudge of God in my heart. I could have responded in unbelief, "Oh! God did not call me to put together a work like this. No way, not me! Those three confirmations were just a fluke, a coincidence." Oh! BUT GOD! He knows me and because of the relationship and the seeking I am led to do, I heard HIM! I responded out of faith and obedience and He led me to get this work done. He assured me that it was HIM calling me by giving me what I needed BEFORE I even asked for it. AMEN!

You do not have to wait for some powerful experience to hit your life before you begin to respond, because the power of the Holy Spirit is with you always. If you know Jesus, then you know the power and life of the Holy Spirit is in you. The more you read the Word the more you will begin to pray. The more you pray the more Word you will read. The more Word you read, the more your faith will increase.

Your ears will then be attuned to Jesus' voice, just as a piano tuner gets tuned in to the pure pitch needed to succeed in his work. Before his work begins, the tuner may play a few chords to see just how out of tune the piano is. If it is out of tune, the harmony will sound chaotic. Enter the tuning fork. <u>When struck</u>, the tuning fork holds the perfect tune. Over time, the tuner's ear is attuned to the correct frequency of that tuning fork. Because of this, he knows the exact amount of tension to apply to the string. When he <u>does the work directed by the turning fork</u>, the "sound" leads him to bring the piano into perfect pitch. The action of "striking" must take place first, before all the movements begin. If the piano tuner just sets the fork on the piano and waits for the correct harmony, then that piano will remain out of tune. He had all the proper equipment but didn't put them to work. He must act upon what he knows, and when he does, the piano is tuned—mission accomplished. This is the way God works in our lives through the Word HE gave us.

God's Word is our tuning fork. It holds the keys to getting into perfect tune with Him. The more we read and seek Him, the more we recognize His plan and purpose for our lives, and respond in faith and obedience to Him. If our Bible is just a coffee table display, or if we are waiting for God to move, our spirit (our piano) will remain out of tune. Our walk will become chaotic, scattered or just plain idle.

This may challenge you to make a big change in your life, and you now wonder how in the world you will meet the challenge. The answer is to take it one day at a time. Your starting point must be the establishment of a consistent prayer life.

"For unto us was the gospel preached, as well as unto them: but the word preached did not profit them, not being mixed with faith in them that heard it" (Hebrews 4:2). The Word did not do them any good because they did not believe. Before we can respond, we need to be able to believe. We need to take heed when we hear His Word then we need to respond to the Holy Spirit by obeying His Word.

When we hear the message, we need to take that message and mix it with faith and then we need to respond. We must respond with faith because that will give us perseverance as we pray with expectation.

This is not saying that you will not ever miss a day; it just means that becomes the exception, not the rule. Your life should consist of a daily prayer life where God gets the best time of your day, the first part of it. This is not about legalism or ritual, it is about building a relationship with God.

One caution: If you get up every morning and pray without expectation, believing that it's not really going to count, then it's not going to. You will not have the perseverance and you will begin to die out after two or three days.

We cannot study the life of Jesus without studying about prayer because Jesus' life was inseparable from prayer. Jesus came to earth, not as the Son of God only, but also as the Son of Man, to be our example of how, by the grace of God, we are to live. If we see Jesus only as the Son of God, then His example to us will become irrelevant. He came also as the Son of Man, saying that the way He lived is the way we should live. One of the main components He had was that He had a deep relationship with His Father through prayer. Prayer must become an integral part of our lives.

Ask yourself these three things:

1. Do I want to change?
2. Do I want to obey Christ?
3. Am I willing to follow Jesus all the way to the grave?

You may see this list and think they are small changes. If you have a routine and are in a comfort zone, you will see just how easy or hard it will be when He begins to move you out of it. It is a struggle between doing what God wants you to do versus what you want to keep doing for yourself. You must be willing to ALWAYS put God first.

"And at even, when the sun did set, they brought unto him all that were diseased, and them that were possessed

with devils. And all the city was gathered together at the door. And he healed many that were sick of divers diseases, and cast out many devils; and suffered not the devils to speak, because they knew him. And in the morning, rising up a great while before day, he went out, and departed into a solitary place, and there prayed" (Mark 1:32-35). Jesus was never too busy to pray. He worked all day and into the night, yet He still got up the next morning, before sunrise, and prayed. He was tired but He got up because He knew He needed to spend time with His Father. Jesus knew He would not be effective in His ministry if He did not pray.

"And it came to pass in those days, that he went out into a mountain to pray, and continued all night in prayer to God. And when it was day, he called unto him his disciples: and of them he chose twelve, whom also he named apostles" (Luke 6:12-13). Jesus prayed all night before He chose His 12 disciples

I believe Jesus spent all night in prayer, not because He was waiting for God to tell Him who the twelve would be, but because He was praying for those twelve men. I believe He already knew who the twelve would be and He spent all night praying for them. He knew the unique purpose for each of their lives because through them the message of salvation would go forth to all humanity.

God has promises for us, but if we do not pray into those promises, we will never see them fulfilled. God gives us glimpses into His will so we will know what to pray. We need to pray into it! Every day we should come before the Lord and proclaim those promises before Him. We agree to those promises for our lives. Once you know what God's will is for your life it becomes a lot easier for you to pray concerning it. When you begin to see those promises line up to His Word, just keep coming before the Lord agreeing with those promises for your life, co-laboring in prayer and agreeing with His Word.

"O God, thou art my God; early will I seek thee: my soul thirsteth for thee, my flesh longeth for thee in a dry and thirsty land, where no water is" (Psalm 63:1). That is the secret, seeking God early. Picture your life as a dry and thirsty land. If you do not have prayer, you will dry out and you will drink anything! When we seek Him through prayer, He refreshes us and we go out to a dry and thirsty land offering "water" to others.

"But seek ye first the kingdom of God, and his righteousness; and all these things shall be added unto you" (Matthew 6:33). Seek first the Kingdom of God and all these things will be added unto you. If you start off your day in "busy work," notice you will never find time to pray that day. If you start your day off in prayer, you will still have time to do everything else.

"But thou, when thou prayest, enter into thy closet, and when thou hast shut thy door, pray to thy Father which is in secret; and thy Father which seeth in secret shall reward thee openly" (Matthew 6:6). Here we see some components of prayer. The word for *room* used here has a number of meanings. It means *inner chamber*. That speaks of a solitary place. I speak and pray to God while going about my everyday chores and errands, but this scripture is not speaking about those times. There is a time when we must stop everything and go into a solitary place, just us and God, a place where we are aware of only God!

When you go into that place, you pray with your heart. This is not where you pray for family members and others, but a deeper, more intimate prayer, where you are in secret with just you and God. Talk to God and share those very intimate things of your heart and listen as He shares intimate things with you.

This verse also instructs us to "shut the door." Shut the door to your soul so that the distractions of your home and the outside world are completely shut out. When you begin to get intimate with God in prayer, your mind will try to wander off and begin to think of all the things you forgot to do. Shut the door, lock it, and pray.

Prayer implies speech! Verbalizing prayer helps to focus our mind and our intentions. If we try to pray just using our minds, chances are, our mind will be scattering all over the place. Verbalizing helps our "hearing" and helps keep us focused. When you move into His presence you will begin to get overwhelmed with wonder and God's love! You begin to feel God's presence in a tangible way! It moves you into praising Him, thanking Him, and worshipping Him! Entering into His presence after your verbalized prayer, you will feel yourself pulled into a reverent place of waiting on God. Your spirit is quietly thanking the Lord, as peace settles over you.

Some people, while in their prayer closet, will keep a pen and paper close by. They will write down the revelations God gives them concerning Scripture. They will also write down things that God impresses on their hearts. Those things that settle into your heart are the things God is trying to speak to you! **"God hath spoken once; twice have I heard this; that power belongeth unto God" (Psalm 62:11).** Big truth alert! Stop! Pay attention! Write it down! If what you hear from God becomes alive to you, write it down! This verse, I believe is speaking about when God reveals His meanings to you. The first time is when you read the scripture or hear it preached. The second time is when God gives you the meaning and life jumps into your bones!

If we do not have that prayer in our secret place, God will seem like a foreign concept. We will not be equipped to minister to others. The cultivation of what God wants us to do will not spring forth.

In Matthew, Jesus says, **"pray to thy Father which is in secret; and thy Father which seeth in secret <u>shall reward thee openly</u>" (Matthew 6:6).** This does not mean just an answer to a specific prayer; it is greater and bigger than that. It is the will of God being manifest in our lives. The greatest consequence of consistency in prayer will NOT be seen in sudden or abrupt change. It will have an effect over the entire course of our lifetime and will affect all whom we encounter in our life. If you pray for a week and do not see any changes, you do not understand that prayer is relationship. It is something of substance the effect of which will be seen over the course of our lifetime. The evidence is seen in the lives of those with a consistent prayer life—the steady, forward progression of their spiritual lives. The believers who do not have a consistent prayer life are seen in the same old ruts, always wondering why "nothing" is happening for them spiritually. I know both sides of this fence.

In Matthew we find this caution: **"But when ye pray, use not vain repetitions, as the heathen do: for they think that they shall be heard for their much speaking" (Matthew 6:7).** It is a caution for us to have the correct attitude in prayer. Prayer is a relationship with God. We do not pray, "Gimme, gimme, gimme, heal me, heal me, heal me." It is about us unburdening our hearts. So what is the difference between "vain repetitions" and persistence in prayer? Our focus and attitude.

We come to God with whatever our needs are, but we focus on Him. We can be persistent in presenting the same prayer for days, weeks or even years, but we keep praying while staying focused on Him. We do not go to Him with the attitude that if we keep praying long enough that we will finally get the answer. We speak with Him knowing that He is at work in our lives. We continue speaking with him, co-laboring with Him, until we see that manifestation to that prayer in our lives. Unburden your soul and look forward to the fulfillment of His promises.

Exodus records a stunning prayer encounter between Moses and God. In it we see Moses talking to God, and God talking to Moses.

[11]And the **LORD** spake unto Moses face to face, as a man speaketh unto his friend. And he turned again into the camp: but his servant Joshua, the son of Nun, a young man, departed not out of the tabernacle. [12]And Moses said unto the **LORD**, See, thou sayest unto me, Bring up this people: and thou hast not let me know whom thou wilt send with me. Yet thou hast said, I know thee by name, and thou hast also found grace in my sight. [13]Now therefore, I pray thee, if I have found grace in thy sight, shew me now thy way, that I may know thee, that I may find grace in thy sight: and consider that this nation is thy people. [14]And he said, My presence shall go with thee, and I will give thee rest. [15]And he said unto him, If thy presence go not with me, carry us not up hence. [16]For wherein shall it be known here that I and thy people have found grace in thy sight? is it not in that thou goest with us? so shall we be separated, I and thy people, from all the people that are upon the face of the earth. [17]And the **LORD** said unto Moses, I will do this thing also that thou hast spoken: for thou hast found grace in my sight, and I know thee by name" (Exodus 33:11-17).

The Lord said to Moses that He would do the thing he asked for in prayer because HE knew him by sight and also by name, (the Bride of Christ). Prayer is a place of intimacy and friendship and in verse 11 the Lord spoke to Moses as a man speaks to his friend. When we do not know God as we should know Him, we struggle with fear and doubt. When we know Him, He speaks to us as a friend!

God has a ministry and purpose for every believer but it is only when we spend time in prayer, consistently, that we will see it fulfilled. Moses' example of prayer stirred up the heart of Joshua so much that he didn't want to leave the presence of

God, **"but his servant Joshua, the son of Nun, a young man, departed not out of the tabernacle" (Exodus 33:11).**

In verse 12, Moses is asking the Lord to let him know who God was going to send with him. Moses is sharing with the Lord that He had stated that He knew him by his name and that he had found grace in His sight and he wanted to know who God was sending with them. In other words, "I know you say you love me. I know you say you know me personally, but if you do, show me whom you will send with me."

What was it that led Moses in the wilderness for forty years? A pillar of smoke by day and a pillar of fire by night. Whom does that represent? The Holy Spirit. There is an angel of the Lord in the midst of the pillars. Whom does the angel of the Lord represent? Jesus Christ. Moses is saying, "If I have found favor in Your sight, then show me who will lead me."

God has given us the Holy Spirit and His Son Jesus. It is through Christ in us and by His Holy Spirit that He is going to lead us! We have found grace and favor and now MAKE ME know them! I want to know the Holy Spirit more! I want to know Christ more! They are the ones who are going to lead us through the wilderness to the Promised Land for the purposes of God. He has extended His grace to each of His children and through prayer we get to know the Holy Spirit and Christ.

In verse 13, Moses is saying, "If I have found grace in Your sight, then show me Your way." What does this mean for us? Jesus Christ is the Way, the Truth and the Light. Then it appears that there is a contradiction taking place. Moses goes on to say, **"shew me now thy way, <u>that I may know thee</u>, <u>that I may find grace in thy sight.</u>"** That is grace upon grace! We receive grace and He knows us. Show me Your ways Lord so that I can have more grace and know You more! It is a growing experience! Amen!

In verses 14-15 The Lord is saying to Moses that His presence will go with him and He will give him rest. God's presence gives us rest. When we come into that place of prayer, we enter into that rest, but if we ignore it we will have restlessness. In verse 15, Moses said, in effect "Do not take us further if you are not going to go with us." Moses' prayer time was in the tabernacle. That is where he spent time with God. Moses would go no further unless God went with him.

Prayer is not a "feeling," it is an experience. Prayer is a relationship. Glory to God!

In verses 16-17 the Lord assured Moses that he had found grace in His sight and that He knew him by name. We come to God because we have found grace and He knows us by name! Then Moses asked a rhetorical question: "How will we know we have found grace in Your sight and that we are Your people? If Your presence does not go with us, how will the nations know that we have found favor in Your sight and that You know us and have chosen us?" By His grace and by His presence we know God is with us.

How can we be effective witnesses for Jesus Christ? Should we take a course in evangelism? It is good to learn things, but without the presence of God, we will have no witness. People will see the presence of God and others will see it through the effectiveness of God working through us. People will sense the supernatural things of God in our lives and will desire to have that as well.

Prayer is a place where God affirms us. We see that in Exodus 33:17, **"And the LORD said unto Moses, I will do this thing also that thou hast spoken: for thou hast found grace in my sight, and I know thee by name."**

We must keep humble before God when He affirms us. We must guard our hearts to keep pride from rising up when we know that God is sending us, because His glory is on us. If we do not, it will lead to our destruction and God will have to lay the stones again. We all struggle with pride. We want to be used in miracles and see God move, praying, "If you do God, I will stay so humble Lord. I promise!" Then when God moves through us, the first thought or thing out of your mouth is, "WOW, look what God did through me!" We must be disciplined and swift to give God the glory!

In the flesh nature, it is impossible to remain humble in the glory of God! WHY? Because the flesh contains the sin nature and the sin nature is the nature of lucifer. What was lucifer's sin? When he saw the glory of God, he wanted it. The sin nature is in our flesh and when we see the glory of God, we want it and it's impossible for us to remain humble. Any man in the flesh who sees the glory of God and lives, it will destroy him.

It does not have to be that way, for there is a place in God that is safe. God can cover you just as he covered Moses in the cleft of the rock, in safety, when He passed by him in all His glory. Where is that place? That safe place is in prayer in Christ. God chooses those who are in that "cleft in the rock." Those that are not looking at themselves, or looking here or there, will see His glory. For their eyes are already focused on Him and seeking Him in prayer.

Some people will "peek" from behind that cleft when they see God moving. Pride, strife, control, ambition will rise up on those who peek! Stay safe in prayer in Christ. Run to that place of prayer to maintain the presence and glory of God in your life, so when God starts using you, you will not be destroyed.

What did He do when He used the bread and fish to feed the five thousand? What did he do to the disciples? He pushed them into a boat and there was a storm coming. These mighty men of God begin yelling, "We are going to die!" Jesus said, "If I would not have done it, you would have died!" Pride would have filled their hearts, turning them carnal, and they would have had to start over. Pushing them into that boat kept them from developing pride, yet it put them into a safe place as they cried out to God.

"And it shall come to pass, while my glory passeth by, that I will put thee in a clift of the rock, and will cover thee with my hand while I pass by" (Exodus 33: 22). And

in Colossians, we find, **"For ye are dead, and your life is hid with Christ in God" (Colossians 3:3).** Our life is hid in Christ; He is our safe place. God will exalt you in due time. Sometimes He keeps a pressure on us to keep us in a place of need. Humble yourself under the mighty hand of God; do not try to run away from it. When God allows the pressures to come upon us, He is just pushing us into that place of protection in Jesus so that He can use us. God keeps us in a place of humility so that we will not exalt ourselves. Even Paul, when he was given a thorn in his flesh, was grateful, because it kept him humble. I can relate to this. The Lord has also given me a thorn in my back and it keeps me humble and serves as a reminder.

"And I will take away mine hand, and thou shalt see my back parts: but my face shall not be seen" (Exodus 33:23). We will be able to see the effect of God's glory on people, but we will never see how God's glory is working through us, or we will be destroyed by pride. When God removed His hand, Moses was able to see the goodness of God's glory as He was passing by.

As we minister to people, God will give us the joy of seeing lives touched. We will witness the affect of what God's glory has done, but we will not be able to see His glory. In other words, we will pray, teach, and spread the gospel and never know the affect it will have on those we touch, because it is not for us to know. But we can rejoice when we see God's glory touch people's lives. It is when we show love to people, pray for people, share the gospel, and reach out to people that we see changes. Our response will not be, "Well look what I did!" NO! We will say, "Oh God, your great compassion has healed people and set them free!"

Going back to Exodus 33:11, how does it say that Moses was able to see God face to face while in **Exodus 33:20** it says, **"And he said, Thou canst not see my face: for there shall no man see me, and live.** In our prayer closet, we are able to see

God's glory. When we see God's glory in a place of prayer, it is all about Him. If we see God's glory within our ministry, it then becomes all about "us." If we begin to lose the discipline of personal prayer, then pride will come upon us like a monster and destroy us. In other words, the more God uses us, the more we have the need to be prayerful, so we are not destroyed by pride. You can see this in those who God has used in a big way in the beginning, but over time, everything falls apart. They needed to pray more to maintain the same level of humility. Their prayer life decreased the more God began to use them because their focus moved onto what was taking place. This caused God's glory to leave.

Know how to get into prayer to connect with God, yet know how to remain humble! This entire chapter is not a comprehensive study on how to develop a disciplined prayer life. It is a challenge to seize the opportunity that the Lord has given us to respond to a new level of prayer. I need to learn to pray more. I need to learn how to get into His presence more! I am so thankful that He has taken me out of my rut and He has placed within me the desire for more of Him. I desire to see such a huge revival in this country where the dead are raised, the sick are healed, and those in sin are freed from bondage!

When a nation's people are a people of prayer, you will see God's hand move upon it! Prayer removes you from that rut because it begins to move the world you cannot physically see, the spiritual world. Do not struggle, just take it one day at a time. Make a fresh commitment every morning. Do not make a prayer board showing what days and times you will pray, because by the time you get to the second week, you will run dry from the legalism of it. Pray as you are led by the Holy Spirit, but know that if you do not seek, you will never feel led.

Building on Home Relationships

I want to touch briefly on another aspect of relationship-building, the building of a family relationship at home. **"For if a man know not how to rule his own house, how shall he take care of the church of God?" (1 Timothy 3:5).** A Jewish custom that has held Jewish families together for centuries is one that Christian families would do well to begin.

On Friday, at sundown, the beginning of the Sabbath, the father, who is the high priest of his home, gathers his family together to honor God. He pronounces a blessing on his wife in the presence of all their children. Then he blesses each of the children. (Do not get caught up in looking at the Sabbath festival aspect, focus on the action that is taking place.) This custom strengthens relationships and affirms identities. Constant affirmation creates strong emotional security so necessary for a healthy society. **"Husbands, love your wives, even as Christ also loved the church, and gave himself for it; That he might sanctify and cleanse it with the washing of water by the word" (Ephesians 5:25-26).** Husbands should hold their wives in the same reverence that Christ holds His Bride. This cements the relationship in love and creates an atmosphere in the home and prevents divorce.

"As arrows are in the hand of a mighty man; so are children of the youth. ⁵Happy is the man that hath his quiver full of them: they shall not be ashamed, but they shall speak with the enemies in the gate" (Psalms 127:4-5). Children who are not ashamed are those who know their identity due to strong affirmation.

I am a personal testimony of how God can change your life through prayer. I am also a personal testimony of being a Christian who did not maintain a prayer life. I know both sides; I drank from both wells. One well led me to a bag of crackers that dried my thirst while the other one satisfies my thirst and moves me forward. I praise God for an ear that finally began to recognize His voice. Remember the three grounds. Desire to have the Lord increase in you so you can become an effective witness for Jesus Christ. Remember, it is all about choice! Amen.

Suggested Books,
DVD'S and Websites

Online resources:

Our website, a work constantly in progress, draws from some of the most informative teachings by Glenn and Robert Ewing.

Glenn Ewing founded Grace Gospel Campgrounds in Waco, Texas. Holy Spirit inspired, he and his son Robert, through spirit-filled teachings, have transformed, and continue to transform, the lives of many. Both men have since passed away. There are photos of these two men of God on the site as well.

You can also contact us through our site. In the near future, there will also be CD's available of our teachings and the teachings of Mr. Ewing.

www.gracegospelwaco.com

A wonderful online bible search tool.
http://www.biblegateway.com

Books:

Which Bible Should We Trust? by Les Garrett.
Currently found on amazon.com

The Seven Festivals of the Messiah, by Eddie Chumney.
http://www.hebroots.org

The Messianic CHURCH Arising! by Dr. Robert D. Heidler

DVD's:

The Star of Bethlehem
This DVD explains the stars and the signs within them at the time Christ was born and crucified.
http://www.bethlehemstar.net/

Endnotes

a Bitter defined in Collins Gem Webster's Dictionary, 2002, n54.

b Hurt defined in Collins Gem Webster's Dictionary, 2002, n272.

LaVergne, TN USA
21 October 2010
201660LV00001B/9/P